THE *NEW* BLUE LINE

Police Innovation in Six American Cities

by JEROME H. SKOLNICK
and DAVID H. BAYLEY

THE FREE PRESS
A Division of Macmillan, Inc.
NEW YORK

Collier Macmillan Publishers
LONDON

The Free Press
A Division of Macmillan, Inc.
866 Third Avenue, New York, N.Y. 10022

Collier Macmillan Canada, Inc.

First Free Press Paperback Edition 1988

Printed in the United States of America

printing number
2 3 4 5 6 7 8 9 10

Library of Congress Cataloging-in-Publication Data

Skolnick, Jerome H.
  The new blue line.

  Bibliography: p.
  Includes index.
  1. Police—United States—Case studies. 2. Public relations—United States—Police. I. Bayley, David H. II. Title.
HV8141.S57   1986   363.2′0973   85-27535
ISBN 0-02-929311-1

To the memory of
GARY P. HAYES
who contributed so much
to police innovation

CONTENTS

PREFACE

Police innovation is usually associated with Robert Peel, who introduced the London Metropolitan Police to the world in 1829. Faced with the problem of reconciling fear of soaring crime rates with widespread apprehension over potential abuse of police power, Peel and his colleagues devised some brilliant and simple innovations. They designed a distinctive but non-martial blue uniform, gave extra credit to recruits who had ties to the local community, developed a rudimentary professional career service, dispersed foot patrols throughout metropolitan London and—most radical of all—disarmed patrolmen. Many ordinary Englishmen remembered and feared the Peterloo massacre, when the Army and yeomanry assaulted a peaceful protest with muskets and bayonets. Peel's police thus generated twin goals, which they saw as complementary: to reduce crime and increase public safety while assuring the public that the police were no "engine of despotism."

Contemporary American police executives face similar issues. (Indeed, so do British police, as the English riots of the 1980s attest.) Such challenges are endemic to policing in a free,

democratic society. The President's Commission on Law Enforcement and Administration of Justice noted in 1967:

The struggle to maintain a proper balance between effective
law enforcement and fairness to individuals pervades the entire
criminal justice system. It is particularly crucial and apparent
in police work because . . . every police action can impinge directly, and perhaps hurtfully, on a citizen's freedom of action.

The demand for public order and safety continues while mistrust of police can run high, particularly in inner-city communities. Cities—the asphalt roots of America—have seen considerable change since the 1960s. Many leading cities now have
black, hispanic, and/or women chief executives. But has policing been affected? Have new visions and strategies arisen in response to the twin imperatives of public safety and public trust?
These are among the questions we set out to answer in our observations of cities across America—Santa Ana and Oakland in
the far west, Denver in the Rocky Mountains, Detroit in the industrial midwest, Houston in the sunbelt, and Newark, N.J. in
the northeast. What we observed offers hope, but not perfec-
tion or complacency. Overall, we saw a shift away from a distant, technically oriented professionalism of the early 1960s
toward a more community-oriented, crime-prevention-ori-
ented policing. This mode was more fully and effectively developed in some departments than others, but it was palpably
present in every organization. The often fascinating historical
and operational details of how this movement developed, what
it looks like in practice, and what it represents for the future of
policing are what this book is about.

When a sociologist and a political scientist undertake a study
such as this we become the students, the police and the local citizens our teachers. We received splendid, generous cooperation
from the police departments in the cities we studied. So many
helped, however, from patrolmen and women to Chiefs, Captains, and Lieutenants that we can't name them all. Mostly,
they were proud of themselves, proud of the jobs they were doing. Moreover, like all police, they were sharp observers and
sometime critics of their environments. This is their book as

much as ours. They were, and continue to be, doers who are our teachers. We are enormously grateful to them.

We wish also to thank the following: James K. Stewart of the National Institute of Justice, and Patrick V. Murphy of the Police Foundation, for subsidizing our research expenses under Grant No. 83–IJ–CX–0003; Franklin Zimring and Norval Morris, for giving of their time to offer comments on the manuscript; Jonathan Simon, for his general research assistance and insightful field observations; the staff of the Center for the Study of Law and Society at the University of California, Berkeley—particularly Rod Watanabe and Margo Martinez; and Lawrence Sherman, who supported us when we conceived of the project. At the time, Dr. Sherman was Vice-President and Director for Research of the Police Foundation. He saw this book as a potential contribution to the Foundation's efforts to produce significant and influential research on American police. We hope that the results will not disappoint.

We should also add that we are grateful to our sponsors for the unrestricted freedom to see and write what we pleased. Any errors of fact, interpretation, or conclusion are entirely our own and certainly not the responsibility of the Police Foundation or the National Institute of Justice.

Finally, we would like to thank Arlene Skolnick and Chris Bayley, for putting up with the intrusions of field research on the reasonable regularities of domestic life.

Jerome H. Skolnick
Berkeley, Cal.

David Bayley
Albany, N.Y.

October, 1985

1

COPING WITH THE URBAN CRIME PROBLEM

THE NATION'S CHRONIC FRUSTRATION with the criminal justice system is captured in headlines that scream at us daily from the front pages of newspapers: ''Third Schoolgirl Assaulted in Two Days,'' ''Wife Shoots Husband in Face,'' ''Nun in Critical Condition from Mugging,'' ''Second Hammer Slaying.'' Fearful and anxious, we feel trapped in an environment that is like a madhouse of quixotic violence and unpredictable threat. We feel not only terror but helplessness. None of the agencies of the criminal justice system—least of all the police—created supposedly to protect us, seem to be effective. ''Police Investigation Stymied,'' ''No Clues in Abduction of Three-Year-Old,'' ''Police Admit Helplessness in Muggings,'' ''Rapist Freed on Bond.'' Institutions of the law appear powerless and capricious. Are they? This book is about how contemporary police agencies are coping with the urban crime problem. Based on field observations of six American police departments—Santa Ana, Houston, Detroit, Denver, Oakland, and Newark—we searched for innovative ideas, strategies, and organizational reforms that might have some success in responding to city crime. Our search was always interesting, rarely frustrating, sometimes splendidly and unexpectedly rewarding. We learned a lot from the police organizations and cops we studied.

The project began when, discouraged and desperate like the rest of us, officials in the Department of Justice decided in 1982 to ask a bold but simple question: Is there anything the police can do to alleviate the public's paralyzing fear of crime? They recognized, of course, that the public has good reason to be frightened. Fear may be deplorable, but it also saves lives and prevents injury by prompting caution. At the same time fear is a problem in its own right. Often exaggerated by the media as well as by word-of-mouth, it disrupts patterns of daily life, immures people, especially the elderly, in their homes, creates debilitating stress, contributes to the deterioration of neighborhoods, causes economic loss to merchants, and leaves portions of cities abandoned to the very criminals everyone fears. So the Federal Government set out to discover whether there was anything the police could do to regain control of the social environment in ways that would reassure the general public.

The Department of Justice, through the National Institute of Justice, asked the Police Foundation of Washington, D.C., to pinpoint the hottest ideas in street-crime control and try them out under controlled conditions in two large cities. The Police Foundation, created by the Ford Foundation in 1971, had become the leading private research organization in the field of policing. Under the vigorous direction of Patrick V. Murphy, former Commissioner of the New York Police Department, the Police Foundation had undertaken studies into the effectiveness of new as well as old police strategies and management practices. It was therefore natural for the National Institute of Justice to give the Police Foundation a grant over a two-year period to come up with hard information about the ability of the police to provide perceptible increases in public security.

In order to decide what ideas should be tried, the Police Foundation brought together a group of national consultants in the police field in January 1983 to assess what was current and choice. That is where we came in. The Police Foundation asked us to visit several cities known for having recently developed innovative approaches to policing and to report to the group about them. At the meeting, which was attended by about fifteen people, the "delphi technique" was employed to make sure that every possibility was considered. The technique, presumably designed to turn ordinary people into oracles, involved having each person succinctly put forward a relevant idea, in this case factors under police control that can reduce the public's fear of crime. After repeated rounds of the group, forty-nine separate factors were listed. That amount of inventiveness was hardly a matter for congratulation. Either the world was very complex, making it unlikely that any single approach to crime control would produce a discernible effect, or so little was known about what would work, even by very knowledgeable people, that any idea was as good as any other. The group hoped fervently that the latter was the case. Better ignorance than complexity, because then at least experimentation in the field, provided substantial rather than trivial ideas were tested, could produce interesting results.

A cropped inventory of promising approaches was eventually produced. It was taken to the police departments of Newark, New Jersey, and Houston, Texas, to stimulate their thinking about what they might do to reduce the fear of crime in local conditions. Newark and Houston had been chosen by the National Institute of Justice as the places where the experiments would be conducted. They were labeled respectively "snowbelt" and "sunbelt" cities. No one pretended they were representative American cities, but they did have the kind of crime problems that many places were encountering. The experiments were to be carried out in four matched areas of each city, with a fifth area used as a basis for comparison. The Police Foundation is in the process of publishing the results of the experiments, along with descriptions of how the strategies were developed in each place and the problems encountered in implementation.

Everyone involved in the project was aware that much had already been learned about what wasn't working in American policing. Prompted by the historic President's Commission on Law Enforcement and the Administration of Justice of 1967, findings had accumulated over the preceeding fifteen years, often as a result of research sponsored by the Law Enforcement Assistance Administration. LEAA had expired in 1978 and had given birth to the National Institute of Justice. The search for successful approaches to crime and the fear of crime in 1982 did not have to begin with a blank slate.

Research had shown repeatedly that traditional police strategies were not working effectively. As with any research, objections were raised about particular studies, but the clear lesson overall was that whenever tried-and-true methods of policing were evaluated, their usefulness could not be demonstrated. That series of almost unrelievedly negative findings was one reason why the Federal Government was anxious by 1982 to find out if anything could work. For by then progressive police administrators, scholars, and even a few politicians had begun to realize that solutions to America's crime problem were unlikely to be found by conducting business as usual.

Specifically, this is what had been found out:

First, increasing the number of police does not necessarily reduce crime rates or raise the proportion of crimes solved. The same is true for budgetary expenditures on the police. The most that could be said was that if there were no cops there would be more crime; however, once a certain threshold of coverage has been reached, presumably long passed in the United States, increments of money and personnel are no longer efficacious. Variations in both crime and clearance rates are best predicted by social conditions such as income, unemployment, population, income distribution, and social heterogeneity.[1] We have learned that you can't simply throw money at law enforcement and expect proportionate results.

Second, random motorized patrolling neither reduces crime nor improves chances of catching suspects. Moreover, it does not reassure citizens enough to affect their fear of crime, nor does it engender greater trust in the police.[2] Regular patrols by police officers on foot, on the other hand, were shown to reduce citizens' fear of crime, although they have no demonstrable impact on the crime rate.[3]

Third, two-person patrol cars are no more effective than one-person cars in reducing crime or catching criminals. Furthermore, injuries to police officers are not more likely to occur in one-person patrol cars.[4]

Fourth, saturation patrolling does reduce crime, but only temporarily, largely by displacing it to other areas.

Fifth, the kind of crime that terrifies Americans most—mugging, robbery, burglary, rape, homicide—is rarely encountered by police on patrol.[5] Only "Dirty Harry" has his lunch disturbed by a bank robbery in progress. Patrol officers individually make few important arrests. The "good collar" is a rare event. Cops spend most of their time passively patrolling and providing emergency services.

Sixth, improving response time to emergency calls has no effect on the likelihood of arresting criminals or even in satisfying involved citizens. One recent and very large study showed that the chances of making an arrest on the spot drop below 10 percent if even one minute elapses from the time the crime is committed.[6] Only instantaneous reaction, in other words, would be effective in catching criminals. Yet that can't reasonably be expected unless a cop is put on every corner. Speed of response makes so little difference because victims delay an average of four to five and one-half minutes before calling the police, even when they have been victims of confrontational crimes.

Rapid response also doesn't satisfy citizens, surprisingly, because what most victims of crime want is predictable rather than quick response. Victims seem to recognize that in most crimes the criminal will be long gone whenever the police arrive. What they want is a police response they can count on as they go about reordering their stricken lives. They would rather wait forty-five minutes, the research shows, for an assured reaction from the police than the uncertainty of waiting for an unpredictable response. They don't want to have to sit around waiting.

Seventh, crimes are not solved—in the sense of offenders arrested and prosecuted—through criminal investigations conducted by police departments. Generally, crimes are solved because offenders are immediately apprehended or someone identifies them specifically—a name, an address, a license plate number. If neither of those things happens, the studies show, the chances that any crime will be solved fall to less than one in ten. Despite what television has led us to think, detectives do not work from clues to criminals; they work from known suspects to corroborating evidence. Detectives are important for the prosecution of identified perpetrators and not for finding unknown offenders.[7]

Those findings are devastating. They mean that the primary strategies followed by American police departments are neither reducing crime nor reassuring the public. Like other public institutions—schools, the Defense Department, prisons—the police often devote resources to traditional but bureaucratically safe approaches that no longer work—if they ever did. That probably explains why additions of money or personnel have slight measurable effect on security. How could they, when existing strategies seem largely bankrupt? The studies clearly imply that protection needs to be provided by citizens themselves, and that their assistance is essential in capturing and prosecuting the people who victimize them. The job for the police, therefore, is to work with the public so as to ensure that those things happen, to develop specific and articulate approaches that can achieve results. Like good, cautious scholars, we feel compelled to say again that the studies cited are not conclusive. Perhaps what has been shown to be true in Kansas City, Peoria, or Los Angeles isn't true for other places. However, until the usefulness of local police strategies has been demonstrated, citizens should take police assurances with a grain of salt.

Although we have continued to serve as advisers to the project, we thought we could make a contribution independently of the experimental assessment of contemporary police strategies. We took our ideas to Lawrence Sherman, then research director and vice president of the Police Foundation, and to its then president, Patrick Murphy. We explained that our brief visits to several cities, in addition to our own field studies over many years, had convinced us that police departments were already grappling reflectively with the problem of fear reduction—and that a few of them had embarked on significant initiatives of their own. We thought it would be useful to immerse ourselves in the operational world of senior administrators to see what might realistically be accomplished in crime control, what local approaches were being developed, what difficulties were being encountered in carrying out new programs, and what results were being achieved. Sherman and Murphy gave us the go-ahead and the necessary financial support.

Our plan was to undertake mini-ethnographic studies of six cities: Denver, Detroit, Houston, Newark, Oakland, and Santa Ana. This was not a scientific sample. The cities were selected because they scattered fairly well throughout the country (the Southeast being the obvious exception); some were already known for innovation; some were recognized as being particularly difficult to police; some we had worked in already; and in all we had assured access. As luck would have it, they turned out to display remarkably well the gamut of strategic thought and practice in contemporary policing.

We visited each city, observing operations at close hand and trying to get into the minds of police officers at every rank level. Cooperation was outstanding in each city, from the chiefs to rookie patrol officers. Night and day, winter and summer, we watched and talked to cops in patrol cars, at precinct stations, on street corners, in private homes, in fast-food restaurants, in jails, at training academies, in headquarters offices, in alleys, in vacant lots, in bars, and even behind bushes. Our concern was with the strategy of policing and not with the tactics employed by individual officers. Thus we looked at the emphasis given to criminal investigations but not to interrogation practices; to patrolling but not to domestic dispute guidelines; to creation of foot patrols but not to surveillance conduct; and to deployment schemes but not the rules for stop-and-frisk. Similarly, we attended to managerial practices and organization, such as training, planning, leadership style, and recruitment, only if they clearly affected the success of strategic programs. We wanted to find out how resources generally were being used to reduce crime and reassure the public.

We sought to capture the institutional character of each of the six police departments and cities we studied. Each city and its department became fascinating to us. In some respects every police department is alike. Each is a classical bureaucracy. Each has a chief or commissioner or director, a hierarchical organization, a paramilitary structure, an assignment of functions, and formal rules for carrying them out. Each has an organizational chart and a set of general orders. But the chart and the general orders often omit key factors affecting the day-to-day operations of the department. For example, no organizational chart explains how higher management and the police union get along. The outcome of that relationship is ordinarily embodied in a legally binding "memorandum of understanding." Still, there are significant issues beyond the formal contract. How do higher management and the rank-and-file perceive the fundamental problems facing the police department? And are they willing to cooperate in carrying out programs to resolve some of those? As we learned through our explorations, the relation between leadership and followership within a police department is often a key factor affecting the capacity of the department to introduce innovative strategies.

Although American police departments exhibit similarities—they are of course much more like each other than they are, say, like the Japanese police—they are also articulably different from each other. They would have to be. The police in a Texas boomtown like Houston must be different from the police in a classic Midwestern industrial city like Detroit. Newark's population may be the most impoverished in America, and the police department resources reflect that poverty. Santa Ana is the county seat of conservative Orange County, California, although, as we shall explain, it may well enjoy the most innovative police organization in the United States. Thus, since our research was organized as a search for strategic innovation as it was occurring nationally in American policing, we considered why there should be more innovation in conservative Santa Ana than in liberal Oakland, California, or in Denver, which in the past decade has experienced almost phenomenal economic growth in high-tech industries.

We present what we found in six chapters, a separate one for each city. Although we avoided a rigid outline, we tried to provide answers to issues that might be considered a paradigm for a causal analysis of innovation. One question involves an assessment of the department's resources. Newark police who visited Houston told us that when they observed that city's largesse of equipment—particularly its helicopters—they were impressed, envious, and paradoxically a bit self-congratulatory. Newark policing is undertaken with a minimum of technical support. When the department pulls itself up by its own bootstraps, it looks down and observes that the bootstraps are tattered.

Other issues flow from other realities. Every city has a unique and weighty history affecting the police department: a tradition of government, an economy, a changing population base, a shifting political climate. We assess those for all the departments. During the 1970s the nation experienced a net migration of nearly 10 million people from cities to suburbs. Most of those who left were white and in the middle and upper income brackets, while those who remained were mostly black and poor. John J. Palen wrote in 1975 that

. . . the most spectacular instance of invasion and eventual succession is found in the racial changes taking place in the central city. Many whites fear the movement of blacks into a neighborhood because they believe it will threaten the stability of the area. By this they mean that their neighborhood will lose its middle-class character, the quality of the schools will decline, street violence will increase, the area will generally deteriorate to the level of an inner-city slum.[8]

Those fears—as well as the pull of newly developed and attractive suburbs—generated a self-fulfilling prophecy. Neighborhoods did become increasingly unsafe and dilapidated. Face-to-face interaction declined among neighbors, and the police became a more immediate and sought-after instrument of social controls. At the same time police experienced declining resources and sometimes serious losses of manpower, with accompanying morale effects. We attempt to assess some of the relationship between the police and associated urban ecology in each chapter.

We do so because it became quickly evident that the interplay between police and locale is a significant factor affecting police innovation. For example, how do they police generally feel about the city they are policing? Do they regard it as a kind of "jungle" and its inhabitants as predatory animals? Whether or not police actually reside in the city they are policing, would they consider living there? Is the city an important place to them? Those sorts of basic attitudes, which cannot be tapped by cold questionnaire, are terribly consequential. They affect the enthusiasm with which police work. They affect their constitutional obligations. They influence street encounters with adult citizens, with juveniles, and with homeowners seeking police services. Our ethnographic investigations try to answer such questions and to identify the differences among the departments in organization, background, and attitude.

Was it possible, we especially wanted to know, for police departments to overcome adverse background conditions? Just as psychologists of human development ask how influential a bad childhood is on adult behavior, we inquire into whether police departments can outgrow a deprived past?

Here and there—particularly in Santa Ana—we found some very good news. We discovered that administrative leadership, an animating philosophy of values, can indeed effect change. It can alter both the structure of police organization and the performance of street patrolmen.

We found, in short, the beginnings of a social reconstruction of American policing. That development is predicated on an understanding of how police need to reconstitute their conception of their role to adjust to novel and emergent social circumstances. Consider the following statement by Chief Raymond Davis of Santa Ana in the *Los Angeles Times* (October 30, 1983):

I believe in the age-old philosophy that a police department must have the support of the community, be involved in the community and serve the community. This position should not be surprising. The real question should be: why did it take so long for us to recognize that neighborhood watch programs, community assistance programs, community advisory panels and strong citizen involvement were really the only available opportunities for success for a local police department?

Or consider the police responses to community pressures in Oakland, California, where at least twenty people were killed in 1984, including a fifteen-year-old pregnant girl shot by mistake, as a result of street warfare involving rival drug gangs. There, police and prosecutors have both reassessed priorities regarding street drug arrests. The police, in particular, responded positively to community campaigns—including public marches and meetings—to focus public attention on the needs of neighborhoods. The Oakland Police Department is thus beginning to move toward heavier community involvement, although it is more reactive to the community than Santa Ana's proactive community orientation. In both Houston and Detroit we observed innovative programs designed to encourage citizen participation in policing and to persuade rank-and-file police that citizen participation was useful and important to the success of the policing enterprise. As shall be seen, such persuasion didn't always work, but trying is also important to the community.

Such change as we report should be considered in the context of a not so distant past history when police were viewed with alarm and suspicion by many people, particularly by the black and Hispanic residents of America's inner cities. The situation has improved in the cities we studied, albeit with some reservations expressed by members of both police and minority communities. Even in cities where mistrust remains high, however, we see glimmerings of new understanding. Thus, the *Cleveland Plain Dealer* quotes from Cleveland Police Chief Jeffrey G. Fox on the importance of addressing the fears of blacks and Hispanics: "There is ultimately more security [for police] in community support than there is in sophisticated weaponry." The *Plain Dealer* adds: "The security of all should be the goal. That cannot be achieved if half of Cleveland's residents fear the police almost as much as they do the city's hoodlums and thugs" (March 28, 1984).

We did not study Cleveland, but we did study Detroit and other large cities. We found success in combating both fear of police and fear of crime. We found also a strong inclination to recognize the significance of community trust and cooperation as a central feature of the police role. We did not find this everywhere, among all administrators and patrol police. Despite resistance, particularly among rank-and-file officers, we did find significant change in the idealogy and organization of policing.

When we found some observable success, we attempted to analyze it. In general we found that success seemed to arise out of the capacity of police leaders to imbue a sense of responsibility and accountability to the citizenry into the policing enterprise. Often the infusion resulted from an evolving recognition that the dominant and stable community—particularly among minorities—shared, indeed demanded, traditional police values of stability and security. We found, in addition, that success required more than altering values. Our observations showed how crucial it was to translate value preferences into concrete organizational changes, such as team policing and subsidiary strategies of decentralized assignment and community mobilization against crime.

So we observed some palpable success stories. We also kept our attention tuned for novel and interesting strategies so as to identify possible future directions for American policing. Some of them we found in the most economically deprived departments, Newark and Detroit.

In our concluding chapter, after summarizing the characteristics of policing in each of the six cities, we therefore discuss (1) how the activating philosophy of police leadership can shape the direction of innovation; (2) what assumptions and experiences lead to innovation; (3) what sorts of factors and trends facilitate or impede police innovation; and finally, (4) what changes—including emerging visions of the police role—we might contemplate as the future of American policing. In sum, we try in this book both to locate innovation and to understand why and how it happens, especially where its occurrence may not conform to original intuition.

2

SANTA ANA:
Conservative County,
Progressive Police

On June 1, 1969 a member of the militant Black Panther party, a young man named Arthur League, shot and killed Nelson Sasser, a thirty-three-year-old Santa Ana policeman. According to Lieut. Joseph Brann, then a Santa Ana police trainee, the killing and its aftermath symbolized the hostile relationship between the Santa Ana police and minorities in the 1960s. The summers of 1969 and 1970 were long and hot for everyone, Brann recalls. "We didn't have the sort of major riots that Los Angeles, Detroit, and Newark had. But we had mini-riots practically every weekend, where situations in the streets would get out of control." At that time Santa Ana was one of the most ideologically conservative cities in the United States. The City Manager and the City Council forbade the Chief of Police to apply for or accept any Federal grant monies. Within the police department itself, a group of officers that became known as the "John Birch Conspiracy" tried to wrest departmental control from Chief Edward J. Allen.

Brann and others describe the crime control strategy of those days as simple, if not simplistic: "Kick ass and take names." Brann adds, "That was it. That was one of the appealing things about it, though. I knew that when I went out on the street at night, starting my shift, there would be a lot of activity. Santa Ana was recognized as a high-activity town. Because we were undermanned, there was always something to keep you going."

Sgt. Dan Carr, a big, ruddy-faced, handsome man in his early thirties, likewise acknowledges vast improvement in community relations since then but also recalls the old days with a certain nostalgia. "In those days," he remembers, "we would have a lot of fights, especially in bars. We'd get in a lot of stick time. I was big, strong, in my twenties, and I loved to fight. Besides, cops always win."

Carr is an old-fashioned cop who likes to mix it up and also enjoys talking with people. He relishes the potential excitement of the street and like many cops is fundamentally gregarious. Although others in the department think Carr possesses the ability to advance to a management position, Carr himself, like many other street-oriented cops, prefers life in the patrol car and the open air. Carr approves of the directions the department has taken to facilitate friendliness between the community and the police—he enjoys his amiable relations with citizens in his area—but he doubtless would have remained had the old ways of "badge-heavy," aggressive patrol continued. For street cops like Dan Carr, fighting can be just another form of human interaction.

According to Joe Brann, however, the situation prevailing at the turn of the 1970s just couldn't be allowed to continue, not for him, not for the department or the community of Santa Ana. It was simply that unpalatable. Like his other "management" buddies, Capt. Paul Walters and Lieut. Pete Jensen, Brann is nobody's stereotype of a cop. Tall, earnest, intelligent, so clean-cut that he looks as if he polishes his buttons, Brann left the Brigham Young University's pre-med program in 1969 to earn some money to continue his studies. On the one hand he found police work enormously exciting—all cops, he thinks, become adrenalin junkies. But Brann possesses other qualifications for police work besides a penchant for adrenalin. He is a four-time police olympic gold medalist in small-bore and high-power rifle shooting.

At heart, however, cops like Brann, Walters, and Jensen are thinkers rather than shooters. All hold advanced degrees and are continually taking courses to upgrade their policing and management skills. All were dismayed by the hostility between the cops and the community and the dismally stagnant quality of the police organization during the early 1970s. All seriously considered alternative careers. The department itself ran perilously by the self-made rules of cops on the job.

Brann recalls how, as a trainee, he was dispatched along with his training officer to pick up and arrest a suspected cop-killer. "If that's really our man," he was told "we don't bring him back alive." Brann knew that the execution of an alleged cop-killer was itself the most serious crime on the books, and he wasn't about to commit a murder. At the same time he was aware of the then prevailing blue code of silence. One did not turn in or testify against a fellow officer. Fortunately, his predicament was resolved when the suspect turned out to be the wrong man. That particular situation aside, the more fundamental problem for Brann and others like him had not been resolved. The Santa Ana Police Department was backward and moving nowhere. Relations with the public were unpleasant and often antagonistic. Police were openly and frequently called "pigs" on the street, and police returned the compliment with epithets of their own or, more likely, with the end of the nightstick.

During the early 1970s even optimistic civic boosters conceded that crime was becoming an unbearable part of life in Santa Ana. When a *Los Angeles Times* reporter, Evan Maxwell, interviewed a police lieutenant about the city's problems, the officer put it this way: "Name any problem of the inner city and we had it—poverty, the highest minority population in the county, a heavy concentration of drug addicts, substandard housing. The city was losing industry, people were moving out, and all because of the crime. We really were in danger of losing the city."[1]

THE CITY OF SANTA ANA

Santa Ana is part of the great megalopolis of southern California, 33 miles southeast of Los Angeles, 20 miles east of the ports of Los Angeles and Long Beach, and 90 miles north of San Diego. The Santa Ana Freeway, connecting downtown LA with

Orange County, is jammed with suburbanites during rush hours. Considering that Orange County's 1980 population was counted as nearly 2 million, highways would of course be jammed. Although Santa Ana is the county seat of Orange County, Santa Ana does not altogether typify the mainly homogeneous and suburban cities surrounding it: Garden Grove, Orange, Tustin, Irvine, Costa Mesa, Fountain Valley. Former City Manager A. J. Wilson, who left Santa Ana for America's highest-paying manager job—in Kansas City—describes Santa Ana as a real city, in contrast to a suburb. "We're a concentrated urban area. We're a business center. We're dealing with issues like rapid transit possibilities for the future, greater densities of housing, much greater densities of office construction—these kinds of things."[2]

Santa Ana might not feel much like a city to an Easterner, because its 27 square miles held a 1982 population of only 215,050. Of those, about 45 percent were white and an equal percentage Hispanic. The remaining population groups were Asian and Pacific Islanders 5.2 percent, black 4.0 percent, and a sprinkling of American Indians, Eskimos, Aleuts, and others. These percentages were derived from official population figures of the U.S. Census. Within the Police Department, however, one continues to hear informal estimates of tens of thousands of illegal aliens occupying residences in Santa Ana. Estimates range from 50,000 to 80,000, extraordinary numbers considering the base population of the city. It is hard to estimate the accuracy of such figures, but consider the following statement of Alan Eliason, who heads the Border Patrol operations for the Southern California area adjacent to Mexico: "Last year [1983] in this sector of the border, which is 66 miles long, we apprehended more than 430,000," Mr. Eliason said. "This year I don't see any letup. The flow is continuing at high, extraordinarily high levels. It's as if we're under siege." Mr. Eliason added that his agents were noticing increasing illegal migration by people from countries outside Latin America.[3]

Observations from a Santa Ana patrol car tend to confirm the migration of thousands upon thousands of Spanish speakers, plus the increasing migration of South Asians, particularly Vietnamese. A Santa Ana patrolman unable to speak Spanish cannot converse with a substantial segment of the population.

In 1984 only one patrolman spoke Vietnamese, and none spoke Cambodian or Laotian. Southern California has become a cosmopolitan, polyglot place, but the non-English-speaking immigrants are from Mexico, Latin America, and Asia rather than Europe. Santa Ana police in 1984 were facing issues comparable to those faced by the New York City police before World War I.

Santa Ana is Orange County's second oldest city, dating back to 1886. More important, it is the county seat. Santa Ana takes pride in an architecturally advanced Civic Center, which houses municipal, state, and Federal offices, as well as the Police Department and state and Federal courthouses. On warm, sunny Southern California days, the Civic Center gleams over a city whose interior can vary abruptly from the ramshackle to the resplendent. As in many American cities undergoing change or renewal, an observer moves from discontinuous pockets of charm and affluence to poverty and shabbiness. Single-family, ranch-style dwellings dominate the residential landscape. Most Santa Ana streets are modest but reasonably well kept, with trees, flowers, and wrought-iron fences. Even the city's worst "slum" area would scarcely be described as oppressive. Like the "slums" of East Los Angeles, those of Santa Ana are blessed with sunshine and spaciousness in contrast, say, to the slums of Newark or Chicago. There is plenty of crime and violence in Southern California, but the pastel streets do not convey the mean intensity of those of Chicago, Newark, or New York City.

There is also some high residential living in Santa Ana, affording prosperous, Beverly Hills–like accommodations to affluent business and professional people. These houses are not set dramatically apart from the rest of the city, and their residents appreciate the rise in safety and property values that the city's progressive police policies have afforded them.

Santa Ana is not a poor city. It provides a congenial business climate as well as an attractive location for skilled workers. As a tourist city it could scarcely compete with nearby Anaheim (Disneyland), Buena Park, or Newport Beach. Its main and now thriving industrial base rests in light industry, such as computer firms, companies maintaining aircraft components, and pharmaceutical companies.

Business, commercial, and ethnic community groups attribute Santa Ana's current prosperity to police innovations introduced by Chief Raymond C. Davis in 1973. Heavy-set, hard-eyed, and fiftyish, Raymond Davis looks as if he might have spent his younger years as an interior lineman—a nose guard or tackle—for the Los Angeles Rams. Seated behind a desk in short-sleeve shirt and vest, tattoos showing on his forearms, he seems typecast to play a redneck Southern—or Southern California—sheriff. In this instance appearance belies reality. Davis held modest but solid academic credentials—an M.A. from Golden Gate and a B.A. from Long Beach State—when he was hired in 1973 by the Santa Ana City Manager, and had a reputation for being a progressive but also tough administrator. Over a period of ten and a half years Davis had risen from street cop in nearby Fullerton to the rank of captain. He already enjoyed connections with Orange County law enforcement officials. "We had heard about Davis before he came here," one sergeant told us, "and we were concerned. We heard that all those cops in Walnut Creek [the Northern California department he headed previously] had Masters degrees. But then we checked around and found out that when he was a young cop in Fullerton he kicked ass pretty good."

Those reports of Davis's earlier years don't describe his tenure as Santa Ana Chief or the sort of department he and his administration have tried to create. Even those who feel uncomfortable with Davis's innovations and attitudes acknowledge that his administration has greatly improved the police department's quality. He himself declines to take full credit for the upgrading, pointing out that the department was so bad when he took it over—so underfunded, undermanned, and undertrained—that *any* reasonable police administrator would have had to point it in an upward direction.

Santa Ana is a charter city, which means it is run by a professional City Manager. The city manager system was intended to insulate government departments from direct involvement in electoral politics, and it has largely succeeded in doing so. The system, widespread on the West Coast, probably more than any other single factor accounts for the general lack of corruption in Western police departments. But perhaps that is the wrong way to formulate the relation between municipal government organization and police corruption. It is perhaps not so much that the city manager system is so good as that its classical Eastern alternative, the mayoral-ward system, is so fundamentally bad.

Where the ward system held sway, the political machine strongly influenced the selection of the police chief, promotion and assignments, and even admission into the police department. The political machine needed funds to reelect its candidates, and a substantial portion of such funds were obtained through illegal activities, classically gambling and prostitution. Vice purveyors kicked back portions of the profits to machine politicians and to cops. Police salaries could remain relatively low, because they would be routinely augmented by weekly pay envelopes divided among and by police themselves. That was the situation Frank Serpico found when he joined the New York City force. Later the Knapp Commission uncovered police corruption involving drugs in New York City in the 1960s. But corruption was not an isolated New York phenomenon; it also was happening in cities like Philadelphia, Boston, Newark, and Chicago. They just didn't happen to have a Knapp Commission investigating them.[4]

On the whole, West Coast police departments have not experienced corruption problems, but they have been charged with being distant and aloof from the communities they serve. Since the police are insulated from politics, their "professionalism" can take on an arrogant style, particularly when dealing with minorities who have relatively little influence under a city manager or a police chief.[5] Moreover, minorities—particularly blacks and Hispanics—do not embody the average policeman's idea of the worthy citizen whose rights and property are to be respected.

When Raymond Davis took over the Santa Ana Police Department, it is true, he was provided with substantial resources as Chief that his predecessors had been denied. They included hiring one hundred new police employees, eighty-eight of them patrol officers. That augmentation would raise Santa Ana's police–citizen ratio above the national average of 1.5 to 1.7. The community also supported the Police Department with additional funding. The voters agreed to impose a citywide utility user's tax, which would raise more than $2.3 million annually.

But Davis brought something more to the Santa Ana P.D.

than the capacity to generate a bigger budget and more manpower. He brought a philosophy of public service policing that
sought to combine community responsiveness with professionalism and high technology. Davis insisted that he had learned a
fundamental lesson during his experience as a street policeman
and police administrator. That lesson was the significance of the
tie between professionalism and sensitivity to the community.
Even the most technologically advanced police department, he
argued, could not perform at its best without community cooperation. The police, he learned and later was to insist, were dependent upon the community for both material support and information about crime and crime control. No matter how
sophisticated a computer is, it is only as good as the information
provided for it. There cannot be a response time to a call when
a woman is too afraid or embarrassed to report a beating or a
rape because of the treatment she expects from the police. When
police alienate substantial segments of the community, they may
lose not only electoral support for material resources but also
information about the incidence of crime and identifications of
criminals. They may even "create" crime by escalating hostility into physical conflict or riot.

Raymond Davis had come to understand those realities very
well. His philosophy happened to fit nicely with the qualities
the downtown business community was seeking in a Police
Chief. "We were looking," a leading local businessman told
me, "for a Police Chief who is up to date. He must combine
management expertise with very strict department controls
over the police." Davis has had several run-ins with the rank-
and-file. He conducts tough internal affairs investigations and
over the years has weeded out cops who haven't fitted into
Santa Ana. In 1984 he received a "no-confidence" vote from
the Patrolmen's Benevolent Association following a dispute in
which he took a hard stand against a work week of four ten-hour
days. The department figured it would be too costly and too inflexible. On the whole he seems to be respected but not entirely
beloved by his officers. Davis retorts: "Any Police Chief who is
beloved by his men isn't doing a good job."

Davis is more concerned with his relationship to the community, a character trait that the community was seeking when
Davis was hired. The same businessman continued, "We

wanted someone who was willing to work together with the residential and business communities. The old guard didn't want to hear from the community. They told us they were professionals and that they didn't want to have anything to do with us. There is a huge difference between Chief Davis and his team and the old guard. The old guard thought they were professionals. These new men are more professional because they understand a whole range of problems the city faces. The old guard were the old professionals. These are the new professionals." When he was appointed Chief, Ray Davis moved as quickly as possible to establish the direction of new professionalism for the Santa Ana Police Department. He called it COP—community-oriented policing.

COMMUNITY-ORIENTED POLICING

Community-oriented policing provides a philosophical umbrella for the Santa Ana Police Department. All of Santa Ana's other programs—which sometimes assume a bewildering variety of acronyms—are related to the philosophy of community service. COP, in turn, has its own roots. It is traceable to the "team policing" concept of the 1960s, an idea rooted in the often unpleasant if not bitter historical experience of that tumultuous decade.

Recall that during the 1960s police encounters with student protestors, antiwar demonstrators, and black militants resulted in a steady escalation of conflict, hostility, and sometimes outright violence. A Task Force appointed by the National Commission on the Causes and Prevention of Violence reviewed studies of the police written before 1968 and concluded that a majority of rank-and-file police were hostile toward minorities. Some of those studies went back to the nineteenth century. Others were from the 1930s and 1940s. Even as late as 1966, when the President's Commission on Law Enforcement and the Administration of Justice invited Albert J. Reiss, Jr., and Donald Black to study police minority relations, the authors found—based on field observations of Boston, Chicago, and Washington, D.C. police by thirty-six observers—that 72 percent of the

officers expressed either "extreme" or "considerable prejudice." Those views were not solicited but were recorded when
voluntarily expressed.[6]

Some police chiefs shared those prejudices toward minorities and did not find them to be a problem. Others, along with
some rank-and-file officers, saw the situation rather differently.
Every observer of cops on the job has concluded that police officers enjoy great discretion in stopping, frisking, arresting, and
charging and that police can never be fully supervised. Moreover, the great majority of patrol work involves noncriminal
matters. Given a situation where most police are racially prejudiced and enjoy great discretion, the results can be most unfair,
if not explosive.

During the same time period, the 1960s, crime rates began
to soar and fear of crime was escalating into the main concern of
many citizens, who felt themselves to be potential victims.
Thoughtful police executives began looking for ways of resolv-
ing the dilemma. They needed to satisfy minorities who were
demanding at least evenhandedness, if not sensitivity to minority needs and aspirations, while reducing crime and fear of
crime in the majority community.

Given the polarization between rank-and-file police and minorities, plus the similar split between minorities and the larger
white community, reconciliation between crime control and
community sensitivities was not going to be easy. The same
Presidential Crime Commission that had studied police–minority relations hinted at one possible strategy: team policing. By
1973, the year Ray Davis took over the Santa Ana P.D., team
policing had been tried with mixed results by a number of
American police departments. A 1973 study of team policing in
seven cities described it as follows:

In theory, the patrol force is reorganized to include one or
more quasi-autonomous teams, with a joint purpose of improving police services to the community and increasing job
satisfaction of the patrol officers. Usually the team is based in a
particular neighborhood. Each team has responsibility for police services in its neighborhood and is intended to work as a
unit in close contact with the community to prevent crime and
maintain order.[7]

The study also warned, however, that in practice team policing had not always been able to accomplish its theoretical goals. Team policing was never "fully developed" in the seven cities studied. The researchers pointed out how difficult it was to evaluate policing strategies unless researchers enjoyed the opportunity to control relevant conditions experimentally. At the same time experimental researchers often find themselves on the horns of a dilemma, since they must organize their experiments around a theory of relevant conditions. For example, the most ambitious team policing experiment was begun in March 1973 in Cincinnati. Under a Community Sector Team Policing Program, or COMSEC, the downtown, inner-city area only slightly increased its manpower but dramatically changed the organization and direction of policing. Except for homicides, which were still investigated by headquarters detectives, virtually all calls (91 percent) were handled by a team assigned to the sector. Moreover, beat officers appeared at meetings offering crime control information and exchanged information with colleagues. The experiment did not prove successful. Citizens' feelings of safety did not change in the area, and the crime rate, except for burglaries, was not very different from the rate for the rest of the city.

But were the relevant conditions actually controlled? Suppose the department had presented team policing as part of a larger vision of the role of police in community and society? That might not have made a difference, but it would have presented a different test of team policing. Thus even if team policing were to make little impact in some conditions, it might make an impact if combined with other conditions. If house plants aren't thriving and we add water, they still might not thrive if what they really require is a combination of water and sunlight.

Even assuming relevant conditions—the independent variables—could be controlled, true crime rates are notoriously elusive figures as a dependent variable. When citizens mistrust police, they may fail to report crime. Victimization surveys have shown substantial numbers of unreported crimes. Ironically, then, a police department that turns the corner in community relations may show a rise in crime because residents are more likely to report crime to the police.

However unproved the results of team policing as a concept, Ray Davis believed it was important to introduce his version of it into Santa Ana and to make it the cornerstone of Santa Ana's community-oriented policing program. He is among the first to acknowledge that team policing may not work in other places, but Santa Ana's team policing is different from attempts at it in the 1970s. There is a much greater commitment to it citywide, and it is part of an integrated plan for both crime control and community relations.[8]

Santa Ana's team policing approach makes the city a smaller, more decentralized place. Davis subdivided Santa Ana into four areas, each of which had previously generated a roughly equal number of calls for police service. Each area was placed under the supervision of a commander, usually a lieutenant, responsible for patrol work in two contiguous districts; and each commander was offered wide latitude in making day-to-day assignments and formulating special projects. Prior to COP, officer assignments would be rotated, and an individual officer might find himself working mostly east one night, west another, and so forth. In those circumstances officers rarely got to know individual citizens. The policeman was a distant, if not forbidding, figure called only in emergencies. After COP, patrol officers were assigned to a team for extended time periods, as much as two years or more. "You get to take a personal interest in people," one officer told me. "You make friends on the street. In the old days, you never knew where you were going to be assigned. Now, I go to the same place every night and I know everybody. That allows me to have snitches who tell me what's going on. I know all the hookers and I know who's dealing dope on the streets."

At the same time that sort of semi-permanent assignment results in greater accountability of patrolmen. A sergeant comments: "When the COP program started here patrolmen were told that they had to be involved with people on a person-to-person basis. And the Chief made it clear he wouldn't tolerate any kind of ethnic slurs, any kind. Also, guys are assigned to an area for eighteen months at a minimum—they live there. So they can't pull any baloney and walk away to a different district the next day." He adds, "But this kind of neighborhood policing can only work when the Chief is behind it all the way, and everybody knows he is. It has to come right from the top all the way down to the bottom."

Civilianization

The "top's" primary values—service, community participation, fairness—are democratic and constitutional. Under the team policing plan, those values logically require that the goals of the police department be set only after serious consultation with the community. When the community is the entire city, a police department is more likely to generate a consensus—if one is possible—out of the give-and-take of pluralistic politics. When the community is subdivided, there is more likely to be a similarity of interests within a particular area. The "community" then becomes more akin to a series of neighborhoods, with more grassroots participation in influencing and shaping the priorities of the department.

Grassroots participation does not just happen by itself. Structural changes need to be made within the police organization. By far the most important change—more important than any single program or crime control strategy—was the civilianization of police personnel. When Ray Davis took over the Department in 1973, 25 percent of the personnel were civilians. By 1984 that had increased to 40 percent, approaching the goal of 55 percent civilian, 45 percent sworn. (Sworn police officers wear guns and make arrests.) A survey of forty-one metropolitan area police departments taken in 1973 by the National Advisory Commission on Criminal Justice Standards and Goals found an average of 16 percent civilians to 84 percent sworn.[9] Nonsworn officers in Santa Ana wear uniforms but no guns or batons. The Santa Ana P.D. calls them Police Service Officers—PSOs. At one time the department considered dressing the PSOs in blazers to distinguish them from sworn officers. But a brief experiment showed that citizens were reluctant to accept them when they were dressed that way.[10] Apparently the blue uniform signifies the only sort of authority citizens are willing to accept.

Students of policing generally agree that in the typical police department the overwhelming majority of the patrolman's time

involves service to citizens rather than direct criminal investigation. In community-oriented Santa Ana, possibly 70 to 80 percent of police work is service-related. The PSOs do most of that
work in Santa Ana at a cost saving of approximately 40 percent.
Their base salary is approximately 70 percent of a patrolman's,
and they are not entitled to similar pension, insurance, an
workman's compensation benefits. The department figures
that nine service officers can be hired for every five patrolmen
and that the service officers provide equally qualified service.
Anybody who has observed service officers in at least half a
dozen different settings, as we did, would probably agree.

Every police department is familiar with the use of civilians
to supplement enforcement officers. Many departments employ civilians in communications and front desk jobs. The meter maid is probably the most recognizable civilian alternative
to the patrolman. But in Santa Ana civilians—86 percent of
whom are women and 21 percent bilingual—are to be found in
almost every aspect of police service, except those specifically
restricted to police officers because of special skill and hazard
requirements. Civilians are not, for example, assigned to the
Santa Ana P.D.'s SWAT (Special Weapons and Tactics) team.

PSOs do ride—alone—in patrol cars equipped only with radio, but that is an important piece of equipment. They can investigate all sorts of situations on the street and call for a patrolman if needed. For example, they can mark abandoned vehicles
and have them towed when appropriate; respond to a variety of
crime reports that are not in progress—e.g. the report of a burglary or a rape that occurred the night before; and can recon-
tact crime victims to obtain further information, not only to
solve the crime—which may well be out of the question—but
also to give victims the feeling that somebody cares. "That's so
much more important," says Ray Davis, "than what so many
departments do—sending victims a PR card, a postcard, saying
the case has been assigned to investigation and if you get any information contact us, when in reality all that happens is that it's
thrown in a corner and nobody does anything with it. It would
be much better for a policeman to come back to and talk to a
victim, even if the crime is only a stolen hose.

"There's value in community contact that's more important
than solving a crime. So-called experts get too caught up in
pure cost-benefit analyses without figuring in the benefit of the

intangibles: perception of service, perception of caring about people, perception of commitment to the community."

Community commitment is exemplified in Davis's concern for traffic investigation, a patrol function performed almost entirely by PSOs, who receive specialized training in it. By our observations, they do it at least as well as patrolmen in other departments, who commonly view traffic investigation as a nuisance task involving considerable paperwork and little real police work. Davis points out: "When a department has a prioritization of calls system, traffic accidents rate a low priority. But to the average person, a traffic accident involving $500 damage to the front end of the car, why, that can be the most significant and traumatic event of the day or month. Our PSO traffic specialists take a lot of satisfaction in what they do and have a real sense of job achievement."

One might question whether the rank-and-file patrolmen accept PSOs. Sgt. Bob Ensley is another big and tall man. When he and the Chief walk down a corridor, there's not much room to pass. During most of the study, Ensley was head of the Police Benevolent Association. Ensley confesses that he was initially opposed to the PSO concept but slowly became persuaded that civilians could perform community organization and mobilization as well as or better than sworn officers. "Today," he adds, "I'm one of the strong supporters of increasing use of nonsworn in this department. But I don't think I'm an exception. Most of us realize that in many instances they do a better job than we would, because they're trained for it."

Perhaps two self-interested reasons also explain why sworn officers are motivated to support civilianization: The department makes clear that the PSO does not threaten the status of the sworn policeman. Both PSOs and sworn police recognize that the higher-status job is the patrolman's. The department defines the policeman as the professional and the PSO as the paraprofessional. Just as the duties of M.D.s and paramedics overlap, so do the duties of the patrolman and PSO, but everybody recognizes the patrolman's higher rank. Second, just as M.D.s earn more than nurses, sworn cops take home fatter paychecks than PSOs.

Some of the PSOs see their job as a stepping stone to becoming sworn police. Gracie Hernandez is an outstanding but not a typical PSO. She was recruited to do clerical work in the Santa

Ana P.D. as a high school student, part of a community out-reach program. Quick to learn, enthusiastic, and bilingual, she liked working in departmental headquarters, and people liked her. After graduation she joined the Department as a PSO and worked in a variety of assignments, from communications to crime prevention. She was a traffic accident investigator in 1983, a job for which she received special training. She earned $1,751 per month as a PSO, plus an additional $100 monthly stipend the department pays to all bilingual officers. When PSO Hernandez becomes a sworn officer, she will earn $2,127 per month plus benefits of $984.00. By the time she is twenty-five Gracie Hernandez should be earning more than $30,000 a year, with ten years of police experience behind her.

PSO Janet Misoguchi is single and doesn't want to under-take the responsibilities that go along with the badge and gun. She doesn't look forward to subduing, handcuffing, and arrest-ing recalcitrant suspects. Instead, she prefers to work in com-munity mobilization, as an organizer of Area B.

Community Mobilization

If civilianization is one structural cornerstone of Santa Ana's COP philosophy, community mobilization is another. Each of the four community areas has 150–250 block captains, who may be responsible for thirty or forty neighbors. There were in 1983 approximately 900 block captains. Although the numbers change from day to day, roughly 30,000 Santa Ana residents have signed up to receive information and attend meetings sponsored by the Santa Ana P.D. Block captains are actively in-volved as liaisons, communicating with the Police Department. The result is something quite extraordinary. The Police Depart-ment has not only responded to the community; it has in effect *created* a community— citywide—where formerly none existed. Neighbors who were strangers now know each other. A sociolo-gist who wants to consider the "positive functions" of fear of crime need only look at the Santa Ana team policing experi-ment. Consider that up to 10,000 residents annually participate in a "Menudo cook-off and dance" organized by participants in community-oriented policing programs. This sort of com-munity support is obviously important for social adhesion. It is equally significant for the Police Department. Community support is not simply an abstraction. It is also a grass roots political base, assuring the department a generous portion of the city budget (of which in 1983 it received 30.7 percent).

PSOs contribute the organizational glue for community involvement in the team policing enterprise. They are, in effect, community social workers under a "crime control" rubric. They work closely with block captains and the Board of Directors to schedule the agenda for monthly meetings. They also organize and distribute COP crime warning and crime alert bulletins, as well as area crime resumés; maintain area crime statistics; coordinate residential burglary seminars and home security inspections; recruit and train block captains; maintain a continuing relationship with block captains and community watch members; and attend the meetings of and advise the area executive boards and citywide executive boards. Finally, they help to organize all manner of special community events, from the aforementioned "Menudo cook-off" to track meets, picnics, and Christmas charities. They perform some of the same functions that traditional grass roots political clubs used to provide in the East.

The Santa Ana P.D. produces a lot of information for its residents, a lot of meetings and community activities. The executive boards of each area meet once a month with a PSO and the area commander in attendance. Members of the board usually double as block captains and are among the more committed members of COP. The issues discussed at executive board meetings are scarcely earthshaking, but they can arouse considerable feeling. For example, we attended a meeting where, aside from the usual housekeeping matters, the issue was whether each area should contribute $38.03 toward the purchase of COP jackets for members of the City Council. The executive boards of the other areas thought that would be good for the community and the Police Department. But members of this executive board objected to the contribution partly on grounds that it would be "political" and therefore inappropriate for this civic organization, and partly because of the feeling that the City Council ought to pay for its own jackets.

That cosmic issue aside, of far more interest were the evident warmth and loyalty between the Police Department representatives and the citizens. It is perhaps not surprising that urban residents should respond positively to the attention they receive from ranking police officers and vivacious women who are serving their organization. Perhaps more surprising are the positive feelings of solid, masculine police toward this sort of assignment. Area Commander Lieut. Hugh Mooney says he fights for the positions taken by his area activists as against those in other areas when they sometimes conflict. He also supports his area in Police Department meetings. "This is my area . . . I am their spokesman," he says. "If anybody says anything bad about any of my block captains, I take offense. I support them 100 percent. If I have to argue with them, I do it here, and we work things out. Then, when I do go before my peers and superiors I tell them exactly what my people feel." And he adds, "I represent them. It's their organization. I don't feel the police should dictate to the people who have volunteered their time and effort as to what they should or should not do."

Lieut. Greg Cooper is Area Commander of Area A, possibly the most active community area in the city. Cooper is a member of the executive board which represents captains and lieutenants in negotiations with the city, and also heads the SWAT team. As a former motorcycle cop and for twelve years a cop on the street, he enjoys a reputation for being tough and street-wise. He says he never thought he could stand being an Area Commander, an administrator, a bureaucrat, someone who works at responding to citizens and attending meetings. To his surprise, like other Santa Ana street cops, he finds he enjoys the positive feedback provided by positive and direct citizen contact. "These," he says "have been the best three years of my life in policing."

Arla Crandall might have been typecast by Hollywood—and played by Jill Clayburgh—as an attractive housewife who got tired of crime and decided to do something about it. Her intelligence and warm personality have projected her into a prominent position in Santa Ana. She is president of COP, elected by the membership. Nevertheless, she says that she is fairly typical of those citizens who have signed up in the program. They are middle-class people who own homes or businesses, or live in apartments, and who are delighted with the police crime prevention seminars and the speakers who talk on such topics as driving under the influence, welfare fraud, career criminality and fire prevention. "The PSOs," she says, "deserve enormous credit. They became a part of the community."

Such activities as area board meetings and crime prevention seminars might be thought of a "proactive" community policing. Community-oriented policing can also be *reactive* at the neighborhood level. For instance, a group of neighbors living adjacent to a park report to their PSO that there is an open and accessible public rest room in a community park especially designed for children's play activities. Homosexuals have been using the rest room as a sexual meeting place, and parents are afraid to send their children to the playground. The PSO hears the complaint, learns the details of the offensive activity: "It's a pretty big park and goes back much farther than it appears from the street. People hide in the bushes, then go to the rest room. It's clear that we need to have a foot patrolman walking that park." The PSO arranges with the Area Commander to assign an officer to patrol the area.

Note well the division of labor between the PSO and the sworn officer. By taking and investigating the complaint, the PSO frees the time of sworn officers to work directly in crime control activities. If we consider that as an allocation of resources issue, nearly twice as many sworn officers are freed for direct apprehension activity. A sworn officer might not actually apprehend the offenders in the children's park, but a uniformed presence might deter them from using the park further and would certainly reassure parents and children of the park's safety.

Hispanic Affairs

Officer José Vargas—"V as in Virgin," he says—is the only Hispanic Affairs officer in Orange County. Hispanics are not as likely to join COP area organizations as are middle-class white homeowners. Vargas is a direct liaison with that Hispanic segment of Santa Ana's population. Vargas does not, he points out, serve as a liaison to the Vietnamese. "They talk funny," he says in heavily accented English, as his face breaks into a smile.

Vargas has recently obtained U.S. citizenship but before

that was deported eleven times as an undocumented alien. Vargas is keenly aware of the divisions in Santa Ana's Hispanic community. Most have Mexican backgrounds, but there are also Salvadoran political refugees, Argentinian Jews, and Peruvian Seventh Day Adventists. Vargas estimates that 75 to 80 percent of Santa Ana Hispanics—which simply means Spanish-speakers—were born outside the United States and have problems with the English language. A stocky, brown-skinned, energetic man in his forties, Vargas himself speaks voluble, sometimes broken, and often humorous English. But he is not being funny when he observes that language problems are also cultural and attitudinal. "When a person is speaking his native language, he is thinking in terms of the way law enforcement operates in his native country. That's how come our Mexicans get to seem so peculiar to American police—the Mexicans think they are dealing with Mexican police, and you know what they are like.

"We ask," he continues, "from the Hispanic community that they learn about the laws of the United States. As far as I know we are the only agency that teaches American law to immigrants, not only to Hispanics, but also Vietnamese, Cambodians, Laotians, Maungs, whatever.

"Irene Jones is a Mexican girl who teaches for Catholic Welfare and comes here once a month with interpreters. She'll tell them in English, Okay, here are some American customs and laws you should be aware of. And they'll turn around and interpret in five or six different languages at the same time.

"This department," he says, "believes in active communication. I am so proud to work with the Santa Ana Police Department, because I know of no other agency that goes out of their way—and a correct way—to assist and educate the Hispanic community. I write a column in the leading Spanish newspaper in Southern California, answering questions about law and police practices, and advising people about any new laws that are coming out. Some of the Hispanic community is maybe better informed even than the people who read English language newspapers.

"For instance, I just wrote a column telling people that after New Year's Eve, if you take your little kid out make sure he has a safety belt or some safety device in the car, because after midnight, if he doesn't, you're going to get a ticket.''

Vargas maintains that the Spanish-speaking community in Santa Ana has the best communication with the Police Department in all of California. ''I have roamed all over the state,'' he says, ''and I know.

''At bottom, it all comes down to the Chief's attitude. If you check the records you will find that the Chief comes down very hard on officers who misbehave against citizens. The philosophy of the top man is reflected through the troops, you know. You have to behave and treat people like they should be treated, or else—and let me tell you, 'or else' means a lot coming from this Chief.''

February 5, 1983, was the tenth anniversary of Raymond Davis's tenure as Santa Ana Police Chief. According to Vargas, the department was contacted by Concilio, an umbrella group for perhaps twenty to thirty Hispanic community organizations. Concilio had been originally organized by the Chicago-based activist and community organizer Saul Alinsky, who was never known to be partial to established urban authorities. Concilio was quite unhappy with the Santa Ana P.D. before Davis's arrival, but in the years since it had grown to admire his leadership, and now it was offering to organize a testimonial dinner for him. The dinner took place on February 10, 1983, attended by nearly five hundred people from the Santa Ana Hispanic community.

Ironically, Davis's responsiveness to the Hispanic community has led to a widely publicized conflict with the U.S. Immigration and Naturalization Service. José Vargas had taken photographs of I.N.S. agents questioning people at bus stops and cruising residential neighborhoods in search of illegal aliens. The I.N.S. was appalled that a local police officer would take pictures of Federal agents in the line of duty. But Davis views the I.N.S. roundups as a threat to his department's relations with the community, and he has refused to cooperate in the sweeps. In a city with Santa Ana's large Hispanic population, such searches inevitably involve the questioning of U.S. citizens or lawful residents who merely ''look'' Mexican. Davis told Los Angeles and Orange County reporters that he hoped the INS agents would "get out of town." The story of the conflict became national news.

A spokesman for the I.N.S., Congressional and Public Affairs Director John Belluardo, defended the agency's policies: "Before criticizing the I.N.S., people should ask how many jobs illegal aliens take away from U.S. citizens or lawful permanent residents. They should also ask how much of a drain illegal aliens are on welfare, health care, and comparable funds. How many are being victimized by unscrupulous employers? How many contribute to the crime rate?"

Davis does not deny that illegal immigration is a problem, nor does he refuse to cooperate with the I.N.S. in apprehending smugglers. But he distinguishes between that sort of cooperation, as well as protection of the safety of I.N.S. agents, on the one side, and residential raids and street roundups on the other. The I.N.S. regards that as an insupportable position. "The laws of the land have to be enforced," Belluardo says, "and it's not sufficient for a police chief to opt for selective enforcement."

Is a local law enforcement official legally—and morally—bound to cooperate with a Federal law enforcement agency, regardless of the circumstances, because of the local official's oath to support the Constitution and all laws made in pursuance thereof? That is uncharted legal territory, but, given the realities of police discretion, the answer would seem to depend on the criteria employed by the local police in pursuing selective enforcement policies. Obviously, for example, a local police chief could not enforce curfew ordinances only against blacks or females.

Chief Davis employs cost-benefit criteria. He argues that immigration enforcement within Santa Ana is woefully ineffective in stemming the tide of illegal immigration. "Illegal immigrants should be stopped at the border," he says. He describes local raids as a form of "cosmetic public relations" and contends that they do much less to reduce illegal immigration than they do to undermine his department's effectiveness in dealing with serious crime—robbery, burglary, rape, and murder—affecting all Santa Ana. "After a raid," he says, "our department is swamped with phone calls reporting missing relatives, kidnappings, and so forth. These raids are costly to Santa Ana taxpayers, and they don't accomplish a damn thing as far as illegal immigration is concerned." He further points out that if the Santa Ana P.D. were seen as an accomplice of the I.N.S., undocumented Santa Ana residents—as well as other Spanish-speakers—would not report being victimized, and they would not come forward as crime witnesses.

It is interesting to note that Davis's arguments were persuasive with the two large Southern California newspapers sold in politically conservative Orange County, *The Register* and the *Los Angeles Times*. *The Register* stressed the reality of the Chief's position: "Except for a tiny minority, most of these undocumented workers are not a law enforcement problem—indeed, most of them strive to keep their noses clean and avoid any activity that would attract the attention of the police. . . . It's not a secret that immigration laws are not well enforced; it's probably not going too far to say that they are unenforceable. When ineffective efforts to enforce them become so disruptive of the social fabric as to alarm a thoughtful public official, it seems logical to turn our attention to the laws themselves."[11]

The *Los Angeles Times* joined in: "We don't like neighborhood raids, either. They are, as Santa Ana police contend, too disruptive. It would be far more efficient, practical, and human if the immigration service concentrated its enforcement efforts at the border."[12]

Substations

When we consider how much effort and resources the Santa Ana P.D. has contributed to community relations, it is understandable that the department is reluctant to jeopardize whatever trust it has so carefully honed. In addition to the PSOs and the Hispanic Affairs Officer, the department maintains four police substations, one in each area. The one in the highest-crime area was initiated in 1978. Officer Joe Magnet, supervisor of the substation, has been with it from the beginning. He attributes the high crime rates to the poverty of the residents: "Well, it's a lower-income area. It's a mixture of just about everything. Predominantly black and Mexican. The income isn't so great. The desire for things that other people have is probably just as great or greater. The only way sometimes they can get it is to steal.''

Magnet explains that the substation was opened primarily to serve crime control needs. ''Because of the extreme high crime rate and the busyness of the officers, we had to do something to take the burden off the shoulders of the patrolmen. They were spending a lot of time responding to insignificant calls and doing a lot of paper work, which prevented them from performing their patrol functions involving heavier crime.''

By having a substation available, citizens could more conveniently drop in and ''register their complaints and file their little reports for insurance purposes or whatever. A field officer would not have to be dispatched to their home. Besides, I had the time to sit here and talk to them about their particular problem. If I couldn't handle it here, I would refer them to our experts or specialized subdivisions or some other public agency. Many times it would turn out to be a civil matter.''

The substation also provides a convenience for field officers. Magnet continues: ''The officers in the field really appreciate it. Many times when they had to pick up a juvenile shoplifter, instead of having to sit with him until the parents came, they'd bring him here. I'd talk with him until the parents came. In the meantime the officers would be relieved to go back out in the field and do their own things.''

The substation also doubles as a community center. In another area, the community center doubles as a substation. In this community-oriented Police Department, the distinction makes little or no difference. Block captain meetings are held in substations. PSOs show films on safety and drug-education films. Helen Peralta is a soft-spoken social worker who runs the predominantly Hispanic Delhi Community Center. A block captain and a member of the area's executive board, she endorses the work the police—especially the PSOs—are doing in the community. Several of the PSOs grew up in the neighborhood, know the local families. Ms. Peralta says there used to be a lot of kids who didn't like cops, but now there are only a few. ''But,'' she adds, ''we're getting to them . . . we try to get to the little ones before they get up to fifteen or sixteen years and then you can't get to them.''

She is delighted, even amazed at community support for the COP program. ''There was just a few when we started and now you have a lot of people interested. We have 176 block captains and about five times as many people involved.''

Yet the residents of this area are predominantly poor. Many are undocumented aliens. Still, crime has declined significantly with the introduction of the COP program, Ms. Peralta says. She attributes reduction in crime to reduction in fear of criminals: "People are reporting the crimes, when at first they wouldn't report the crimes. . . . They were afraid. They would be robbed at gunpoint and they would be threatened. They wouldn't dare. They just wouldn't do it, but now they are doing it. Now they come in and report whatever they can. If they see a suspicious car, if they see an abandoned car, they are calling it in. We used to see abandoned cars all over the place. We don't any more. This community watch has done a fantastic job in this area.''

Burglary is a widespread crime here among poor people. Often the burglers are drug addicts, stealing from other poor people. Officer Joe Magnet is not unsympathetic, however. He says there isn't enough manpower to keep up with it. "For every two that we put away,'' he says, "maybe ten will take their place. That's why this center is so beneficial. People out there know who is dealing in drugs, but they feel uncomfortable taking the information to the main station, so they'll come here and talk about it. They won't be afraid of being turned in or being identified to the neighbors as to who gave us the information.

"Also, if someone is in trouble, they can come here and talk to me about it. I'll put them in touch with the proper person regardless of whether they have marks on their arms. If someone genuinely wants to straighten out, this is the place where they can come and talk to us. We won't just lock them up and let the courts take care of it.''

The Santa Ana residential substation seems to offer considerable advantage as a crime control institution. Combined with an active COP program, it is the logical extension of the team policing concept. As we have seen, there is more to the substation than some vague notion of "community relations." On the contrary, two quite distinct crime control benefits flow from the substation. First, its presence affirms the value of an orderly community. At the same time, it performs a second function. By repeatedly defining itself as a "service" agency, the Po-

lice Department appears to be subordinating its authority to
community values. In fact, it turns out that there is little, if any,
difference between the underlying values of most of the residents and those of the Police Department. Helen Peralta offers
a short and pointed expression of those values: "Nobody, it
seems, likes to be ripped off," she says. When the P.D. acts out
a service role, it facilitates expression of values affirming the integrity of persons and property rather than values that challenge authority. The tangible expression of property protective
values aids crime control activities in ways that are both essential and familiar to all policemen. Similarly, citizens—and, importantly in Santa Ana, non-citizens—who have a positive relationship with the police department are more likely to report
crime. Thus, police are channeled into more effective enforcement activities.

Downtown Renewal

Of the four areas of the city, downtown was most important for
demonstrating the success of Raymond Davis's theories. The
downtown area had been prosperous during and after World
War II. As the county seat Santa Ana attracted the larger retail
establishments and drew customers from surrounding and
booming towns in Orange County. Business declined as those
towns themselves began to develop shopping centers and facilities. Besides, Santa Ana was older than its surrounding towns,
and age has its disadvantages. Its retail facilities seemed more
dated and less attractive to Orange County residents. Moreover, as the suburban towns became more inviting, Santa Ana's
middle-class white residents began to migrate to them. By the
time Ray Davis took over, nearly half of Santa Ana's population
was nonwhite, mainly Hispanic and mainly low-income.
    Being a county seat offers certain benefits to a city. It brings
government business resulting in construction, jobs, contracts,
and economic growth. It can also have unwelcome side effects.
One is the presence in Santa Ana of the Orange County jail, a
well-run but overcrowded facility that houses two thousand
prisoners. Jails are relatively short-term incarcerative places,
with lots of turnover. On an average day 150 to 200 prisoners

from all over Orange County are released into the streets of Santa Ana.

Drunks posed even more of a percentage of the released population during the 1970s. According to both police and businessmen interviewed, Santa Ana had become a favorite stopping place for itinerant street inebriates. Judges tended to hand out relatively short sentences for drunkenness-related offenses, and the downtown area was turning into a Skid Row. When drunks were released from jail, they would wander downtown and become part of the street scene. There were also several halfway houses, a mission, and three blood banks in the vicinity of the jail and the downtown business community. It became, said one businessman, "a daily routine to pick up the wine bottles and beer bottles that the drunks left behind the night before."

Drunks rarely threaten public safety—they do not usually commit armed robbery, rape, or murder—but they do pose public order problems. Drunks loiter and sleep in front of stores, urinate in alleys, panhandle, and otherwise annoy the sort of person who might be interested in purchasing a meal, a pair of shoes, or a floor lamp in downtown Santa Ana. The more the downtown area became a haven for habitual drunks and transient street criminals, the more precipitous its decline.

The habitual drunk may not be taken very seriously by local courts. Judges may feel a certain empathy for the public drunk. Alcohol problems are not unknown to members of the legal profession, even among those sitting on the bench, and it is not very difficult to find a judge empathizing with drunks who would lack similar compassion for shoplifters.

The principal U.S. Supreme Court case on public drunkenness upheld the constitutionality of a Texas conviction for "being found in a state of intoxication in any public place."[13] Four Justices dissented on grounds that "the particular defendant was accused of being in a condition which he had no capacity to change or avoid."[14] In short, drunks are often regarded as sick rather than criminal, and doubtless many are. Municipal court judges in Santa Ana and elsewhere tended to release such offenders within a few hours, usually with only a forfeiture of bail or with credit for time served.

But the police and the downtown merchants came to regard

the just-deserts theory of punishment—drunks are sick and
therefore don't deserve punishment—as inappropriate for
chronic street inebriates. They came to favor other justifica-
tions for punishment, including incapacitation, deterrence, and
hope of rehabilitation. The just-deserts theory, they argued, resulted in the reappearance of the drunk and the encouragement
of others. Raymond Davis says that parts of downtown Santa
Ana were beginning to resemble a hobo jungle. His idea of
"community" did not extend to drunks, especially to transients. He encouraged judges to impose substantial sentences,
partly to deter transients who thought Santa Ana might be soft
on drunks, and partly to rehabilitate drunks—to the extent that
a long period of drying out might help in that process. Mainly,
he wanted to rid downtown of its drunks.

The Police Department enlisted local businessmen to put
pressure on the courts. Public meetings were called to discuss
the problem, attended by judges, police, the District Attorney,
and various citizens groups concerned with the image and realities of downtown Santa Ana. The Police Department established a case-tracking system to review the disposition of convictions for drunkenness-related offenses. Local judges became
sympathetic to the business establishment's problems and modi-
fied their sentencing assumptions and practices. As a result, according to Capt. Paul M. Walters: "Within a nine-month
period, there was a reduction in public offenses of over 70 percent. Between January and September 1980 every long-time
vagrant familiar to area shopkeepers was either in jail or gone.
The transients and drunks were rapidly disappearing. Santa
Ana was no longer a haven."[15]

The Downtown Substation

The success of the Skid Row cleanup was only partly attributable to case-tracking and public meetings with judges. Another
part could be traced to the opening of a downtown police substation in February 1984. The Santa Ana Police Department is
housed next to City Hall in the Civic Plaza, which might also be
described as a gigantic parking lot surrounded by large and—to
the first-time visitor's eye—fairly indistinguishable government

buildings. The department headquarters itself is not particularly forbidding; as entrances to police departments go, Santa Ana's is quite pleasant. The front desk is staffed by young, smiling, attractive women—in uniform—some brown-skinned, some black, some white. Nevertheless, there is no mistaking this for anything but a government office. However pleasing it might be made by the people within it, it is concrete and steel and hard to find. It is remote, and it is a bureaucracy. By contrast, a substation is located where people live and work and eat. Even though the substation is only blocks away from City Hall and Police Headquarters, it is symbolically miles away. The downtown substation has since moved, but the original location, where we spent five nights observing, was a former photography studio on a main shopping street. The station is ordinarily staffed by two uniformed female PSOs. The women are bilingual and can answer questions and take complaints from people frequenting the forty blocks of stores, rundown hotels, movie theaters playing mainly Spanish language films, bars, offices, and restaurants that make up the downtown area.

The substation also houses four foot patrol officers during the day who amble down the sidewalks, duck into alleys, walk slowly through the bars and restaurants, and check the hallways of seedy hotels. During 1983 we had also been observing patrolmen out of the Ramparts district station in Los Angeles, next to Watts. We observed a distinct similarity between the seedy hotels in East Los Angeles and those in Santa Ana. Garbage litters the alleys. Cooking and other smells emanate from the rooms. California slums are worse when you can see them up close and smell them.

As night falls, a new team of six patrolmen take over in downtown Santa Ana. The business people leave the area for ranch homes and suburbs. Those who remain, and those who arrive, are overwhelmingly Mexican. At night East Fourth Street is transformed into a "Corso," a customary feature of Spanish life. The quality is almost that of a stage set. Mariachi bands play in the bars. Guitarists and singers emerge and play in the street. Lines between inside and outside, public and private are blurred. Some bar customers are legal residents, some are not, but no attempt is made to check legality of residence. The patrolmen do not ally themselves with the I.N.S. police, the border patrol, often referred to by residents as the "green gestapo."

Foot patrol maximizes police discretion. The citizen (or illegal alien) comes to understand what is considered as crime on these streets. Legislators may make the law, but the foot patrolman defines it. The officers prohibit murder, rape, robbery, theft, and public intoxication. Many customers of Fourth Street bars reside a few miles away in the city's worst slum area, Minnie Street. If a man is seen weaving down the street, he is arrested. I am told that most of the drunk driving in Santa Ana occurs when people leave the Fourth Street bars for their Minnie Street residences.

Foot patrolmen are symbols of authority. As the foot patrolmen walk past, people on the street, mostly under thirty, seem to ignore them. Surely they know the police are there, but people who prefer to be ignored by the police pretend inattention. Young women lounge in front of bars. We are told some are hookers. Santa Ana hookers do not seem to advertise themselves with the audacious clarity of LA's spike-heeled ladies of the night. Santa Ana hookers look almost like high school seniors dressed up, but only a little, for Saturday night. Prostitution is tolerated by the foot patrolmen, but only under certain conditions related to drug use and dealing.

The foot patrolmen are benevolent and paternalistic. The idea of "serving" the people takes on many meanings in practice. People who own or work in businesses are served when drunks are taken off the street. People who loiter on the street are presented with different standards of service. Police develop their own rules as to which street crimes will be enforced, which will not.

"Sugar" is allowed to work on the street. Pretty, petite, dark-haired, and dark-eyed, Sugar dresses in a gray alpaca jacket and jeans. At 5 feet tall, with an unblemished face, she looks years younger than her actual age of twenty-four. She is the mother of four small children. A babysitter cares for them while she works the street. She is bright, articulate, and good at bantering with men. Her "old man" sometimes cares for the kids, but he is now in jail. He is a burglar.

Sugar says that on a good night she can turn fifteen tricks at

$20 apiece. Most nights she averages more than $200. The money is not reported as taxable income. I ask what she does with it, and she smiles coyly. One of the patrolmen fills me in. "She blows most of it on dope, uses five to seven ballons a day." She knows the rules. She says, "Everybody on the street knows the rules. If you work the street loaded (under the influence of drugs or alcohol) you will be arrested."

A young man approaches Sugar while we (the observer and two policemen) are speaking with her. He asks to talk to her privately. They walk away, make an arrangement, and stroll around the corner. We walk a few blocks, turn around, see Sugar and the young man returning. The Anglo patrolman asks him loudly in Spanish so that other bystanders can overhear, "How was it?" The bystanders laugh, the young man blushes. "We don't arrest these people," the officer explains. "These are young men. They work hard and are saving up money to bring their families from Mexico. In the meantime, they're gonna have sex. There just isn't any point in arresting people for having sex."

Clearly, the foot patrolman exercises considerable authority and personal discretion. From the point of view of those who are being policed, the officer's conduct might be perceived as arbitrary, even baronial. Foot patrolmen "own the street" and make the rules for those who spend much time on the streets. Usually the officer's discretion is exercised in the walker's favor. Moreover, Santa Ana officers apparently do not gratuitously harass and certainly do not employ racial or sexist epithets. The norms developed by the patrolmen seem consonant with departmental priorities, which, downtown, are primarily those of the business community. As we have seen, other substations are not as enforcement-oriented as the downtown station. In them, one gets a stronger sense of community participation.

Crime Prevention and Victim Assistance

Hilda Gabelman is a trilingual—Spanish, French, English—Community Service Officer who is a specialist in commercial security. The Santa Ana City Council has passed an ordinance requiring police inspection of all new buildings on the sensible theory that buildings not properly secured will encourage criminals whose apprehension will be costly to taxpayers across the board. Any construction that requires a building permit, conditional use permit, variance, minor exception, or anything of that nature must be approved by the Police Department.

In general, crime prevention rates a very high priority in Santa Ana's COP scheme. The department maintains a crime prevention van, a former library bookmobile, which is taken out about once a week and displayed in shopping centers. Hilda Gableman and other CSOs offer demonstrations on home security in the parking lot and also take the van around to the neighborhoods. If members of the Vietnamese community are to be addressed, a Vietnamese officer will accompany the van. Police and other students of crime—including insurance companies— have long recognized that much property crime occurs as a result of opportunity. By reaching out to the community, the Santa Ana P.D. is able more than most to undercut those opportunities.

The elderly are another population group singled out for special treatment by the Santa Ana Police Department. Part of the job of the elderly assistance detail is to offer crime prevention information to older people. When the department is unsuccessful in preventing crime, it goes out of its way to assist older victims on the assumption that crime has a greater impact when experienced by an older victim than by a younger one. "If a person loses their entire month's salary and say they're seventy-five or eighty years old, they can't get loans, they can't get overtime, they can't get advancements on their paycheck— all things that are available to a twenty-four- or twenty-five-year-old," says Officer Gary Adams, who heads the elderly assistance unit.

There is no set pattern for assisting the elderly. The officer in charge of the elderly assistance unit complained in 1983 about the decline of the economy and budget cuts in programs that were designed for older people, but they do what they can with available resources, will contact the Social Security office to assist the elderly victim in getting the next paycheck, will direct them to senior counseling programs, and so forth. Not surprisingly, older people are active in neighborhood watch programs and are among the Police Department's most vocal and consistent supporters.

CRIME MANAGEMENT

It is hard in Santa Ana to distinguish between community-oriented programs and those directed primarily at managing crime. The two are closely related, and the official goal is an "Integrated Police Service Delivery System." Although it is analytically possible to distinguish between COP programs and crime management, the strengths of the Santa Ana Police Department's crime control programs are largely derived from its philosophy of community-oriented policing.

Technical Reserve

One dramatic example is the development of a special reserve unit composed of technically qualified professional people— accountants, engineers, lawyers, and computer scientists. One of them, Michael Sokolski, a computer scientist and vice president of the SCAN-TRON corporation, provided the department with a SCAN-TRON Optical Mark Reader (OMR). Instead of using traditional handwritten logs of officer activities, officers now record their activities on scoring devices such as those used in school testing. Forms were designed on which officers could simply mark by pencil their daily activities. The OMR converts pencil marks on a special form directly transmitted into a computer. That provides a data base from which to evaluate officer performance.

The department figures that the system saves seventeen officer paperwork hours per month, in addition to enhancing the department's capacity to compare officers on the basis of performance norms provided by the officers themselves. Most important, the department has been able to mobilize and utilize the services of citizens to improve the internal administration of the department itself, an aspect of policing that is often jealously guarded by police administrators.

Uniformed Generalist

The Santa Ana P.D. envisions the patrolman as a "uniformed generalist" enjoying considerable investigative responsibility. The ideals of efficiency and community responsiveness are tied together in the uniformed generalist approach. Under it the patrolman who takes the initial report is encouraged to investigate the crime. The field officer performing the initial investigation classifies each case as having an A, B, or C priority. As any police investigator is aware, probably half of the reported cases are generally considered to be unworkable. There is little or no evidence pointing to a suspect and no way of getting it. Some analysis is done of those cases to see whether geographical or *modus operandi* patterns can be detected. Most such cases are dead ends.

About half the cases include evidence that may lead to a suspect or the stolen property, based on information that can be obtained shortly after the initial investigation. The longer it takes for such information to come to light, the less likely it is to prove valuable. Where there is fresh information with workable leads that can be followed up by the patrol officer, he or she is encouraged to do so. Some kinds of cases require specialized expertise to be investigated (e.g. homicides, missing persons, gang-related), although other police departments also have patrol officers engage in investigation. Under the COP team approach in Santa Ana it makes particular sense for officers to investigate as many crimes as possible. That way, even when the crime isn't solved, contact between the local patrolman and the local resident is enhanced. Santa Ana P.D.'s community-oriented policing philosophy holds that contact between officer and citizen is time well spent, even if the crime isn't solved.

The Gang Detail

The gang detail is another important unit. In 1983 the Santa Ana police counted twenty-seven gangs. Some gang members are white, black, or Vietnamese, but most of the 500 or so gang members in Santa Ana are Mexican Americans who claim a geographic area with boundaries defined by natural and constructed features of the environment, as well as graffiti. Gang members typically wear their colors, sporting jackets or logos. Often the criminal acts of gangs are directed primarily at one another, but innocent bystanders and passersby can become inadvertent victims.

Gangs can intimidate whole neighborhoods. According to Lieut. Reinertson, ''We did a door-to-door survey of neighborhoods where we knew gangs were active. Our results were very interesting. We found out that people who live in little pocket communities where gangs are, live in terror. . . . They didn't call us because they feared word would get out and the gangs would retaliate against them. That's what gangs do, they retaliate.'' The ''gang unit'' doesn't work standard hours. To be a member one must maintain a genuine commitment to obtaining convictions. ''The rules of the game on the street,'' Lieut. Reinertson says, ''were that if you just stonewall it, if you don't say anything, the police will give up, they will go on to something else. But we found that if we simply stayed on the case, interviewed people over and over again, maybe offered a little extra effort to protect witnesses, we could win our cases.''

One of the more interesting enforcement innovations of the gang unit was to use civil abatement proceedings in areas where the gangs hung out. ''We took a printout of every time the police responded. We included the individual crimes, like where a kid was shot off a tricycle when they were aiming at another gang member. We took our information to civil court and got a temporary restraining order against the owner of the property as well as the people who were living there. It kept people from congregating at that area, because if you have such an order you can then arrest people who violate it.''

CONCLUSION

How effective has the Santa Ana Police Department been? Measures of Police Department effectiveness continue to baffle those inside departments as well as those who try to write about them. One measure is the crime rate. Santa Ana P.D. statistics show crime rising less than had been projected between 1970 and 1982. It is possible, however, that overall rise in reported crime rates is attributable to citizen willingness to report having been victimized. Another indicator of Santa Ana success is the willingness of banks to provide loans on residences where they would not have been so willing a decade earlier.

We were not able for this study to undertake anything like a systematic survey of Santa Ana citizens. It would probably be almost impossible to do such a survey anyhow. In a city where thousands of undocumented immigrants reside and where thousands of legal residents live with or next door to undocumented immigrants, survey researchers are probably not going to get pure cooperation.

Nevertheless, a participant observer can sense, by looking, interviewing, and reading the newspapers, how the community feels about the Police Department. During the eighteen days spent observing Santa Ana, this participant observer did not see, hear, or read anything negative about the Santa Ana P.D. That was not true in other cities studied, as will be reported later on.

It seems that insofar as the community of Santa Ana or, rather, the subcommunities within the community—the businessmen, Hispanics, blacks, women, the elderly—are concerned, the unique combination of the values of community orientation and high technology suggest a rare and resounding police success story. By 1983 the Santa Ana P.D. had been the beneficiary of substantial Federal and state grants. It had attracted numerous visits by U.S. and foreign police executives, students of police, and journalists. It was documented by "60 Minutes" as an exemplary police department. Orange County and Los Angeles newspapers have written uniformly positive stories about the Santa Ana P.D. In private interviews LA reporters rated it well above its LA counterpart, especially for innovativeness in community relations. One Philadelphia TV producer heard about the department and planned to visit for a couple of days of shooting film. Instead, he and his crew hung around shooting and interviewing for a couple of weeks. The program's narrator is seen on the resulting videotape commenting, "A lot of communities have baseball teams and then root for those baseball teams. It seems to be that in Santa Ana everybody is rooting for crime prevention."

Everybody agrees that the change in Santa Ana's Police Department is attributable to the policing philosophy and administrative direction of Chief Raymond C. Davis. Davis is unusual, because he has changed so much. When asked directly if he had "kicked ass" as a Fullerton cop, he admitted he had. But when asked what made him change over to the values he now holds, he answered, "You change when you have to change, when conditions call for it."

Not all officers in the department have changed. There is still a small but influential group who, Davis recognizes, would like to "thump heads." The question remains, then, how did Davis succeed in transmitting his values to the majority of police employees. As a captain in another police department asked, "How did he get the clowns on the street to go along with his philosophy?"

First, by *civilianizing* nearly half of the employees, Davis was able to recruit people who could naturally be more sympathetic to a community-oriented policing philosophy.

Second, as new positions opened, Davis *recruited* laterally across the state. In the process Davis found himself in a battle with civil service. For him, however, affirmative action requirements were a blessing, a way to win. He was able to generate separate minority and bilingual lists, under civil service, for lateral transfer. That meant he could recruit people who went along with the program.

Third, he *reorganized* the department so as to create opportunities for bright and energetic officers. Davis, who plays his cards shrewdly, well understood that when you create opportunities, people who are otherwise reluctant will join the effort. Reorganization thus permits a strategy of co-optation: You don't beat the opposition, you reward it for joining the team.

Finally, those who remain recalcitrant go unrewarded. If they misbehave, Davis has no hesitancy in using all his considerable muscle to punish them. He likes to tell the story of the old chief of police who said, "I'd love to be respected by men, but in the absence of respect, fear will do nicely."

All of those strategies have resulted in a ship tightly run, technologically advanced, and unusually sensitive to the local community.

3

DETROIT
No More Nightstick Justice
in Motown

DETROIT IS AN IMPROBABLE PLACE to encounter one of the most exciting attempts at strategic innovation in contemporary American policing. Detroit is a predominantly black city with a bitter history of violent race relations. Blacks and whites fought pitched battles at Belle Isle in 1943, and the black ghetto exploded in fire and looting in July 1967, one of the worst riots in any city during that strife-torn period. John Hersey's brilliant book *The Algiers Motel Incident* laid bare the pain, bigotry, frustration, and agony of relations between police and blacks at that time.[1] The infamous motel where three black men were killed and two white women brutally beaten during an investigation by police was on Woodward Avenue, several blocks north of downtown. The incident and the riots occurred at a time when, as older officers remember, nightstick justice was dealt out on the street by police and when the few black officers were assigned together to a cruiser known in the department as the "coal car." "Sure there was prejudice," one officer told us, "but there was respect too, and that's been lost."

Detroit's curious history is written on its face. Dotted with French names like River Rouge, Belle Isle, and Beaubien Street (pronounced "Beau-be-in"), where police headquarters is located, Detroit has changed in the last twenty years from a white city with a large proportion of blue-collar workers who had migrated from the Deep South to a black city. Not a black ghetto, but a black city. In many neighborhoods, all jobs are held by blacks, from custodian to bank president. Billboards feature black men and women advertising prominent brand names. Martin Luther King, Jr. has given his name to a high school, a park, and a boulevard; Rosa Parks Boulevard has replaced Twelfth Street, which was devastated in the 1967 riots. A police officer laughingly complained of people who say the police single out blacks to arrest. "Who'm I supposed to arrest?" he said, gesturing out the patrol car window at the crowded streets without a single white person in sight. Another officer threw up his hands when the radio dispatcher broadcast a message to be on the lookout for a black male, eighteen years old, wearing a blue T-shirt, levis, and tennis shoes. Apart from the color of the T-shirt, twenty people could be found within two blocks on that warm summer night who fitted the description. Detroit now has a black Mayor, elected in 1974, a black Chief of Police, several black senior command officers, and a black majority on the Board of Police Commissioners.

Race relations remain unstable, because a mosaic of white ethnic neighborhoods, often built around churches, are being gradually squeezed out by blacks. The whites have gradually been pushed into enclaves in the far northeast and northwest, where, incidentally, many of Detroit's white police officers have their homes. An important exception is the Chaldeans. Though to most of us Chaldeans are barely remembered people from the Bible, they exist in greater numbers in Detroit than anywhere outside the Middle East. Clannish and shrewd at business, the Chaldeans own many retail stores throughout Detroit. Angered by repeated armed robberies, several Chaldean merchants took matters into their own hands and shot back. In a short period they killed several would-be robbers who happened to be black. The police department was considering creation of a reaction task force to handle Chaldean–black relations.

Detroit is also a desperately poor city. Unemployment has been running about 20 percent, almost double the national average. One out of every three people is on some form of public

assistance.[2] An enormous billboard advertising an automobile
agency presented this message in large red letters: "We're
happy when you're happy." In smaller letters a line below:
"And your check has cleared." Forty percent of Detroit's
households are headed by women, and median household income is about two-thirds the national average.

After being seared by the flames of social violence of the
1960s, the Detroit Police Department was battered by man-
dated changes throughout the 1970s. In a bitterly contested case
that went to compulsory arbitration, police officers were compelled early in the decade to live within the boundaries of the
city. Then in 1975 a Federal court ordered preferential treatment in hiring for minorities and women. Roughly 80 percent
of every rookie class had to be black and 50 percent female.
Only 20 percent could be white males. That practice was declared unconstitutional by the Supreme Court in 1983 in a suit
supported by the Reagan Administration.[3] The department
was also hard hit by the recession in the automobile industry.
Since 1978 the number of police officers has declined through
layoffs from 5,800 to just under four thousand. Since no new
hiring has occurred since that time, the police force is composed
entirely of veterans.

Crime in Detroit is high by national standards and is increasing. In the early 1980s the rate for serious crime in Detroit
was 50 percent higher than for other urban areas and double the
national average.[4] The murder rate was three times higher than
in other cities. Not for nothing is Detroit called the "murder
capital" of the United States. As police officers ruefully comment, "We're having to fight 1980s crime with 1947 manpower."

Considering the city's social circumstances and its recent
history, one would expect the Police Department to be shell-
shocked, defensive, and unimaginative, shackled to the essen-
tials of traditional police practice. Amazingly, however, the department has deliberately and self-consciously reoriented its
strategic approach to emphasize crime prevention through the
mobilization of the community. Rejecting the view that police
on their own—the heroic thin blue line—can successfully fight
crime, its leaders have argued that the police must seek out the
public in order to involve them in responsible crime prevention.

By forming a partnership with the public before crime occurs, the police sought to demonstrate that security can be improved, even in the inner city, and that fear of crime has been exaggerated. That shift in strategy, many officers believe, has accounted for Detroit's ability to preserve law and order during the city's crippling depression. As one sergeant said, "When manpower is cut, crime prevention becomes more important." "Crime prevention is not a frill," said another. "It is crucial when manpower for traditional services has been cut back." Spoken matter-of-factly, such statements would be heretical in most of the country's police departments, even those that would appear to be freer to innovate than Detroit. Detroit seems to prove the rule that necessity is the mother of invention.

In this chapter we shall examine Detroit's experiment in strategic innovation in four parts: (1) development of the basic program, (2) an operational view of the program in the field, (3) evaluation of the program's effectiveness, and (4) prospects for the future.

THE PROGRAM

The essence of Detroit's plan has been to deemphasize reactive policing and follow-up criminal investigation in favor of intensive community mobilization for self-defense. In effect, police personnel have been disconnected from the emergency 911 radio dispatch system and assigned to work preventively with the public. That philosophy has been implemented in two primary ways.

First, thirty-five officers were formed into a Crime Prevention Section responsible for coordinating citywide crime prevention activities, particularly in designated high-crime "target areas." It was an independent command whose importance was signaled by its placement within the office of the Chief of Police. Physically the Crime Prevention Section was housed in the downtown headquarters building, which also served as a precinct station. The building could have been used as the set for "Hill Street Blues." Though lacking the milling frenzy of "Hill Street," it was old and cavernous, with tiled floors, nar-

row stairways, ancient toilet facilities, and glacially slow eleva-
tors. The large office of the Crime Prevention Section was a
rabbit warren of desks, cabinets, and tables. When we were
there air conditioners were stuffed under desks, awaiting instal-
lation in large, old-fashioned windows that could actually be
moved up and down. The location enjoyed one great advantage: Historic Greektown, where eating was exceptional and
cops were well known, was only one block away. The department maintained foot patrols in the area and briefly experimented with outfitting them in turn-of-the-century uniforms.

The officers of the Crime Prevention Section organized
people into Neighborhood Watch for residences, Business
Watch for commercial establishments, Apartment Watch for
high-rise apartments, and Vertical Watch for office buildings.
Officers inspected premises and recommended ways to increase protection. In some cases security hardware, such as
deadbolt locks and safety catches for windows, was provided at
no charge to qualified people, such as senior citizens and people
on public assistance. Special attention was given the elderly, including arranging for transportation to banks, grocery stores,
and medical facilities. Rosters were compiled of senior citizens
living alone. The seniors were telephoned regularly to check on
their needs, demonstrating, the police hoped, that someone
cared. The Crime Prevention Section conducted programs for
schoolchildren, private security personnel, and people whose
occupations exposed them to street crime, such as meter read-
ers and delivery truck drivers. Visual aids and slide-tape shows
were produced by the section. Finally, a well-organized referral
service was provided for anyone contacting the department
about a noncriminal matter.

Twelve full-time crime prevention officers were also assigned to the city's twelve precinct police stations, serving as
staff to the precinct commanders.

Second, fifty-two mini-stations, devoted exclusively to community mobilization, were established throughout the city.[5]
Each of the city's precincts had at least three, more commonly
four. The mini-stations were organized into an independent
command that reported directly to the Chief.

The mini-stations were like rocks scattered in a very large
pool, their effect felt only in the immediate area. Detroit is a

city of 147 square miles, completely surrounding the municipalities of Highland Park and Hamtramck. One of Detroit's precincts alone covers an area as large as Cleveland, with a population half that of Denver. Laid out like a fan radiating northward from the Detroit River, its spine, as John Hersey called it, is "rod-straight" Woodward Avenue, dividing East and West Detroit. Both precincts and mini-stations are subject to direction from east and west command bases. The city's far-flung boundaries are marked by East and West Eight Mile Road.

Unlike most old, large Eastern American cities, Detroit gives the appearance of having suburban neighborhoods. These are composed almost entirely of one- and two-story detached homes. The skyline is low and green, with a profusion of trees everywhere. The only concentration of tall buildings, apart from a few public housing projects, is the stunning Rennaissance Center downtown, which seems to anchor the city like a spike driven into the earth. Because of the contrast between the soaring downtown and the rest of the city, Detroit belies its size and seems a much smaller place.

A mini-station is a base for an officer assigned permanently to the work of community crime prevention. Mini-station officers don't answer radio calls, though they are equipped with personal radios, and don't patrol beats. Mini-stations encourage walk-in calls for police service, especially filing of reports about crimes, although most requests are then referred to the precincts or a headquarters office.

Until recently the bulk of the mini-station section's 148 officers were not assigned to mini-stations, although they were the unit's most distinctive feature, but to mobile eastside and westwide crime prevention task forces. Those officers were also decoupled from the 911 system. Half their time was spent in organizing neighborhood self-defense, the other half in patrolling, either in traditional marked cars or under cover in surveillance of known offenders or suspicious persons. The undercover officers thought of themselves as headhunters trying to catch perpetrators in the act of committing a crime—"search and destroy," as they said.

Implementation of Detroit's crime prevention program required a significant reallocation of personnel within the department. Though most American police departments have learned

to talk about the importance of crime prevention and community involvement, few have actually committed resources. Detroit, however, did more than talk. A decade ago no Detroit officers specialized in crime prevention, unless one counts a small
headquarters detail that supervised the Police Athletic League.
Sixty percent of the force was in patrol and 10 percent in criminal investigation. By 1983 the proportions had changed: Patrol
declined to 44 percent, crime prevention increased to 5 percent,
and criminal investigation stayed about the same.[6] It would appear that crime prevention grew at the expense of patrol. That
is not the case, however, because in the same period total force
strength declined by almost one-third. But it would be fair to
say that the Detroit Police Department was willing to favor
crime prevention while traditional patrolling, the mainstay of
most police departments, was deemphasized. What is remarkable is that Detroit's field operations changed character during
the past decade despite drastically reduced resources.

The new program was not built in a day. Its inspiration
came from Detroit's first black Mayor, Coleman Young, who
had sharply criticized the Police Department in his election
campaign in 1974. He had singled out the lily-white character
of the force, the low proportion of officers living in the city,
and the controversial Operation STRESS (stop the robberies—
enjoy safe street), in which fourteen blacks had been shot by
undercover officers posing as "marks." He had promised if
elected to establish mini-stations, an idea patterned on Japan's
neighborhood police posts and Britain's village Bobby. Young
was thoroughly committed to making the police, as well as government generally, accountable to the community. One of his
first acts as Mayor was to create a Board of Police Commissioners with supervisory authority over all aspects of police activity.
He also established small neighborhood city halls so that people
could make requests and take care of routine business at decentralized locations.

Coleman Young's election had an immediate impact on the
police department. In 1975 a Community Relations Section of
twenty-seven officers was created within the Administrative
Service Bureau. It was renamed the Crime Analysis/Crime
Prevention Section after William Hart became Chief in 1976,
and it reported directly to him. Hart is the first black Chief of

Police in Detroit's history. He is an urbane, affable man of middle height, with a kind, deeply lined, avuncular face. Hart works in a large, high-ceilinged corner office—not behind the desk, where one expects to find him, but off to the side at a long table. His desk is entirely covered with police memorabilia from his considerable travels throughout the United States and abroad. Besides being Detroit's first black Chief, Hart also enjoys the distinction of being the longest-serving Chief in Detroit's history.

The mini-stations were created initially in 1975 under a grant from the Law Enforcement Assistance Administration. Hart expanded the number of officers assigned to them from sixteen in 1976 up to 102 by late 1977. They were viewed as neighborhood police stations, small-scale versions of precinct stations, manned around the clock and providing every kind of police service. The precinct commanders, who were responsible for them, quickly came to see them as inflexible, costly, fixed beats. The officers and their vehicles were tied to the mini-station; they couldn't be assigned wherever action was heavy. Moreover, mini-station officers had little to do, because walk-in demand for service was small. As one officer remembers: "We'd drive by and the mini-station officers would be sitting on their asses." As a result the precincts dumped expendable personnel into them—"report-writing deadheads," one officer called them—including pregnant females and officers awaiting disciplinary hearings. Many mini-stations were never fully staffed.

The critical moment in the development of Detroit's program came in 1980. Hart and his senior commanders decided that the mini-stations could not do full-range policing. Rather, they were to become fixed bases devoted exclusively to crime prevention. They were to be bridges to the community. In order to accomplish this goal, Hart indicated, a functional division had to be created between enforcers and preventers. The precincts were to enforce; the minis were to prevent. Accordingly, the mini-stations were taken from precinct control and made a unit supervised directly by the Chief. They were not, however, attached to the Crime Prevention Section, as one might have expected. The Crime Prevention Section remained at roughly the same strength it had been in 1977, about thirty-five officers. Chief Hart still hoped in 1983 that the number of minis could be expanded from fifty-four to between 100 and 125.

Larry Holland, a balding, voluble man in his mid-forties, was selected to command the Mini-Station Section. Although appointed in 1977, he wasn't really in charge until the mini-stations were separated from the precincts. That—in terms of organizational politics—was when Holland got his empire. Holland is a cop's cop: energetic, tough, profane, cynical, and shrewd. Offhand in speech and manner, Holland is capable of discussing passionately and articulately the need for a police force involved in nonthreatening ways in the community. Holland combines the ''soft'' vision of policing, based on a thorough knowledge of police research, with the street cop's hard exterior. Maybe that is what is required if rank-and-file police are to be made believers in any new strategy.

In summary, between 1975 and 1980 the Detroit Police Department shifted to a strategy of community-based crime prevention by creating two specialized crime prevention units, by deploying some of this personnel in fixed posts, by separating crime prevention from other line operations, and by diverting substantial resources to it.

FIELD OPERATIONS

What do crime prevention officers actually do in order to promote community self-defense? What practical problems do they encounter? What does community crime prevention look like in practice?

Officers of the Crime Prevention Section work standard eight-hour days, usually from 8 A.M. to 4 P.M., although they frequently reschedule to attend evening or late afternoon meetings when people come home from work. About half the section's personnel support the field officers throughout the city—preparing visual aids, coordinating activities with the precincts, organizing the Chief's monthly crime prevention meetings, evaluating nominations for awards, telephoning senior citizens, or lecturing on specific topics. The other half of the section's staff are assigned to the two ''target areas'' located on the East and West sides. Working out of field offices in those areas, officers go door to door, block by block, offering to make security inspections and enrolling people in the various watches. If people aren't at home, officers leave Courtesy Security Awareness "tickets" that list points of vulnerability—unlocked doors and windows, open garage doors, entrances concealed by shrubbery, bicycles not locked, and accumulated mail or newspapers. Residents are invited to make an appointment for personal security surveys. Responding to one of those, an experienced black crime prevention officer with fourteen years on the force calls at the modest, one-story brick home of a widow, white, about seventy years old. The officer, dressed in green sports jacket, black tie, and dark slacks, takes about thirty minutes inspecting the house inside and out, trying windows and doors, turning lights on and off, and pointing out precautions that might be taken. At the end, he and the woman sit companionably at the dining room table discussing the measures he recommends in his security report. He displays hardware for windows and doors. A copy of the report is left with the woman, very grateful for the advice.

Another crime prevention officer works with an inner-city Southern Baptist mission. In exchange for the use of an office, the officer advises the staff about security and lectures regularly at various meetings of the parishioners. For the most part these are senior citizens living in dilapidated old apartment houses, and on Social Security incomes of about $350 a month. Finding out that locksmiths often exploit those people, the director of the mission and the crime prevention officer recruit fifteen to twenty volunteers from the congregation to install locks free of charge. Two hundred are installed over three years, most of them donated by the city. Senior citizens, often with tears in their eyes, hug the volunteers for providing them with peace of mind. Deadbolt locks are not put wherever requested: In apartment buildings frequented by transients and prostitutes, security hardware may be ripped out and sold.

By the end of 1982 about a third of Detroit's twelve thousand blocks had been organized into crime prevention associations. The department then became concerned with maintaining their activity and interest. Associations were threatened with "decertification" if they did not hold at least one meeting a year.

That seems neither an onerous nor an especially meaningful requirement.

Meetings are the life-blood of crime prevention, and they involve all levels of the police force. Neighborhood meetings are the most common, attended by crime prevention officers and beat personnel from the precincts. They are held in basements, living rooms, apartment house rec rooms, patios, business offices, and backyards. One precinct circulates a trophy among the clubs for highest attendance at regular meetings. In addition, each precinct has a Police–Community Relations Council that meets monthly to review crime trends, propose activities, and discuss police priorities and performance. Also, each month the Chief of Police convenes a citywide meeting of block captains and interested citizens. The department's top brass are required to attend. Lectures and seminars on crime prevention are given, and the Chief present awards for unusual contributions to crime prevention. Each recipient is given a photo of the occasion. Twenty-six people make up a citizen's advisory council that supervises the department's entire crime prevention program. It meets with the Chief every two months. Finally, the Board of Police Commissioners holds open meetings periodically at different locations, with the public invited to attend and to raise matters of local interest.

Detroit's crime prevention program does not treat the public as a passive audience to be mobilized according to a police agenda. The department has the courage to open itself to extensive and often unpredictable interaction with the public. It acts on the premise that effective community self-defense involves the demonstration of genuine reciprocity between police and public, even if that means exposing the police not only to endless meetings but also to unwanted criticism. Community crime prevention in Detroit involves the potential for the exercise of grassroots accountability of the police.

The Crime Prevention Section also supervises the city's citizens' band (CB) radio mobile patrols. There were eighty-five of them in 1983, involving approximately two thousand volunteers. The Section's CB-liaison officer took us to a meeting of the Greenbrier's CB Patrol, just being organized. It was held in the half-finished basement of a one-story house in a middle-class white neighborhood in northeast Detroit. The evening was an uphill battle against the elements. The slide show presented by the crime prevention officer kept being interrupted, because the electrical circuits were overloaded by electric heaters stuck around the basement to keep out the fierce cold of a January night. Peering murkily at one another through a thick haze of cigarette and cigar smoke, we were alternately too hot and too cold. The dark periods were marked by embarrassed curses as the host stumbled to find the fuse box. Despite those odds, the group read out twenty-nine questions for the officer, dealing with such matters as their constitution (required by city ordinance), reimbursement (a token from the city for gas and a few items of equipment used by all), background checks on members (required), training (required and provided by the Police Department), and equipment for cars (decals but no sirens or overhead lights). Food and drink were plentiful, and the enthusiasm of the group contagious. They could hardly wait to get out on the street. The officer had to caution them repeatedly about what they could and could not do. They were told to think of themselves as eyes and ears for the police. They could look and listen but were not to intervene in any situation. Their obligation was not more than that of any other citizen: If action was required, they were to call the police. The prime commandment, repeated over and over by the crime prevention officer, was "Never leave your cars."

Members of the CB patrol agreed to a weekly schedule of patrols, usually in the early hours of the night. The officer apologized that the precincts would only occasionally and haphazardly supply them with information about local crime or "hot sheets" of stolen vehicles. They would not be given lists of wanted persons, although precinct officers sometimes did so privately.

Since CB patrols work in cars marked with emblems, they are considered a deterrent to crime. One mini-station asks a CB patrol to concentrate on shopping centers at Christmas time to discourage muggers. It also gives the patrol the names of suspected youths. The muggings immediately decline. Sometimes CB patrols uncover ongoing criminal activity. One patrol hears that a martial arts studio is dealing drugs, so it informs the precinct, and the place is successfully raided.

Undoubtedly the most distinctive feature of Detroit's new strategy is the fifty-two police mini-stations. A mini-station is a police office whose primary function, in the words of a departmental memorandum, is "to stimulate and improve citizen participation with the police . . . this increased citizen participation to be achieved through crime prevention activities.[7] Specifically, they are directed to document crime in the area; make contact with community leaders and organizations; canvass and organize blocks, businesses, apartments, and public housing units into appropriate "watches"; advise schools; supervise CB patrols; reassure the elderly; and generally serve as a catalyst for any crime prevention initiative. Mini-station officers do not investigate crimes, do not patrol, and do not answer 911 calls, although they provide backup to other officers in an emergency.

We find mini-stations sited in all sorts of premises and in every conceivable kind of neighborhood. While most occupy unused storefront property, four are in ground floor apartments of public housing projects, one in an interior office in the lovely new Youth Recreation Center on Rosa Parks Boulevard, and another is in a small corner room with large plate-glass windows on two sides just across the street from General Motors World Headquarters. At the other end of the scale, one mini-station is smack in the middle of Skid Row, surrounded by bars, pawn shops, and dilapidated hotels used by prostitutes. The cost of premises for all the mini-stations runs to about $100,000 a year. Space for about a fourth of the minis is donated free or at nominal rent.

Mini-stations consist minimally of one room, with a reception table, desk for the assigned officer, telephone, supply cabinet, coffee-making equipment, and a toilet. The toilet poses a problem: should the officers allow anyone to use it? The mini-stations, officers say, are not intended to be thought of as comfort stations. Officers apply a rule of reasonableness, which means they give a hard look at who is asking. One mini-station, however, takes advantage of its ability to supply physical shelter to do crime prevention. It is located at an important transfer point between two bus lines in the inner city. On cold winter days people keep coming in to get warm. The mini-station officer put benches inside, encouraging people to use the station's large front room and to read the piles of crime prevention information. The toilet was not advertised.

Most mini-stations have a distinctly makeshift, down-at-the-heels appearance—linoleum-covered floors, metal folding chairs, scarred desks, sprung swivel chairs, and paint-peeled walls hung with faded notices. A very few are comfortable, even posh, depending on the support of the local community. One even has carpets, a leather couch, and two armchairs, all donated by local businesses. The one adjacent to the General Motors Building is carpeted and air-conditioned, making it a favorite stopping place, on hot days, for patrol officers whose vehicles are air-conditioned only by four windows (as they ruefully say). The mini also serves as a great place for girl watching, since it is located right next to a modernistic vest-pocket park where modish secretaries eat lunch on warm days. In another mini, long and cavernous, the community has constructed a paneled interior office for the officer, complete with ceiling and observation window. A few minis even have television sets.

What a mini-station becomes depends less on circumstances, most officers agree, than on the imagination and drive of the officer. The key problem is to fit crime prevention to the needs of the local community. It doesn't do any good, one officer says, to show people on Skid Row a crime prevention film featuring tract houses in Southern California. Another officer flatly refuses to do security surveys because he knows that people in his area can't afford the gadgets he might recommend. People in poor areas of the city won't hold crime prevention meetings in their homes because they are afraid of being ripped off later. Their neighbors are the very people they fear. Another officer explains how difficult it is to convince residents of a housing project that calls to 911 are anonymous and cannot be traced. Residents are convinced that criminals will know if they've called the police and will retaliate.

Yet some mini-stations clearly do succeed. Officer Bob Adams' mini-station—"Friendly Bob" as his business card rather defiantly says—is used as headquarters for the crime prevention activities of the Warren Street Commercial Association. The association staffs the mini-station with a volunteer, refurnishes it, transfers its files to it, and installs a telephone. The mini is also used for an evening class of retarded adults, for meetings of a local Girl Scout troop, and for coordination by a senior citizens' transport van.

Officer Paul Jackson, who is black, runs the 14-mini-2 on West Grand River located in a pepper-and-salt neighborhood.

When he wants to launch a summer project using teenagers to clean up trash in the streets and weeds in vacant lots—"signs of neglect" that diminish pride in a neighborhood—he gains agreement from the Burger King across the street to contribute 10 percent of its gross sales over three days, provided he can persuade a popular disc jockey to broadcast one day from their location in behalf of the project. Paul Jackson also combines crime prevention education with holidays. He gives candy, donated by local businesses, to children at Halloween and dresses up as Santa Claus and the Easter Bunny for the mini's annual holiday parties. On those occasions he gives short lectures on crime problems and distributes crime prevention pamphlets.

Another mini-station officer awaits approval by the city of a "mini police force" composed of youths eighteen to twenty who, wearing distinctive arm bands, will escort senior citizens depositing welfare and Social Security checks on the first and fifteenth of each month. Officer Bob Dawson, who played safety for the Kansas City Chiefs in the mid-1960s ("Everyone likes a jock."), sets a record for organizing a housing project when he forms an elected executive board for the project's watch committees and opts a local television station to cover the first meeting. The next day twenty-five other project buildings ask to join.

The "Cass Corridor," Detroit's Skid Row, is notorious for prostitution, drug-dealing, alcoholism, and grinding poverty. Even it has a mini-station. The Corridor is an area of cheap hotels, shabby apartments, and boarded-up buildings. Several of its large old homes have been converted into halfway houses for the mentally ill. Neighbors frequently complain about hearing weird screams at night. Pedestrians amble listlessly, their expressions furtive and hangdog. Most of the cars parked on the streets seem abandoned, although every now and then someone drives one away. Ma-and-Pa convenience stores advertise "dream books," the local name for the numbers game. In the liquor stores, which draw crowds even at midnight, counters are completely screened by transparent bulletproof plastic. Money and bottles are exchanged through a rotating panel. On warm evenings noisy groups of craps shooters gather in lighted parking lots, stacked six-packs of beer nearby. Late into the night people lounge outdoors, the men without shirts, the women in baggy house-dresses, sitting on porches, steps, curbs, automobiles, and folding chairs on the sidewalks, quietly talking, smoking, and drinking. During the summer Good Humor men ply the streets, bells jingling cheerfully, many of them still using the old-fashioned tricycle with the ice chest mounted on the front.

This unprepossessing area, nonetheless home to many, is the responsibility of mini-officer Dagmar Lane. Approximately thirty years old, white, and eight years on the force, Officer Lane loves her assignment, because it allows her to do what she calls "creative customized police work." She digs deep into the community in ways that could not have been done from a patrol car. She organizes a business watch and a CB patrol. When several incidents of child molestation occur at a nearby school, she immediately develops a lecture for children on avoiding pedophiles. She is able to pinpoint drug-dealing in neighborhood buildings, triggering raids by precinct personnel. She says that many problems are brought now to her before they became criminal incidents.

In a nearby public housing project, Officer Wyman Turner faces a different challenge: to capture the attention of the residents, 80 percent of whom are over sixty-five and on meager fixed incomes. To get people in one six-story apartment building to a morning crime prevention meeting, he takes the elevator to the top floor and bangs on each door on each floor with his nightstick, announcing, "This is Officer Turner. Do you know that there's a crime prevention meeting at ten o'clock in the laundry room? Bring a chair. We'll wait for you." Eventually fifteen people turn up, all black and only three under sixty-five. In sweltering heat, they listen to the apartment watch captain's presentation on how to use an engraving tool to mark valuables. Officer Turner offers to do a security survey of every apartment. Then he talks about cashing Social Security checks. The best practice, he advises, is to deposit them directly. But don't, he warns, cash them on the day they arrive. Muggers know the schedule and are more likely to victimize them. Wait a day or two, he advises, then do the shopping. Sweat trickling down their lined faces, the people quietly punctuate his presentation with "Yes," "That's right," "We'll do it," as if it were a church meeting.

One old woman complains about the muggings around a check-cashing machine outside a nearby bank. The bank thought it was providing a convenient after-hours service; the residents think they are being set up. The officer tries vainly to interest them in smoke detectors, since fire is a greater danger to them than burglary. The residents counter with complaints about unnamed people in the building who loan out keys to the outside door, thus allowing strangers to roam the halls. Officer Turner ends the meeting with the announcement of a rape prevention film to be shown next week at the mini-station. The rapes in the project are almost all of elderly women.

On the way back to the mini, Turner asks what we think of the meeting. We say it was like spooning water with a sieve. He chuckles.

Turner takes advantage of free lunch programs for both the handicapped and senior citizens to show films on crime prevention. He learned early on, however, that people would leave immediately after dessert, not waiting for the presentation. So he now turns the lights off during the meal and shows the film. He organizes five separate presentations that focus on the problems of his particular clientele: how to put off winos, avoid drug-dealing locations, and be safe using buses.

Some mini-station officers sell crime prevention by contacting crime victims, especially those who have been burglarized. Not only does that provide an opportunity to do a security survey, but it shows sustained concern for the plight of the victim. Rather than taking a report and leaving, usually never to be heard from again, these officers help victims reorder stricken lives. That kind of follow-up is not done systematically in Detroit, however. It depends on individual mini-station officers' getting lists of victims from the precinct stations.

Successful mini-stations create neighborhood networks, as one officer put it, of "enthusiastic busybodies" concerned about crime prevention, ready to help mobilize the public on the mini-station's behalf. Some officers accomplish that by becoming active in local service organizations, such as mental health clinics, community boards of schools, residents' associations in housing projects, and neighborhood councils. They become unofficial security advisers and frequently use the groups' newsletters to publicize information about crime patterns and suggest protection strategies. One mini-station even publishes its own newsletter. In addition to crime information it gives notice of community metings, recipes for seasonal foods, household hints, and even astrological predictions.

Many of the mini-stations have become all-purpose referral agencies. Modern society is bewildering to people who haven't the skills, let alone the money, to complain effectively about city services, obtain medical entitlements, replace stolen Social Security checks, or get legal advice in disputes with landlords. Mini-stations help with those mundane but important problems. Most often mini-station personnel simply refer citizens to the Crime Prevention Section, where referral has systematically been organized. Some minis develop their own local referral networks. One recruits volunteers from among retired business people to assist people in filling out government forms, including income tax returns.

Mini-stations that successfully embed themselves in the life of local communities are called upon to handle situations that would normally fall through the bureaucratic cracks, situations that in some cases could generate serious crime or safety problems. For example, when neighbors complain about a semi-trailer rig regularly parked in a residential street, a mini-station officer arranges for it to be moved to a nearby vacant lot. Later, when a young boy falls off it and breaks his arm, the officer matter-of-factly tells the driver to keep the rig at the terminal.

A crime prevention block captain from a working-class neighborhood of single-family houses talks at a mini-station meeting about a vacant house, recently sold, where heavy auto traffic disturbs neighbors throughout the night. The neighbors suspect the property is being used as a drug house. The mini-station officer agrees with this assessment and alerts narcotics officers. He also calls the realtor and learns that keys to the house had been loaned out but would be returned that day. The block captain is instructed to inform the police if occupancy continues.

Similar suspicions develop in another neighborhood around an owner-occupied house located in midblock. The mini-station officer, told of the problem, finds out from narcotics officers that the suspicions are well founded. Taking advantage of the neighborhood's concern, he immediately organizes a block watch. At the first block meeting 75 percent of the residents sign a petition, which is sent to the offending residence. That is followed by a second meeting, held on the lawn of a house directly across the street. The mini-station officer had assured a large attendance by personally going door to door to announce the meeting. Both he and the beat officer speak at the meeting, after parking their marked patrol cars directly in front of the "drug house." Discussion is lively, accompanied by scowls and accusatory gestures at the house across the street.

Drug-dealing is a constant preoccupation for Detroit police, because it is so pervasive, open, and well organized. In the inner city small crowds gather daily on specific street corners, several in the housing projects, waiting for drug deliveries. Dealing is so flagrant that even uniformed patrol officers in marked cars can make busts. Kids nine and ten years old, who can't be prosecuted as adults, have been organized into Young Boys, Inc., to act as runners. Drugs are even peddled under brand names like "Murder One" and "Rolls Royce," marked with decals on plastic envelops. Deliveries are sometimes apparent even to the casual observer. We saw one delivery made by a sportily dressed young black man, not more than nineteen years old, hung about with gold chains like Mr. T and driving a black Mercedes sedan. His dress and demeanor were a virtual advertisement for his drug-dealing activities.

Mini-station officers in heavy dealing neighborhoods are concerned less with making felony drug arrests than with recapturing the streets for the residents. They know that local residents are frightened of the waiting packs of addicts, who are unpredictably violent when not panhandling or simply nodding and sprawling. We observed the mini-officer patrol the area, letting the dealers and their clients know they are being watched. He is often watched in turn by relays of kids, so that if he leaves the mini-station as a delivery is being made, the cry of "Off the hook, off the hook!" is shouted up the street to alert the dealers. The officer frequently orders the waiting addicts to move on so that they don't obstruct walks to apartment houses. In this way he hopes to reassure residents that somebody with power is keeping order on their behalf.

Mini-station officers also keep friendly watch over people who need reassurance and light supervision. For instance, a retarded forty-five-year-old man with a seamed, perpetually un-shaven face lives with his very elderly mother in an apartment across the street from the mini-station. He pops in and out of the mini-station as he pleases. Sometimes he simply flops down on a chair and says, "Want talk you." Good-natured and un-demanding, he runs errands for the mini and shovels its walk in the wintertime. In this way the mini-officer keeps tabs on the family and offers sympathy and reassurance.

In another neighborhood a twenty-year-old man paces rest-lessly about the mini-station most of one morning, his eyes star-ing fixedly into space. The officer explains to us that he is from a family of fifteen children, ten of whom are still living at home. The father works two and a half jobs. The young man had tried to commit suicide and is now on antidepressant drugs. His drug use explains his condition this morning. Knowing all this, the mini-station officer gives him money to buy orange juice for the officer's breakfast as well as milk to help the man digest the medicine. As it turns out, the youth vomits the milk into the toi-let, but soon calms down, and goes home to take a nap.

Because mini-stations are open twelve hours a day, usually from nine in the morning till nine at night, seven days a week, officers need to recruit civilian volunteers to cover them. Most officers, in fact, with their heavy outside meeting schedules, spend only a small proportion of working time in the mini-station. Volunteers open and close the mini-stations, keep a visi-tors log, sweep and clean, make coffee, take preliminary re-ports of offenses, and issue bike licenses. If they show capacity and inclination, they are trained by officers to type correspon-dence, schedule speaking engagements, undertake simple medi-ations, and organize such ancillary services as van pools or referrals. Officers spend heavy time finding, training, super-vising, and motivating volunteers. There are two sorts: (1) vol-unteers with manifest skills, such as local business people, re-tired professionals, Police Reserves, and Explorer Scouts, and (2) people on public assistance who are required to volunteer under the state's "Community Work Experience Program." The proportion of public assistance "volunteers" varies from mini-station to mini-station, generally depending on the char-acter of the neighborhood. In one inner city slum the mini-station has seven public assistance volunteers out of nine; in a black but middle-class neighborhood there are only three out of fifteen. Public assistance volunteers keep a monthly record of hours served and receive bus tickets for transportation to the minis. Most of the public assistance volunteers are women. Though friendly, they appear dispirited and apathetic—smoking cigarette after cigarette with a slow concentration that suggests it is an important consolation in bleak lives.

Despite what the department says, the amount of unsolicited walk-in work at mini-stations appears small. The department touts figures based on each mini's log, but those report every entry and exit, including those of the mini-station officer and observers such as ourselves. Many logs show less than one genuine visit by a citizen per day. These are usually for bike licenses, some breaking-and-entering reports, and complaints of minor violations. Four times during one week we are told by mini-station officers, "Today is slow. You should have been here last week." This refrain has become a standing joke among observers of the police throughout the country. And it doesn't matter what assignment is being studied. Patrol officers, too, are always busier last week. If police are overburdened in the United States, one can't find out by looking.

The important point is that the work of the mini-station officer does not come to them; it must be created by them. That is why it takes unusual officers to make mini-stations succeed. They have to be committed, self-directing, and able to deal effectively with all sorts of people. Most mini-station officers work odd hours scattered over evenings and weekends. They accumulate a lot of uncompensated overtime. Some even keep in touch with their minis by telephone when they are on vacation, just to see how things are going and to encourage volunteers. One can scarcely imagine a patrol officer doing something like that. Perhaps the mini-station officer's most important trait is the capacity to show concern over and over again for the specific, petty, undramatic problems of ordinary people. That kind of work is not intellectual, glamorous, exciting, or uplifting. But it is serious and important to the people involved. Whether a mini-station works at all depends in large measure on the empathy, patience, and understanding of officers in handling the mundane problems of individual lives.

To acquire officers with the necessary aptitudes, the mini-station command recruits only carefully chosen volunteers. "We want people who've seen the light," Inspector Holland says. Even so, mini-stations have sometimes failed under a succession of officers, until exactly the right person is found. When officers don't work out, they are transferred. This policy engenders problems with the Detroit Police Officers Association, the union of the rank-and-file. It insists that mini-stations are not exempted from the requirement to select among volunteers by seniority, even if, as one senior administrator said, they have had "six citizen complaints against them."

Mini-station officers display a great sense of camaraderie as well as high morale. That undoubtedly grows out of their status as officer volunteers, largely self-taught about running mini-stations. Although mini-station officers are given two weeks of special training, mostly they learn from one another. The brass encourages mini-station "superstars" to visit newcomers and offer them pointers. Help, as one officer said, is only a phone call away. Perhaps more important, the group recognizes that they are mavericks in the department because they share the uncommon belief that proactive crime prevention is more important than reactive patrolling. That commitment often has intense personal meaning for them. Almost without exception, mini-station officers tell of the frustration they felt year after year as patrol officers arriving at scenes of crime with too little, too late. They were sick of cleaning up blood after crimes had occurred. They felt "burnt out," helpless, ineffective, frustrated. As mini-station officers, however, they believe that at last they are helping people *avoid* injury. They are truly preventing crime, doing what people really want the police to do. Some officers say that transferring to mini-stations saved their careers.

Because mini-stations organize people, they develop considerable political clout—as the COP program has experienced in Santa Ana. Not only do they help give voice to the security concerns of local residents, but they assist in representing communities before various public and private authorities, such as zoning boards, developers, and the sanitation and public works departments. As a result, mini-station officers develop the kind

of grassroots connections politicians labor over. Those connections could easily be converted by an ambitious mini-station officer into a personal political career. Some, in fact, have been
approached by political parties to run for office. So far that has
not happened. Nor have local politicians shown resentment
over the representational activities of mini-stations, as one
might expect. Politicians do not appear to see them as invaders
of their own prerogatives. On the contrary, the politicians
sometimes use the mini-stations as allies in improving the quality of life.

Equally interesting is the leverage that mini-stations develop's within the Police Department itself. Through just a
few phone calls to community supporters, adroit mini-station
officers can exert pressure on command officers to approve
mini-station proposals or simply to stay off their backs. That is
playing with fire, and most mini-station officers know it. Senior officers can strike back in dozens of ways. Nonetheless, the
more useful a mini-station becomes to a community, the more
independent it becomes within the Department. Just as mobilization of the community for crime prevention creates opportunities for grassroots accountability, so the development of
mini-station networks changes the top-down nature of police
command. Mini-station policing represents not only a new
strategy, but threatens traditional command practices. Precinct
patrol commanders who are especially preoccupied with coverage and emergency response, tend to view mini-stations as indi-
gestible lumps in the system.

Because mini-stations did not work well when used as small-
scale police stations—subordinated to precinct command—they
were reorganized in 1980. Since then the mini-stations and precincts have operated complementarily: The mini-stations deal
exclusively with crime prevention; the precincts handle
traditional patrol and criminal investigation. But it was obvious
to people in both commands that the precincts and mini-
stations could not go entirely separate ways. Unfortunately, cooperation was haphazard. For example, the mini-stations' detailed knowledge of particular localities was rarely tapped. The
precincts didn't rely on them for criminal intelligence or refer
calls to them for follow-up after initial emergency response.
("Precinct," by the way, is a word almost nobody in the Police

Department can pronounce. The most common variants are "precin," "presink," and "precint.") When talking about mini-stations, one commander says, "They don't tell me what they're doing." Another says, "Shiiit, we don't know they're there." One patrol supervisor can't remember where the four mini-stations in his area are located and asks us to tell him what mini-station officers do with their time. When mini-station command asked patrol inspectors in the precincts to meet with local mini-station officers at least once a month, the precincts begged off, pleading pressure of work. Inspector Holland takes that to be calculated disdain on the part of the precincts: "We're saving their asses and they know it."

Mini officers complain continually that precinct personnel look down on them for not doing "real police work." Mini-station officers feel demeaned by front line patrol officers. They even describe themselves as doing "soft" police work, compared with the "hard" policing of the patrol units. They need to reassure observers that they are real cops, saying over and over, "I was a beat officer." That refrain is, of course, a plea for understanding that they had once done "hard" policing too.

Whatever coordination does occur between the patrol units and the mini-stations appears to result from mini-station initiative. Mini-station officers go out of their way to promote informal contacts—some do it by attending precinct roll calls periodically. Others encourage beat officers to visit their minis by providing free coffee and donuts. A few give keys to the night cars so that patrol officers can rest out of public sight, use the telephones to call girl friends, or write reports at the mini-station's desks. As a result beat officers do sometimes stop by to inquire about particular situations, and mini-station officers offer criminal intelligence to beat cars or detectives. But by and large, such integration of activities rarely happens.

EFFECTIVENESS OF THE DETROIT PROGRAM

Has Detroit's shift of resources from "hard" to "soft" policing worked? Has it made sense to assign police officers, who cost about $50,000 a year when all fringe benefits are included, to mini-stations instead of patrol cars? Are people in Detroit now safer, less fearful, and more cooperative with the police as a result of the crime prevention program?

No one really knows. There has certainly been no dramatic turnaround in criminality. According to official statistics reported in the *Detroit Free Press*, between 1978 and 1983 reported offenses rose 26.9 percent, arrests fell 18.1 percent, and cases cleared by arrest went down 21 percent. Things would seem to have gotten worse, though it could be argued they might have been even more dismal without the new program. Moreover, during the same period the number of police officers employed declined by 27.5 percent.

The only other information about the success of Detroit's crime prevention program comes from three surveys. The Michigan Office of Criminal Justice studied victimization, fear of crime, and attitudes toward the police throughout the state, including a random sample from Detroit, in 1973, 1976, and 1980. The survey showed a rise in the incidence of crime in Detroit, a slight decline in fear of crime, and a decline in regard for the police. The trends are generally the same in Detroit and the rest of Michigan. Maddeningly, the state terminated the studies just as Detroit's program was getting well off the ground. Two studies by the Detroit Police Department show that crime prevention activity probably did reduce crime and reassure the public at least in the short run. In 1979 total crime declined by 58 percent in the target areas (61 percent for burglary), as opposed to 10 percent generally in the control areas (12.6 percent in burglary). A survey of residents before and after introduction of Neighborhood Watch in 1977 showed that fear of crime declined substantially and that participants were not only more active in home security but had more positive interactions with the police.

The amount of activity undertaken by crime prevention personnel has certainly been impressive, work that wouldn't have been done had Detroit followed traditional strategies. In 1982, for example, more than 5,000 residential security surveys and 339 business surveys were conducted. Almost 3,400 crime prevention programs were held, attended by about 215,000 people.

Detroit's strategic innovations attract considerable national and even international attention, putting Detroit very much on the map. Articles have appeared in *Reader's Digest* and *National Geographic*. Many police departments have sent teams of officers to study the mini-station and crime prevention operations. Toronto, for example, decided to create its own mini-stations after extensive observation in Detroit in 1982. The department receives a constant stream of inquiries by phone and letter. That shows, Chief Hart says, that America's many police departments aren't independently reinventing the wheel but are increasingly willing to learn from one another.

None of the statistics marshaled with pride by the Detroit Police Department offers a test of whether the new strategy enhances public safety more than customary practices. On the other hand, none of them shows that investment in community mobilization doesn't work. One could use the same figures given by the *Detroit Free Press* to argue that traditional patrolling also fails. After all, crime prevention is still a relatively small program in relation to patrolling and criminal investigation. Possibly nothing at all that the police have been doing is working. It is the *relative* efficacy of "hard" and "soft" policing that must be tested. Crime prevention might, in fact, be the finger in the dike that holds back an even greater flood of criminality.

Detroit has undertaken one of the most extensive and carefully planned shifts in operational strategy among large American police departments, and under extremely difficult conditions, yet the success of the entire venture has remained unevaluated, forfeiting an opportunity to inform hard-pressed police managers in other places. The reasons for the crippling lack of reflection are all too understandable. Impact studies are costly, and Detroit, already strapped financially, is more concerned with doing than with studying. That attitude could be considered a given in policing. Outside agencies, especially of the Federal government, are essential if natural experiments are to be evaluated. When serious innovations in policing are undertaken, they should provide resources and, if necessary, expertise. In that way the country as a whole could learn from the inventiveness of courageous departments.

THE FUTURE

Although Detroit has the most extensive community crime prevention program of all large American cities, its future is far from assured. Pressure has increased sharply on the police to "do something about crime." In particular, the department has been criticized for lack of a uniformed presence on the streets and for failing to respond adequately to telephone calls for service. That criticism, while not directed explicitly at the new strategy, has worked in favor of a reemphasis of traditional patrolling.

In mid-1983 the *Detroit Free Press* published figures showing that although crime was up 26.9 percent since 1978, hours on patrol decreased 46.6 percent, and police dispatches fell 18.2 percent. During the same period demand for police service, measured by the number of 911 calls, declined only slightly, by approximately 10 percent.[8] Politicians feel such heat and pass it on to the department. The chief complaint seemed to be with dropped "runs," as they were called in Detroit—unanswered calls for police assistance.

It was certainly true, as the newspaper figures indicated, that raw police protection declined since 1979. After all, the number of sworn personnel declined by almost one-third. At the same time the ratio of police officers to population in Detroit was second highest among the country's ten largest cities. Specifically, there is an average of 2.5 police officers for every one thousand people in cities with populations over 250,000. In Detroit there are 3.3 officers per one thousand people. Detroit had suffered a decline in personnel, but from a level considerably higher than comparable cities.

Dissatisfaction with current operations also has grown within the Police Department. Precinct commanders, responsible for answering 911 calls, complain that they simply haven't the bodies to do the job. Officers are overworked, they contend, and morale is falling. The added stress is producing "burnout." Every patrol officer passes on stories about backup that never arrived, refusals to handle dangerous situations alone, and willful disregard of calls for service because of exhaustion.

None of those things happened to officers personally, they all say, but the stories are accepted as fact. Curiously, no one in the department from top to bottom can actually produce figures on the rising number of calls per patrol unit. But that doesn't stop people in patrol from casting covetous eyes on the number of officers doing "soft" policing. The Mini-Station Section has more personnel, department critics say, than any precinct. The Detroit Police Officers Association asks for consolidation of some of the Department's "elite" and "specialized" units, code words for minis and crime prevention. Help must be provided, as they put it, to the "front-line grunts." Crime prevention personnel, too, feel frustrated by the many "special events," such as fireworks shows, ethnic festivals, and athletic events, that diverts them to crowd control.

By the spring of 1983, criticism from all sources was so intense that the department felt it had to respond in concrete ways. It began by reassigning the East Side and West Side mobile crime prevention task forces to uniformed patrol duties in the precincts. At a stroke, crime prevention lost about one-third of its strength. Task force personnel were organized into squads that could be shifted to hard-pressured precincts for short periods. They worked peak hours, seven in the evening until three in the morning. The special patrol task forces remained in a precinct until the number of "runs" per patrol car returned to ten, which was the department's standard for the number that a car could responsibly handle in an eight-hour shift. They immediately produced impressive figures for numbers of calls handled, felony arrests, juveniles detained, personnel investigated, and property recovered. Clearly it seems, there was "work" to be done by additional uniformed patrol officers. That raises the question police analysts have recognized but never measured: How elastic is the supply of police work? That is, how intense must patrol coverage be before diminishing returns set in? As experienced police officers know, there is an almost unlimited number of offenses to be found.

Other experiments were adopted as well. In the late spring of 1983, many personnel were ordered to wear uniforms to and from work, thus creating a more visible police presence. In every unit plans were drawn up for replacing sworn officers with civilian personnel. A civilian earning about $17,000 a year could do the work of a $50,000 police officer (including all fringe benefits). That doesn't mean, of course, that police costs would fall. In order to increase patrol coverage, officers would be reassigned, meaning that the total police budget would rise by the amount of civilianization. Two units were also consolidated—auto theft and organized crime—again leading to reassignment of personnel in patrol's favor. Finally, the department established a telephone crime reporting unit. Many crimes, like burglaries and auto thefts, are discovered long after the criminals have fled. Rather than send patrol cars, police now encouraged victims to file reports by phone. Calls are followed up by an investigating detective. Patrol units can then concentrate on true emergencies, as in confrontational crimes. By August 1983 the telephone crime reporting unit was handling 125 calls a day.

In addition to redeploying its personnel in favor of patrol, the department experimented with several specialized solutions to the dropped runs problem. As one would expect, most dropped runs were matters of very low priority. Interestingly, neither patrol officers nor their supervisors could identify the number of priority categories, let alone what each contained. But they could give examples of low-priority calls, like parking violations, abandoned vehicles, complaints about juveniles playing in the street, and hot-rodding cars and motorcycles. Central dispatch, which was responsible for assigning priorities, said that the dropped runs were primarily nonemergency requests where there was no threat to the safety of a responding officer.

Different precincts tried different things. In two precincts a single car was assigned to handle all low-priority calls throughout the area. Another precinct began broadcasting all low-priority calls to all cars, expecting that cars with nothing to do or nearby on another matter would volunteer. Other precincts assigned all nonurgent calls to a "specialist officer," usually someone without enough to do at precinct headquarters. Usually the calls were sent to the precincts by interoffice mail, which took two or three days. The specialist officers thus arrived a long time after action was needed and expected. In most cases, the reported activity could not be found. Even worse, when complainants could be located, they were furious at the delay. One log we saw showed that officers were searching for incidents four days after they had been reported. While those runs were technically no longer being dropped, they were certainly being muffed.

The upshot was that by 1984, roughly four years after Detroit's crime prevention and mini-station program hit its stride, the Police Department was scrambling to meet the familiar burdens of traditional policing: telephone calls for service and uniformed patrol presence. One way or another, additional personnel were being made available for patrol duties. Though the solution need not have come at the cost of crime prevention and mini-stations, the temptation to draw upon them was irresistible. The precincts naturally coveted reservoirs of manpower whose functions they often did not take the time to understand. "Me first" is a bureaucratic imperative. The union disliked units that fought seniority. Precinct commanders didn't like sharing their turf with another command. So crime prevention was cut back. Few senior officers thought the crime prevention personnel would ever be recaptured from the precincts.

Did that mean the gradual collapse of Detroit's strategic innovation? Chief Hart said emphatically not. The mini-stations would remain and so would the downtown crime prevention unit. Moreover, public reaction to the reassignment of task force personnel was immediate: Are you doing away with mini-stations? The Mayor remained committed to them, as he had been from the very first.

In our view, however, given the pressures for more "hard" policing, it seems unlikely that the crime prevention program will be expanded. Indeed, it has contracted and could be abandoned altogether under other leadership. The community crime prevention program can be successfully defended against its numerous detractors only if unambiguous evidence of its usefulness can be produced. That too is unlikely, unless assistance can be provided from outside the department to underwrite an evaluation effort. The deck is stacked, therefore, against Detroit's unprecedented program. Without convincing evaluation, a remarkable experiment in police innovation is in danger of succumbing to the very pressures it was designed to alleviate. That would be both ironic and tragic.

The Detroit Police Department, like most police forces in the United States, still flies by the seat of its pants. New ideas jostle with old, innovation with tradition, until a strategic plan emerges from the interplay of forces inside and outside the department. Inevitably eclectic, strategy adjusts year by year without any evidence that one thing works better than anything else. Detroit adapted boldly and seriously during the late 1970s, challenging deep-seated police traditions in the most harrowing circumstances. Crime prevention and mini-stations may have been the right plan for the time and place. Perhaps not. We will probably never know. In the meantime all that can be said is that the Detroit initiative shows that radical inventiveness in American policing can occur in the most unlikely places.

4

HOUSTON:
Old Habits Are Changing

ONE BRIGHT SPRING AFTERNOON two Houston patrol cars are
called to a low-rent, predominantly black apartment complex
to locate a man who reported that he had been shot by police
the night before and needed medical treatment. The officers
who respond are grateful for the help of one of the estate's private security guards, a neatly dressed young black man, in
searching for the complainant's apartment. After two anxious
visits to the caller's empty apartment, the officers conclude,
partly on the testimony of the security guard, that the man is a
mental case. As the four officers and the black guard walk back
to the main office, they discuss a series of stickups at nearby
Seven-Eleven stores carried out by a black youth armed with a
shotgun who escaped on a twelve-speed racing bike. One of the
older officers, all of whom are white, says unguardedly, "When
one of them niggers—ah, dopers—gets on a bike, he's gone!"
Though the officer covers himself quicky, everyone hears what
he says, including the black security guard at the back of the
pack. The forgetful officer tries to make awkward amends a
moment later when he holds the office door open and gestures
expansively for the guard to enter ahead of him, lightly patting
him on the back. Outside later the officer laughingly acknowl-

edges his gaffe, saying he'd "just forgot." The sergeant in charge chuckles at the officer as he leaves and says, "Twenty-five-year-old habits die hard, huh?"

The point in telling this story is not that Houston police are unusually racist and callous. Denigrating racial remarks are common throughout the country in many occupations when people are talking informally. What is significant here is that the police themselves perceived that old habits were changing and that a new era had begun in Houston policing. Responsibility for the recognition and the real changes that it reflects can be traced in large part to a single event: the appointment of Lee P. Brown as Chief of Police in 1982. Against very long odds Lee Brown is developing a crisp new vision of what policing in Houston needs to be, a vision that encompasses not only programs but the values that should permeate all police activity. Because of Brown's leadership, the Houston Police Department has become a fascinating case of harnessing moral imperatives to operational plans in a bureaucratic setting. Innovation in Houston has involved the transformation of the climate of action as well as the nuts and bolts of strategy.

That the Houston Police Department was long overdue for change was obvious to almost everyone. The misdeeds of the Houston police had become a scandal of national proportions by the end of the 1970s. The Houston police officer was seen, newspaperman Rick Nelson reported, as "someone who'd bust your head open and ask questions later." Nelson is a former police reporter and author of a lively book, sympathetic to the police, entitled *The Cop Who Wouldn't Quit*, about a controversial murder investigation.[1] One event that brought the department to national attention was the case of Joe Campos Torres, who had been found drowned in a bayou in 1979 after having been taken into police custody. About the same time a teenager named Webster was killed after being struck by a nightstick at the end of a high-speed chase across the city. The pursuing officers swore that Webster had brandished a pistol found beside his body. It was later revealed that the gun was on the inventory of the police property room. A dramatic TV movie was made of the episode. Another teenager was shot to death in similar circumstances shortly afterward, again prompting strong suspicion that police had covered up brutality by planting a gun—a "throwdown," as such weapons are called. No wonder Nelson could write that the "Houston police were branded a bunch of gun-slinging and trigger-happy killers. People were becoming as fearful of the cops as they were of the street thugs."[2] And it was not just brutality that made the police outcasts. The smell of corruption also hung in the air. The most notable case was the conviction of a former Chief of Police, C. M. Lynn, for extortion. His picture no longer appears among the photo portraits of former Chiefs in the corridor outside the Chief's office.

Such was the department that Lee Brown was appointed to command, an appointment that constituted a dramatic double challenge to the entire force. Lee Brown is black, and he became the first black Chief in Houston's history. The appointment was remarkable in another way: Brown was the first black chosen as Chief of Police in a large American city by a white Mayor. The Mayor, by the way, was a woman, Kathy Whitmire. Houston was not a white city slowly tipping toward black domination, like Detroit or Washington, where one might expect a black Chief. It was a solidly white city whose police force reflected that composition. Brown was also a challenge to the department because he was an outsider. He had not risen through the ranks; he was not a Texan; he had not even served elsewhere in Texas. Outside appointments are deeply resented in big-city police departments, because they upset promotion expectations and imply inadequacy in senior commanders. On that ground the two largest police organizations in Houston immediately protested the Brown nomination, although undoubtedly less expressible feelings prompted them.

Contrary to expectation, out of this meeting of unusual man and hostile circumstances a clear and comprehensive vision of policing has emerged in Houston. The Houston Police Department embarked under Brown on a process of radical transformation. We shall now examine what that involved, how it was accomplished, and how effective it has been.

VALUES AND POLICY

One year after Brown became Chief, the Police Department issued a forty-one-page booklet entitled *Plan of Action, 1983.* Lee

Brown's name appeared on the cover as its author. The booklet presented detailed plans for the development of each of the principal branches of the police: field operations, which is what the department calls patrol, investigations, management and administration, and support services. The plan was noteworthy not only for its range and specificity but for the explicit linking of operational plans to values. The Houston program, as the document stated, was designed to create a particular kind of police, police who were committed to particular normative objectives. To ensure that the point was not dismissed as window dressing, Brown issued an "administrative notice" later in the year entitled "Departmental Value Statement." In both publications the department was committed to delivering "its services in a manner that preserves and advances democratic values." That overarching goal was to be achieved through "involving the community in all aspects of policing which directly impact the quality of human life." Reference was repeatedly made to working with "neighborhoods," indicating concern for ethnic and economic diversity. For example, the department promised to deliver "police services in a manner which will best reinforce the strengths of the city's neighborhoods," to allow "public input into the development of those policies which directly impact neighborhood life," and to work "with neighborhoods to understand the true nature of the neighborhood's crime problems and to develop meaningful cooperative strategies which will best deal with those problems." In terms of overall strategy for dealing with crime, the department said it had "a responsibility to react to criminal behavior in a way that emphasizes prevention and is marked by vigorous law enforcement."

Brown believes that policing is more than a set of practices for fighting crime whose success could be measured in terms of crime rates, arrests, and speed of police response. Of course, the police must protect the community. But doing that involves enlisting the active support of the community. That, in turn, requires the police to gain the trust of all sections of the community by continually acting in an exemplary way. In Brown's view policing is more than doing; it is also being fair, honest, candid, and concerned. Policing has to be permeated with moral, and not simply tactical, objectives.

Brown wanted to create a different kind of police. The department would protect people, but in a way of life that nourished them. Officers would have to learn to accept responsibility for displaying appropriate values in all that they did. Brown asked for more than mechanical conformity to the detailed prohibitions of a rule book—which is how most police departments in the United States are managed. Each officer had to be imbued with the department's values so that they could translate them into the reality of life in the unpredictable situations that would be encountered. Management's job was not to make choices for officers; it was to instruct officers about what was expected of them in all situations.

There is tremendous risk in Brown's approach, not only because it is ambitious but because it is easy to dismiss as a public relations gimmick. Constant invocation of values may strike many as too glib. Police officers, like the general public, are often skeptical about people who wear values on their sleeves. While they expect preaching on ceremonial occasions, they aren't accustomed to finding policy directives encumbered with moral commitments. Americans in general react very much like the working-class English boy in grade school who was asked to write a one-sentence description of the police. To the teacher's considerable consternation, he wrote, ''The police are bastards.'' The teacher immediately decided that something had to be done about such a negative attitude. So she arranged with the local police to have the class visit a police station, climb in and out of police cars, visit the radio room, and get to meet officers over cups of tea. Then she again assigned a one-sentence description of the police. Hurriedly leafing through the papers, she found that this time the boy had written, ''The police are clever bastards.''

The close connection between values and policies can be seen most dramatically in the department's recently announced policy on the use of deadly force. The policy was prompted in large measure by the well-publicized events of the late 1970s already mentioned. Change in the use of deadly force came in two waves. In late 1983 the department began to standardize the firearms carried by officers. Although officers were allowed to use almost any caliber of handgun, even automatics, long guns were limited to approved pump-action shotguns. Before that officers had armed themselves with rifles, carbines, shotguns, and even Uzi machine guns. Even though the new rules could hardly be called drastic, many officers resented the change. One even wrote a letter arguing that banning heavy weapons took away the "intimidation factor," which he said was the department's only edge over the criminals in the war against crime.

The second phase came in the summer of 1984 with the publication of rules governing the discharge of firearms by police officers. Once again, Houston officers were not simply given a list of dos and don'ts. They were provided with a moral framework for understanding how deadly force was to be used. Human life was to be considered supremely valuable. Police officers were entrusted with the power to use firearms solely for the purpose of protecting it. As the policy stated, "the use of firearms is never to be considered routine and is permissible only in defense of life, and then only when all other means have been exhausted."

Having provided a context for understanding, eight concrete rules were laid out:

1. Police officers shall not shoot except to protect themselves or another person from imminent death or serious bodily injury.
2. Police officers shall discharge their firearms only when doing so will not endanger innocent persons.
3. Police officers shall not discharge their firearms to threaten or subdue persons whose actions are destructive to property or injurious to themselves but do not represent an imminent threat of death or serious bodily injury to the officer or others.
4. Police officers shall not discharge their firearms to subdue an escaping suspect who presents no immediate threat of death or serious bodily injury.
5. Police officers shall not discharge their weapons at a moving vehicle unless it is absolutely necessary to do so to protect the life of the officer or others.
6. An on-scene supervisor may authorize police officers to discharge their weapons to disable a vehicle only if the continued operation of the vehicle is a direct threat to the life of the officer or others.

7. Police officers shall not fire warning shots.
8. Police officers shall not draw or display their firearms unless there is a threat or probable cause to believe there is a threat to life.

Most of the rules are self-explanatory. Warning shots are prohibited because they may injure bystanders. Vehicles are not to be shot at because if the driver is hit or the vehicle damaged, it may go out of control. Firearms are not to be used to achieve compliance because any use is potentially so dangerous and may cause violence to escalate.

Many police departments in the United States have adopted policies with respect to the use of firearms in the last few years. In enacting its own, the Houston Police Department was aware that research had shown that clearly articulated and rationalized policies did lessen the number of occasions on which deadly force was used and did reduce civilian casualities. As one study concluded, "public criticism, combined with a restrictive written policy and continued administrative pressure, can reduce gun use overall and in questionable situations."[3] Police shootings are not compelled by circumstances; they are matters of judgement. In similar objective conditions related to threat to officers, policy directives can make a difference in firearms use. Early data from Houston support that conclusion. Because the deadly force policy was so thoroughly discussed in the department, its actual publication was almost anticlimatic. So, though the policy wasn't promulgated until March 1984, the number of firearms discharged was down 45 percent during the first six months of 1984 as opposed to the same period in 1983.

Race relations was another policy area where fundamental values had an immediate impact on practice. Brown's appointment itself was, of course, a symbol that behavior toward minorities had to change. It also challenged the minority communities' own abiding suspicion of the police. On both scores Mayor Whitmire's appointment was brilliant as well as courageous.

Houston is a Southern city where racial feelings are frankly expressed. In racial composition it was 61 percent white, 28 percent black, and 18 percent Hispanic, according to the 1980 Census. The Hispanic population is undoubtedly much larger, considering the presence of an unknown number of illegal ali-

ens. Houston exhibits the South's peculiar ambiguity toward
race. Human contacts tend to be warmer across race and class
lines than in the North. That is part of the South's preference
for informality, for an air of laid-back ease, for "down home"
detachment. A "yankee personality," by contrast, is direct, as-
sertive, and too candid. As one black professional woman in
Houston said, Houstonians are more comfortable in the kitchen
than in the dining room. At the same time there are clear limits
to the expression of warmth across race lines. Race prejudice is
predictable at certain points, not hidden behind social dis-
tances, as it is in the North. This has the paradoxical effect of
making blacks more uncertain and more vulnerable in the
North than in the South. In the South, blacks say, at least you
know where you are and how friendly you can be.

Although local cynics say that Houston represents the worst
of two cultures—Southern and frontier—it should not be lightly
dismissed as redneck. Houston has another aspect overlying the
redneck. Many of its inhabitants, especially the legion of mi-
grants from the North, are professional, cosmopolitan, upscale,
and concerned about being progressive. Mayor Whitmire's
election has been attributed by many to a solid coalition of gays
and blacks. The city has a reputation for being where mega-
trends are happening, where people may find jobs, homes, and
opportunity. Like the shoulder patches of police officers that say
"Space City, USA," Houstonians wear technological modernity on their sleeves.

The city's downtown is twenty-first century all the way. Its
showcase skyscrapers, thrusting upward from the flat, tree-
covered plain, are linked underground by air-conditioned tun-
nels, many lined with expensive shops and restaurants. Above
ground, too, wide glass walkways stretching between buildings
make it possible to eat, shop, bank, exercise, drink, and do
business throughout the downtown area without ever setting
foot in Houston's crippling heat and humidity. Houston may be
one of the few large cities where one can play touch football in
the downtown streets at noontime. Joining buildings at first-
floor level, the skyways create an expansive world: more than a
collection of different places, a transition from space used for
one purpose to space used for another. Though accessible to everyone, the posh, sheltered downtown is essentially private, be-

longing to those who work there. People don't come downtown casually to use its impressive facilities. The businesses housed there regulate the skyways, and private security guards close it down promptly at seven in the evening. This futuristic downtown is a classic case of what has been referred to as "mass private property"—public space under private ownership—a late-twentieth-century phenomenon whose impact on policing has not yet been assessed.[4]

In this complex world that defies easy stereotyping, Chief Brown proclaimed a respect for neighborhoods and a willingness to consult with them. His oblique language signaled to Houstonians a commitment to minorities. So far that has meant changing the old "kick ass" approach of the department, especially as it was directed at minorities. Racial disparagement of all sorts has been discouraged. Although changing that kind of behavior has been "like giving birth,"in the words of one sergeant, the corner seems to have been turned. Officers frequently muse about the way it was, either critically or appreciatively. "I don't know if its better to PR 'em like now or get 'em to respect you like ten years ago," one veteran patrolman said. That a change has occurred, however, is no longer in doubt. How deeply it has penetrated remains a question.

The department has been slower to develop programs directed at the particular needs of minority neighborhoods. Officers have a hundred reasons why policing is more difficult in poor, minority areas. They are probably right, but it doesn't follow that nothing can be done. Because the department is predominantly white, its officers don't have the expertise to know what might work. Their lack of understanding, Brown says, has made them uncomfortable trying. The solution so far has been to increase contacts between police and minorities, so that officers could develop more empathy for the world in which minorities live. Commanders, for example, have regularly attended a variety of community meetings. The department established a class in conversational Spanish, one result of which has been to introduce officers to a variety of Hispanic people. Chief Brown has also asked educators at Texas Southern University to help the department develop a program for officers to get to know the culture of the black community, in the sense of how blacks live and think.

Minority recruitment into the Houston Police Department has improved since Brown became Chief, but not dramatically. The force has remained about 77 percent white, 12 percent black, and 11 percent Hispanic. If one compares the proportion of minorities in the police with the proportion in the general population, police recruitment in Houston has a long way to go. Using figures from late 1983, *Law Enforcement News* calculated that Houston had hired 35 percent of the blacks and 49 percent of the Hispanics needed to achieve proportional representation. Among America's fifty largest cities, the best record for hiring blacks proportionately as police officers was achieved by Washington, D.C., at 70 percent of parity. The best record for hiring Hispanics was in Toledo, Ohio, at 120 percent of parity. Among the other cities studied in this book, excluding Santa Ana, Oakland has the best proportional record for blacks and Hispanics together, followed by Denver, then Houston, Detroit, and finally Newark.

Women make up just over 8 percent of the force, up slightly from 1982.

Although only small gains have been made in minority recruitment, including women, affirmative action has been very much in the air—and deeply resented by many white officers. Time and again, officers could be heard complaining that educational standards had plummeted since Brown took over. Officers had all sorts of spurious figures to demonstrate that tests scores for reading comprehension had been lowered to allow virtually illiterate blacks and Hispanics to enter the department. Chief Brown categorically denied that he changed educational standards for recruitment, pointing out that since the mid-1970s the department had been under court order to integrate on the basis of particular procedures. The press, too, he ruefully noted, repeatedly raised the same specter despite all his disclaimers. Fear produces strange logic in people, especially when they feel that qualifications they don't possess will be valued highly. One experienced officer bemoaned the growing inability of young officers, especially minorities, to read and write. A scant half-hour later, however, he complained with equal vigor about the department's growing emphasis on higher education under *Doctor* Lee P. Brown. Whatever the facts might have been, this man felt left out and passed over. With complete lack of self-consciousness, other officers would say, "I'm not prejudiced, but I think people ought to get what they earn, not be given things." "I'm not against anybody because of their color," one officer assured me. But he went on to describe mixed-race areas: "It's a United Nations in there, real turdsville." "Turd" is the favorite term of abuse in the Houston Police Department.

Brown's managerial style in changing the Police Department both programmatically and normatively has been forthright, considered, and participatory. In discussing his managerial objectives, he cited the Peters and Waterman book *In Search of Excellence*, which argues that excellence in business organizations is achieved through participatory management based on commitment to a few general goals. Although deeply committed to certain objectives, he has been cool and thoughtful in his implementation, not depending on emotional fervor or rhetorical flourishes. When developing policies, he consults extensively at all rank levels, soliciting reactions time and again to the various drafts of policy. In the case of the new patrol strategy, called DART, he met with all the department's three hundred sergeants. He met them in groups of thirty for as long as three hours apiece. Brown has made a point of periodically attending roll call on every shift in every police station.

Brown seems to have been accepted by the personnel of the department. For the most part they think him fair and candid. Hostility of the rank-and-file, after the initial upsurge against Brown, has been deflected at the Mayor for freezing salaries for three consecutive years and at some of the civilian experts Brown has brought in as consultants and staff.

Brown is an intellectual as well as an experienced administrator. A tall, large man who wears rimless glasses, he was born in 1938 in California, where he earned four university degrees: a B.A. in criminology, an M.A. in sociology, an M.A. in criminology, and a Ph.D. in criminology, the latter two at the University of California, Berkeley. After serving for eight years in the San Jose police force starting in 1960, he held university appointments at Portland State University and Howard University. Then in 1975 he was named Sheriff and Director of Public Safety for Multnomah County, which encompasses Portland, Oregon. In 1978 he became Commissioner of Public Safety in

Atlanta, Georgia, where he directed the investigation of the ter-
rifying abductions and murders of black children. Decisive and
experienced, Brown is direct in personal conversation. At the
same time he is willing to think out loud and to admit he doesn't
have all the answers. In one conversation he said that police
chiefs need to plan for the year 2000. When we asked how he
did that, he smiled and, opening his hands in a deprecatory
shrug, said simply, ''Think.''

Brown scored a unique triumph in late 1984 when he was
elected sixth vice president of the International Association of
Chiefs of Police by an overwhelming margin. As a result, he will
automatically become IACP president in 1990. Not only was he
the first black to hold that office, he was a "big city" chief in an
organization that had been dominated for years by representatives of small-city and county policing. Brown's election indicated that the IACP might be ready for winds of change to blow
through its conservative corridors.

Brown has the reputation for being a fair but strict discipli-
narian. Reprimands, suspensions, and disciplinary termina-
tions rose sharply during his first year. While Brown's appointment was a message in itself, especially with respect to race
relations, those actions coupled with the public emphasis on
values has let the department know that new standards are being applied.

Because Texas is a right-to-work state, Brown has not had to
negotiate with a union about new policies. A police officer who
even threatens to strike is guilty of a felony, and no one convicted of a felony can be a police officer. That does not mean
Brown didn't have to win the support of the rank-and-file, but
their power was informal rather than statutory. On the other
hand, Brown has had to work through senior officers over
whom he has virtually no control. Promotion in Houston has
been based entirely on performance on written tests. When a
vacancy occurs at any level below that of Chief, the Civil Service Commission notifies people who have served at least two
years in the rank immediately below that an examination for the
position will be held. The individual who comes out at the top
is guaranteed appointment. Theoretically a person could rise
from patrolman to assistant chief in ten years, provided an
opening occurs at the next rank level every two years and the

person is a whiz at taking written examinations. Examinations cover material contained in several designated books. Performance on the job, leadership, and skill are not considered. As a result, the Police Chief in Houston has no control over the membership of his management team. If a vacancy occurs, it is filled without reference to him in any way, and from an increasingly restricted applicant pool, namely those in the rank immediately below. The Chief must make do with whoever is served up, although he may shuffle them about among positions at the same rank. Four assistant commissioners made up Brown's senior command staff in 1984, two of them former Chiefs of Police. J.P. Bales, Director of Field Operations, had been Acting Chief just prior to Brown and had every expectation of being named Chief. To his great credit, he has proved to be one of the most energetic, resourceful, and loyal members of Brown's staff. He is, as we shall see, author of some of the strategic reforms that have been pushed by Brown.

PATROL STRATEGIES

The most significant change in Houston police operations has involved patrol. The innovation goes by the name DART, for Directed Area Responsibility Team. Essentially DART is team policing based on decentralized management and emphasizing community involvement. It began in March 1983 on a one-year experimental basis in District 16, located in the near downtown. Known inexactly as the Third Ward, the district is generally a low-income area, 69 percent black, with a moderately high crime rate. It includes the notorious Cuney Homes public housing project. For the most part yards and vacant lots are unkempt, often littered with old furniture, rusted wheels, parts of cars, and trash of all sorts. People lounge out of doors, especially in the evening, talking, playing games, and furtively drinking out of brown paper bags, even though drinking in public is not against the law. Many of the houses are narrow frame dwellings sagging and tilting in sections on uneven cement blocks. Cars on the street look as if they had been abandoned; many are up on blocks with their wheels removed. Socially, it's "doag eat doag," as one officer said of the environment of drug dealing, hustling, street violence, and killing.

Formulation of the DART idea began under Acting Chief Bales. Chief Brown seized on it as the operational format for professional, self-directed, community-oriented policing. DART provides police services for District 16 through a team of approximately 110 patrol officers, ten detectives, two community relations officers, and ten crime analysis specialists. Those totals include eight supervisors. The evening shift from mid-afternoon until just before midnight has almost twice a many patrol officers as the day shift. Community services officers work generally in the daytime, as do crime analysts. Detectives work all shifts, though fewer late at night. The captain in charge is responsible for providing full-range police services to the area's 67,000 people. He can use the personnel anyway he sees fit. The traditional pattern, still followed in the rest of Houston, is for command to be delegated to five divisional police commands directing patrol officers exclusively. Investigations, community services, and crime analysis are located and commanded at central headquarters. Under DART only a few functions remain with central units, such as the investigation of homicide, forgery, and organized crime.

Not only are districts to operate as integrated teams under DART, involving all the specialists of the department, but patrol officers on each shift and beat are to formulate plans that fit the needs of their area. Those plans, drawn up under the supervision of sergeants, are based on information provided by the crime analysis unit and their own experience on the ground. The experimental district is divided into somewhat smaller beats than before, and to each from two to five patrol cars are assigned on each shift. Officers are required to stay strictly within their beat—"beat integrity"—rather than speeding all over the city wherever they think action is happening. Patrol officers also compile "Beat Books" containing ready reference material on people, places, and problems.

The self-directing team concept is designed to produce "structured" or "directed" patrol rather than the random patrolling whereby officers cruise aimlessly until sent somewhere by the radio dispatcher. Though officers in Houston complain about being overworked, as police officers always do, analysis shows that the average number of calls for service is only three to four per shift. The number of calls to be handled by patrol may be further diminished by creation of a telephone crime-reporting unit. Based on his experience in Atlanta, Chief Brown calculates that 30 percent of all calls for police service can be handled by telephone without the dispatch of a patrol car.

Through DART the department hopes to recapture and focus the uncommitted time of patrol units, which amounts to almost four hours per shift. DART is an explicit attempt to make reactive patrolling more proactive. DART patrol officers are allowed to take themselves out of service, meaning unavailable for radio calls, in order to investigate suspicious circumstances, stake out likely criminal locations, and follow up leads on past crimes. They are also encouraged to do more criminal investigation themselves, using the team's detectives as advisers and keeping in touch with cases throughout their processing. Under DART, therefore, the expectation is that patrolling will become "problem-oriented," allowing police resources on the spot to deal with whatever problems occur based on analysis of local needs.

To be successful this kind of teamwork among patrol officers and specialists requires a radical change in traditional management style. Decisions must be made from the bottom up rather than the top down. The supervisor's job is not to produce conformity with a preordained plan but to help develop a plan out of the insights of the many people doing the work on the street. That is called participatory management, and it is uncommon in police circles. Not only will policing become more purposeful this way, but, it is hoped, officers will develop greater enthusiasm for their work. No longer are they spear-carriers in someone else's drama; they become responsible directors in their own right.

The plans developed by beat personnel are not to be based solely on analysis done by the police themselves. DART calls for involvement of the public encouraged by beat personnel. DART teams are to help the community organize for self-protection and to draw out of them suggestions about things that need police attention. Much of that work falls, naturally, to the community service officers. But beat officers, too, are supposed to use their uncommitted time to develop contacts and to get to know

people instead of driving by impersonally in air-conditioned
shells. In this connection the Houston Police Department is unusually candid about its own capacities: "The implementation
of DART will constitute at least an implied admission that the
ability of the police to 'solve' the crime problem is extremely
limited. . . . Yet there is much the police can do to improve
their relationship with the communities they service and reduce
citizens' feelings of vulnerability and frustration resulting from
fear of crime and lack of confidence in the police."[5] In effect,
the police can do very little on their own. As the research cited
in the first chapter has shown, policing is not done for communities; it is done with them.

The DART system for delivering police services dovetails
with plans for construction of four "command stations" in
which DART teams will be housed and for refurbishing the
downtown headquarters to act as a fifth DART base. By late
1984 Houston had one large, overcrowded police headquarters
and six substations. The substations were not large enough to
house the number of DART teams with their support staffs that
were needed to cover the entire city. Each substation might at
best have accommodated one DART team. The proposed command stations would house three DART teams serving together
populations of approximately 300,000. By the turn of the century planners projected that Houston would need eight to
twelve of those if DART was to become the operational model.
Each command station would be a self-sufficient police station
containing all the facilities DART officers and the involved public might need, including maintenance garages, prisoner holding areas, and public meeting rooms. Branches of the municipal
court would also be housed in them. Only the crime and photo
laboratories would remain at a central location. In this way an
enormous amount of time would be saved for both police and
public, time now spent commuting between far-flung beats and
downtown facilities. The estimated cost of each command station was $20 million at 1983–84 prices. Ground was broken for
the first, in west Houston, in September 1984. A bond election
in the fall of 1984 provided funding for the four new command
stations, thus ensuring the facilities for an expanded DART
program. They are scheduled to be completed by 1990.

Houston is made to order for decentralized policing. It is one
of the largest cities in the country, covering 565 square miles. It

is almost 30 miles from one side of Houston to the other. The population in 1980 was 1.6 million, not counting illegal aliens. It grew by about one-third from 1970 to 1980. By 1980 Houston had 2,867 people per square mile on the average, as against 4,242 in Oakland, 4,452 in Denver, 5,435 in Santa Ana, 8,874 in Detroit, and 11,662 in Newark. To people from the Northeastern part of the United States, Houston doesn't seem like a city at all, except for three widely separated areas where clusters of skyscrapers mark commercial areas. Even in what Houstonians call the "inner city," many streets look like country roads because they don't have sidewalks or curbs and are lined with open fields. "Inner city" has a peculiar meaning in Houston, referring to the area bounded by a freeway loop 9 miles across that circles the core of the city. It is a geographical rather than a sociological characterization.

Houston is a mosaic of place names linked by freeways. The places themselves are large and ill-defined in terms of social character. Houston seems to have no neighborhoods, only mile after mile of houses and isolated shopping centers. If there is a common social reality connecting Houstonians, it is the necessity of driving on the simmering, gridlocked freeway system. Because the city is so extensive, people are funneled into the criss-crossing freeways. Each day hundreds of thousands of people shut themselves alone into air-conditioned cars, turn on the radio or tape deck, and venture into the melee. They would no more walk to their destinations, even if they were nearby, than they would fly. Even when the weather is not hot, Houstonians take it for granted that a person would want a lift rather than walk to places only a few blocks away.

Houstonians hate and dread the freeway system that imprisons them. Not only is it frustrating, it is dangerous. More than three hundred people were killed in motor vehicle accidents during 1982 and 1983, and almost fifty thousand were injured. Houston's traffic fatility rate per capita is one-third higher than Denver's and twice that of Detroit. Houstonians are convinced that the highways are filled with aggressive lunatics, and their fears are fed by stories of minor accidents that have resulted in fights and even shootings between motorists. Texas allows motorists to keep loaded rifles and shotguns in their cars and trucks, although not handguns. Rather plaintively, signs along the freeways admonish people to "drive friendly." The city takes violations of traffic regulations very seriously. The over-the-counter payment for running a red light is $107, for driving without a license $107, for being uninsured $100, and for driving 10 miles in excess of the speed limit $57.

The incidence of crime in Houston in 1982, based on the FBI's seven catagories of serious crime, was slightly higher than New York City's: 9,990 per 100,000 people. Among the nation's twenty largest cities, Houston ranked ninth in serious crime per capita. Detroit was second, just following Boston. Denver, Newark, and Oakland, which are not among the twenty largest cities in population, all have higher crime rates than Houston. Among the cities studied in this book the ranking is as follows based on 1982 data: Detroit, 12,952 serious crimes per 100,000; Oakland, 12,209; Denver, 11,406; Newark, 10,830; Houston, 9,890; and Santa Ana, 9,234. Such figures should be taken with a giant grain of salt. Crime rates in large American cities are doubled or halved with changes in police administration. For example, it strains credulity to believe that in 1982 Philadelphia had only half the crime of Detroit, Newark, Denver, or Houston—but that's what the numbers show. Accepting the figures at face value, Houston had a significant crime problem that was high by national standards. Houstonians certainly thought they had a serious crime problem, and many were ready to take the law into their own hands. Twenty five suspects were shot and killed by private citizens in 1981, seventeen in 1982. The courts found all of those to be justifiable homicides.

The DART strategy has been implemented in the experimental district without additions of personnel. Patrol coverage was more intensive, but that was achieved through reassignment of officers from two-person to one-person patrol cars. Personnel have been assigned to the DART district according to the same criteria applied throughout the city—calls for service in the case of patrol officers, and crime rates in the case of detectives.

The Houston Police Department has been growing steadily in the last few years simply to keep up with population. This has nothing to do with strategic changes. Although the department has been taking in about 560 new officers a year, the net increment has been between 250 and 280. By national standards Houston is underpoliced. In 1983 Houston had 1.9 officers for every thousand persons, up from 1.4 in 1970, as opposed to 2.5 per thousand in comparable cities.[6] Washington, D.C., has a rate of 5.8 officers per 1,000 population, Chicago 4.6, New York 3.3, Los Angeles 2.3, Detroit 3.4, and Denver 2.6. In territorial coverage the contrast is even more dramatic. Houston has six officers per square mile, as against seventy-three in New York, fifty-five in Washington and Chicago, twenty-nine in Detroit, fifteen in Los Angeles, and eleven in Denver. Whether the Houston Police Department will continue to grow depends on economic conditions. Because of a downturn in the economy in the early 1980s, city workers, including police officers, were denied pay raises for three years. In 1983 the city came very close to laying off nonpolice municipal employees. Houston has not yet established a formula for the "authorized strength" of the Police Department but is adding personnel piecemeal and examining results as it goes.

Because Brown believes that patrol is the most vital sector of police operations, he quietly strengthened it relative to other branches. Patrol operations accounted for just over 50 percent of departmental personnel in 1982–83, up from 39 percent before Brown took over. The strength of criminal investigation also rose slightly. The increases in patrol strength came mostly by reassigning people from inside jobs to street work. For example, the number of personnel in support services fell by almost 40 percent. One device for accomplishing that has been civilianization of about three hundred "inside" jobs previously held by sworn officers, such as the supervisor of the police garage, head of the computer center, director of research and planning, and public information officer. Civilianization is also one way in which Brown can "wire around," in the words of a former Chief of Police, the senior commanders whose appointment he cannot control, by putting people of his own choosing in important managerial positions. Unlike Santa Ana, however, the Houston Police Department wasn't making plans to inject civilians into outside police work, such as community organizing or traffic accident investigation. Since some of the jobs affected in Houston were quite cushy, sometimes held by deputy chiefs, grumbling about "fuckin' civilians" was often heard in police headquarters.

DART was not costly, then, in terms of personnel, even though it was labor-intensive. But it was not cost-free either. The biggest additional item was for patrol cars. DART officers did not double up on patrol; each officer had a car. That aggravated an already acute problem: There had not been enough patrol vehicles for existing operations, and district commanders frequently complained that they had to send officers home because vehicles weren't available. In order to meet the problem, which would grow more intense if DART were expanded, Brown decided to eliminate one of the treasured perks of supervisory officers, namely, that they could take their official cars home if they lived within 30 miles of headquarters and did not use them for private errands. Almost 700 cars were involved, including 350 marked cars driven by sergeants. The new policy was implemented gradually. A few patrolmen had been given cars, such as those assigned to the police academy and to special investigations, and those were returned in early 1984. Sergeants were ordered to give up their cars in October. Other ranks would follow, leaving only deputy and assistant chiefs with cars. Departmental planners estimated that the policy would solve the shortfall in patrol vehicles, even under DART.

Another cost was training. Officers assigned to the DART experiment were given two weeks of special training at the police academy in early 1983. Officers subsequently introduced to the DART district, by the way, received no supplemental training. Departmental planners were beginning to think that one week of intensive training might be sufficient in the future when DART was expanded.

Finally, enhanced computer facilities would certainly be necessary to manage and control police operations based entirely on the DART model. Each DART team needs current information about local events and conditions; radio dispatchers need to know the availability of DART units, which could change status on a discretionary basis; and senior commanders need to know what each team and command unit is doing and accomplishing. Accordingly, plans are drawn up for installing a new, upgraded computer system by 1986.

Like many big-city departments, Houston's is well down the road in installing computer terminals in patrol cars so that an officer can immediately identify stolen cars, wanted persons, and persons with criminal records. They can also use the terminals for sending messages to other units without fear of being overheard by people with police-band radios. The terminals increase enormously the amount of relevant information patrol officers have. For example, they can determine before they step out of their cars if the vehicle they have just signaled to a stop is stolen or if its owner, who may be the driver, is wanted in any connection. Officers cruising down the street often idly type in the license plate numbers of cars driving ahead or parked at sleazy motels or private clubs in the faint hope that something interesting will turn up, like hitting a jackpot in a slot machine. The public is generally unaware just how much Big Brother is watching through the new technology.

From the viewpoint of the DART patrol officer working on the street, DART's most salient features have been "beat integrity" and one-person patrol cars. Giving every patrol officer a car and insisting that they all stay within designated beats, officers say, made policing more visible, and they can respond more quickly to calls for service. "It's the extra cover that works, that put the lid on here," said one officer. In fact, response time did fall in the experimental district. Estimates were that the elapsed time between dispatch and arrival was about three minutes on the average in the DART areas, as opposed to about six minutes in the rest of Houston. In the past, patrol cars had roamed all over the city, responding to action wherever it occurred. DART commanders required patrol units to stay within their beat areas unless expressly redirected.

DART patrol officers were relieved to discover that they had "backup" or "cover" when they needed it. Like officers everywhere, they were worried that they would be more at risk patrolling alone, especially at night. Although research elsewhere had shown that the incidence of injuries was not greater for one-person as opposed to two-person patrol cars, a serious injury early in the DART program could have been a severe blow to morale and could have raised resistance to an essential element of the strategy. In fact, the most serious injury occurred during the second year of the program when an officer had his ear almost bitten off in a struggle with a drug dealer. The ear required thirty-seven stitches, and the officer soon returned to work. DART officers monitored the radio frequencies of their beats very carefully and noted locations where colleagues had been called. No matter how trivial the incident seemed, they altered their patrolling to drive by in case the officer unexpectedly needed help. That was part of the reason DART teams seemed to travel in "wolf packs," which they were warned not to do.

Apart from staying within beats, it is doubtful whether DART officers conduct patrol differently from patrol officers anywhere. It doesn't appear, for example, that they are making more than *ad hoc* plans for the use of uncommitted time. "Structured patrol?" one sergeant mused. "It happens very little." Patrol officers appear to do what they always do, patrolling areas where they think crimes will occur or where they can make a good arrest. They cruise the hooker strips, corners where drugs are dealt, convenience stores that have repeatedly been "hijacked," and bars where fights occur. They are guided by their street sense rather than by elaborate crime analysis. Officers seldom interact with members of the crime analysis unit and know of its work largely through the standard circulars of wanted people handed out at roll calls. So structured patrolling actually has little plan to it.

One unexpected problem is that team plans—even when made—don't carry over from one shift to the next. There is simply no mechanism for ensuring continuity. When one shift goes home, the next starts afresh. A few officers did ask for permission to go under cover on their beat at the beginning of the program, but enthusiasm wore off rapidly. "To tell you the honest truth," says one young officer, "DART's no different from regular patrol." And that seems to sum it up for most officers, apart from the fact that more patrol units were around to do the work.

To some extent structured patrol has developed into a special operation in DART. The evening shift has formed what is called a Supportive Response Team, composed of volunteers. The Supportive Response Team does the focused undercover crime prevention work of the entire shift. Several officers have volunteered for the team permanently; others have joined for short periods as part of "job enrichment," which means for the fun of it. The Supportive Response Team concentrates on drug dealing primarily, although it staked out the bus station after a series of street robberies and busted prostitutes when things got dull. Several people in positions to know said that the team sometimes poached outside District 16, violating beat integrity, in order to enhance its record. Though it occasionally works during other time periods on request, it is an evening shift invention. The day and late night shifts have not developed similar units. As a sidenote, team officers were surprised that although they had worked the Third Ward in uniform previously, they were not recognized or their cover blown when they went in plainclothes. They thought there might be two reasons. First, uniforms had obscured their individuality. Cops, like nuns, are faceless, difficult to recognize when they wear civilian clothes. Second, street criminals are not a settled population. They are a transient group that turns over fast.

Since structured patrol remains largely a matter of individual discretion, participant management has never developed either. "If the papers say it's there, I guess it must be," says one cynical veteran. He goes on to argue that patrol operations always had participant management in the sense that they always had fairly close relations with the street sergeants. In that respect DART didn't really change anything.

An important objective of the DART program is to increase patrol officers' knowledge of the local community. "They are supposed," says a lieutenant "to develop a territorial imperative," a more intense identification with what occurs on the beat. They are to assume responsibility for events. Most officers in DART did think they knew people better than before and, conversely, were better known in the community. A few officers even had street names given by local inhabitants, such as Matt Dillon or Mr. Red. DART officers give tersely graphic running accounts of things that had happened at particular places on every street: That's where we busted a fourteen-year-old for selling dope; here's where the whores take their tricks; that house was burned out after a war among dope dealers; we were called to that apartment because a woman had "cut" her husband; that bar was raided last week by the Supportive Response Team; this convenience store has the cleanest toilet in the ward. That kind of knowledge is not, however, unusual among patrol officers, and there is no way to tell if DART officers were in fact better informed than their colleagues elsewhere. They believed they were getting more information from the public about past crimes than before DART. Some of this, they cynically added, might have been due to the Crime Stoppers Program, which paid rewards for information leading to arrest and conviction of suspected offenders. Some ghetto people, they maintained, were living off tips given to the program.

It was also not clear whether increased contacts with the community came from changed activities on the part of the officers or simply from more intense coverage. Chief Brown said that DART would succeed to the extent that it got officers out of their patrol cars and talking to people. If that was happening, it was not dramatically apparent. Officers were invited to attend more community meetings than before, meetings that were organized by the community service officers attached to the team. "DART is just a word," one patrolman noted, for doing what experienced officers have learned to do already—slowing down, watching, talking, and not jumping right back into the car to answer another call. At scenes of incidents officers talked mostly to themselves, as they do everywhere, with the public standing well back. Or they would pull up alongside people and pass the time of day without budging from the front seat. "You workin'?" one asked a black prostitute with a cast on her lower left leg who was sitting against a building, crutches leaning against the wall. "Un huh, have to." Her pimp came over and hunkered down next to the driver's window and tried to appear cooperative in answering questions about a wanted white prostitute who was passing bad checks. Nothing was learned. It was a social occasion that had happened before and would happen again. Some officers joked about needing to put a mechanical hand in the window of the patrol car to take care of the friendly waving.

None of the officers carried the Beat Profile books that had been worked up during the early months of the program. One found a portion of his in the trunk of the patrol car. They knew more from cruising than from the beat books, and they complained that none of the information about people was current enough to be useful. Nor did they carry the cards they were to fill out on informal contacts. "I don't carry any of the DART stuff," one officer admitted candidly.

The work of the community service officers assigned to DART teams appeared to be unrelated to field operations. They did arrange for patrol officers to attend community meetings from time to time, but officers were hard put to think of any useful operation intelligence that the community service officer had relayed to them. ''Blowin' smoke,'' was how their work was characterized. Community service officers were responsible for organizing ''Houstonians on Watch,'' though few of its signs were to be seen anywhere in the Third Ward. Security surveys of premises were not carried out by those specialists but by patrol personnel who had been trained for it. Officers responding to burglaries would offer the service and then notify the appropriate patrol officer.

Close interaction with detectives emerged as one of the most popular aspects of DART from the standpoint of the patrol officer. Convenience was part of it. When DART patrol officers made an arrest, they brought the suspect to the detective office at DART base. There a detective helped them with the often complex paper work, summoning up information about identity and past offenses with the help of a computer terminal. They would jointly assess the evidence, plan the next step in the investigation, pinpoint witnesses, compare *modus operandi* with similar crimes, and even photograph the suspect to facilitate the discovery of witnesses on the street. DART officers didn't have to go to the congested offices of homicide or burglary detectives, which they described as a ''zoo'' where one couldn't even find a place to sit down. It was like trading the precinct station of ''Hill Street Blues'' for a physician's office. Furthermore, patrol officers were not simply numbers standing in line for help. They worked with the same detectives every day, whatever the crime. In that way they developed a sense of joint ownership of cases with detectives. The team concept also allowed patrol officers to remain in contact with cases throughout their disposition. They could find out what had happened, which gave them greater satisfaction, and could answer questions about the case that they might be asked on the street.

It was originally thought that patrol officers might do more of the actual investigation of cases at opening stages. That appears not to have happened, although they are more involved in subsequent investigation because of their constant interaction with the same few detectives.

The Houston Police Department had ambitious plans for evaluating the impact of DART. These involved a survey of public opinion before and after DART was implemented as well as

the collection of information about police activity, such as arrest rates and response time between DART and non-DART areas. Unfortunately "the evaluation fizzled," in Chief Brown's
words, for a variety of reasons, one of them being cost. The bits
of comparative data the department collected on its own activities indicated that DART had worked: Street crime was down,
arrests were up, response time was quicker.

Some of the success of the program may have been due to its
exemplary status. Everyone was aware that DART was a special
project of high priority closely watched by the Chief. Sergeants
and Lieutenants who weren't persuaded of its usefulness transferred out of the district. Patrol officers tended to be young and
very energetic. Several of them, for example, wore black leather
running shoes on patrol. The detectives were hand picked. All
DART officers received two weeks of special training. Even the
kidding that DART officers got at the beginning—"Here come
the real police"—underscored the unusual status of the program.

Despite the lack of systematic evaluation, the Police Department has decided that DART will be the operating mode for delivering police services throughout Houston in the future. "It
just makes sense," said Chief Brown. Accordingly, DART was
expanded to the entire Central Bureau, one of three principal
commands, in early 1985. As the command stations are built,
DART will be expanded again. Barring unforeseen glitches, the
transformation should be complete by the early 1990s.

COMMUNITY POLICE STATIONS

A key element in Brown's strategy was the development of
closer relations between police and public. DART was designed
to encourage that. So too was another device, the storefront or
community police station. When the department applied for a
state grant to fund the DART project, it included money for the
establishment of four "Police Community Stations." These stations were to function in the DART-patrol way, but from fixed
locations. That is, officers in them were to analyze crime patterns, develop proactive patrol plans, compile beat information
books, patrol in one-person cars, and meet citizens informally

to assess their needs. Detectives were not, however, assigned to the community stations, nor were DART personnel required to respond to all dispatches. Instead, they would encourage citizens to bring problems to the community police station and would train civilian staff to cover the station when the officers were working in the field.

The creation of Community Police Stations was an unusual move, considering Houston's vast expanse and low population density. The common wisdom in police circles has been that fixed posts tie down too many people and forfeit mobility. The Houston P.D. was willing to invite that risk in the hope of gaining more intensive interaction with the community, out of which might flow information directing police operations more discriminately.

As it turned out, the DART storefronts dovetailed neatly with one of the "fear reduction" experiments being carried out in Houston by the Washington-based Police Foundation under a grant from the National Institute of Justice. The Police Foundation began year-long experiments in 1983 designed to test the efficiency of several "fear reduction" strategies. The National Institute of Justice chose Newark and Houston as representative "snowbelt" and "sunbelt" cities. Consultants for the Police Foundation worked with police department task forces in each city to select strategies. The experimental strategies chosen by Houston in the spring of 1983, just as DART was getting under way, were the following:

1. Formation of police–citizen teams to organize neighborhoods for crime prevention (CORT, for Community Organizing Response Teams)
2. Telephone callbacks by police officers to victims of crime to check on their welfare and help with problems of adjustment
3. Door-to-door visits by police officers to determine community opinion about needed police activity in the neighborhood
4. Establishment of a storefront police station
5. Circulation of newsletters containing accurate information about local crime and suggestions for protection

The first four strategies were tested in separate areas that had been matched according to socioeconomic criteria. Newsletters were distributed in all areas, because they were such a

useful device for informing the public about each activity. The
Houston Police Department was responsible for implementing
the programs; the Police Foundation provided rigorous scientific evaluation of their impact. The results of the experiments
were published by the Police Foundation in late 1984. We shall
not discuss them here, since our purpose is to describe what
form innovation has taken in Houston under its own auspices.
It is too early to say whether the Houston Police Department
will conclude that it has anything to learn from the Police Foundation's work.

What is significant in terms of the development of Houston's
own strategic plan was that five storefront police stations were
established within months of one another in 1983, one of them
as part of the Police Foundation's "fear reduction" experiment.
Although all storefronts were funded under the DART grant,
they constituted a separate program with its own logic. None of
them, for instance, was put in the DART experimental district.
They were simply another "good idea" that the department
wanted to explore. In particular they were a device for serving
neighborhoods, one of Chief Brown's stated objectives. They
were also a response to public pressure to do something visibly
special. Whereas DART was in a predominantly black ghetto,
the storefronts were distributed more widely through the city,
including one in the Hispanic barrio of East Houston.

In fact, the department didn't really know what to do with
the storefronts. There was no concrete plan, as there had been
for DART, apart from the general notion that they were to combine patrolling with community involvement. District commanders who were not a part of DART in effect got a gift, but
they didn't know what to do with it. The result has been enormous unevenness in performance. Even what they were to be
called remained unsettled. The Police Foundation's "storefront" was called a "Police Community Center." The one in
the Spanish-speaking barrio was called a "Community Service
Center." Another erected a sign identifying it as the "Heights
Service Office," though the stickers distributed to the public
with its phone number referred to it as the "Heights Service
Center." Its own officers call it "the center." Even more con-
fusing, "storefront" was what police officers called the several
police offices that had been attached to multipurpose commu-

nity centers in several parts of Houston, such as Ripley House, back in 1977. Staffed usually by two officers, they linked the clientle of those community services to the police when need arose.

Because three of the new community police stations were placed in the North Shepherd area, they were able to learn from one another and coordinate activities. The Nordling Community Police Station gradually emerged as the flagship of the storefront experiment. There were two reasons: (1) It had more room for experimentation because it was protected by the Fear Reduction Task Force that had been established under the Police Foundation's sponsorship, and (2) it operated under a departmental commitment to let it do its own thing insulated from routine operational pressures. Furthermore, the officer in charge of Nordling was a remarkably dedicated, energetic, and skillful police officer, Robin Kirk, who inspired his brother and sister-in-law, both police officers, to take over the Heights storefront. In fact, storefronts in North Houston were "all in the family," since Robin's uncle—known far and wide as "Unc"— was Nordling's Civilian Coordinator, and his sister was an unpaid volunteer.

All the storefronts except Canal Street's were in vacant stores. "Canal Street" occupied half of a one-story house it shared with a senior citizens' groups. The storefronts were essentially offices, sometimes with several rooms connected front-to-back, with a reception area containing chairs and couches, desks and phones for the officers, filing cabinets, modest kitchen facilities, and a toilet. Reflecting its milieu, Nordling looked like a posh real estate office. It had a room divider, comfortable couches, a large plate-glass window, and fancy office equipment, including a computer terminal. Canal Street, on the other hand, was rundown and had no air-conditioning and a single battered manual typewriter. Except for phones and office supplies, furniture and materials for renovation in all the storefronts were donated by local citizens. The officers themselves fixed up the premises in their spare time.

There was no set schedule for storefront operation. Nordling was open from 9:30 A.M. to 10 P.M. every day except Sunday. The Heights was open from 10 A.M. to 6 P.M. except Sunday. Canal Street was open 10 A.M. to 10 P.M. seven days a week.

Two officers each were assigned to two of the storefronts, Hiram Clark and Canal Street, four officers to each of the other three. Officers worked overlapping shifts singly or in pairs. Unlike Detroit's storefront personnel, Houston's were young in service, generally with less than seven years' experience.

In the larger storefronts, officers spent their time patrolling in standard marked cars. In the Hiram Clark and Canal street storefronts, because only one officer was present most of the time, officers on duty felt obliged to stay in the office. For a while, in fact, Hiram Clark wasn't even provided with a patrol car. Officers admitted that staying in the storefronts all day was deadly dull. They also knew that they were disappointing the public when they refused to leave the office. In the other storefronts, officers generally patrolled in pairs, which was ironic considering that DART had moved to one-person units and most of the storefronts' patrolling was in the daytime. There weren't enough cars for every officer, however, and they didn't want to be seen sitting around all day in air-conditioned offices. Although storefront officers were not required to answer dispatches on their beats, most of them tried to. They wanted to demonstrate to their patrol colleagues that they were pulling their weight. Each storefront beat was also covered by regular patrol units based at the substations.

Storefront patrols concentrated on what the department considered low-priority matters but, as the officers knew, were issues of burning concern to local residents. Patrols did a lot of ticketing of illegally parked cars, arranged for towing of abandoned vehicles, mediated disputes between neighbors, checked up on people living alone, helped to mobilize community pressure informally against disorderly or neglectful people, and assisted in bringing pressure to bear on municipal services to correct problems concerning road safety, health hazards, vacant buildings, and trash disposal.

Houston's storefronts were fairly expensive facilities, not at all like the shoestring operations of Detroit. Not only were several officers permanently assigned to them, but three different types of paid civilians were employed. Each storefront was managed by a Civilian Coordinator, who worked full time and was paid about $1,300 a month. The Civilian Coordinator ran the office itself, supervised the other civilian employees, and did the storefront's crime analysis. Most storefronts also had at least one Community Service Officer, a young person partially trained in police procedures serving an internship in the department. Most of them planned careers in the police. CSOs wore uniforms of white shirts with CSO shoulder patches, black ties, police trousers, and black shoes. CSO in the storefront was a full-time job paying about $1,000 a month. (Civilian CSOs should not be confused with the functional position, also called "community service officer," filled by sworn officers working either for the Community Services Division of the department or assigned to DART teams.) Finally, storefronts employed several Police Aides, who worked twenty hours a week at minimum wages. Police Aides were mostly high school students, many of them young women. A few were enrolled in Houston's High School for Law Enforcement and Criminal Justice, a magnet school for students throughout the system interested in careers in criminal justice. They wore gray and black uniforms with Police Aide patches and silver stars on their shirt fronts.

Storefronts encouraged people to bring problems to them, no matter how trivial or unrelated to crime. During the first year of operation, "walk-in" work varied a great deal from place to place. After the storefronts became established, Nordling and Canal Street were getting ten to twelve walk-ins a day. The Heights had less than ten a day, and Hiram Clark not more than five. The log at Canal Street showed that people came to report crimes, give information about past incidents, ask help in replacing lost keys, report missing children, ask questions about Police Department procedures, and seek advice about obtaining essential papers, such as insurance forms, visas, or ID cards.

The Canal Street storefront had an important advantage in drawing people: All its officers and civilian aides were bilingual in English and Spanish. The storefront solved barrio problems of where to get help in a predominantly English-speaking society. Spanish-speaking people will sometimes wait for days until they see a police car driven by an Hispanic-looking officer before filing a complaint about a crime. The civilian coordinator at Canal Street said she spent most of the time telling people how to obtain documents of one sort or another. For example, a

woman came to complain about a private "immigration service" that promised to help obtain visas for a fee of $700. She
and four other immigrants had paid the money and then waited
for months as nothing happened. The duty officer called
around and found out that the "service" was already being investigated by the city's consumer fraud office. In another instance an elderly woman tearfully reported by telephone that
her grandson had stolen her transistor radio over the weekend.
The officer called the mother and got a promise that the radio
would be returned immediately. No charges were filed, and the
delighted grandmother called back to thank the officer.

The Canal Street storefront was located near Houston's
docks, not far from the ship-turning basin up the channel from
Galveston. The area was filled with cheap wooden homes, some
set on cement blocks, interspersed with unattended lots filled
with trash. Abandoned cars littered the streets, and bums collected along the railway tracks and around vacant buildings.
Roosters could be heard crowing during the day, because many
houses kept chickens. Day laborers waited listlessly in groups
on street corners for someone to drive by and offer a job. The
crime problems centered on sleazy motels used by prostitutes,
unruly bars and cantinas, private drinking clubs, and drug
houses. A few of the better homes had metal grills on their doors
and windows. All business signs and billboard advertisements
were in Spanish. Illegal immigrants could be found everywhere.

Some storefronts actively reached out to the community,
trying to develop permanent patterns of interaction between
police and public. For example, exploiting national publicity
about stolen or missing children, several storefronts undertook
to fingerprint children, providing a copy of the prints to the
parents. Nordling and the Heights sponsored monthly clinics
where people could have their blood pressure checked and individual records kept. Officers made a point of attending meetings of civic clubs, like Rotary and Lions, and giving lectures on
crime prevention at schools and businesses.

Some of the storefronts also held monthly community meetings themselves. The meetings were publicized through fliers
put in shopping bags at local supermarkets. In addition, the civilian staff telephoned every person who had given a name and

address at any past program of the storefront. One of Nordling's community meetings, for example, was held at the Living Word Church, just down the road from the storefront. About seventy-five people attended on a Tuesday evening, mostly middle-aged and dressed informally, as if they'd just gotten up from the dinner table. Amid lilies left over from Easter and under a long banner proclaiming "The Foundation of Love in a Dry and Thirsty Land," Robin Kirk and his colleagues reviewed recent crimes in the area, warned people about a swindle known as a "pigeon drop," and announced forthcoming activities of the storefront. The massive Kirk, who stood 6 feet, 3 inches tall and weighed about 220 pounds, had a deft touch with the people who attended, a talent that is essential in such work. Blond and fair-skinned, he was the personification of the "down home" Texas kind of "boy." With a drawl as big as all outdoors, he invited the people early in the meeting to join him in saying the Pledge of Allegiance. When it was over he said, with moving sincerity, "Didn't that make y'all feel good?" The answer was a soft chorus of, "Yes, yes."

The main event of the evening was a speech by Assistant Chief Bales, who praised the work of the storefront and answered questions from the audience. With abundant thanks to everyone who contributed to the evening, including "the women in the kitchen," the evening concluded with a short prayer by the church's minister. People then stood around for some time drinking fruit punch and eating cookies supplied by a civic club. The tone of the evening was warm, concerned, and practical. It made policing an enterprise carried out by approachable people. Officers in that setting could be perceived as individuals, some so ill-at-ease they had to be coaxed to speak. The meeting also showed the officers that a community is composed of hard-working people who don't necessarily resent the police—people who have vague but real fears about crime but are willing to do what they can to make the neighborhood safer.

By the end of the experimental year the storefronts were beginning to receive information that was useful to the police. For example, officers at Nordling heard that teenagers were cutting school and hanging around game parlors where drugs were being sold. The officers organized a bust and got the local police substation to send officers to round up truants. The merchants near the game parlors were quite relieved when the idle teenagers went back to school. Most storefronts gave some attention to truancy, since the Houston Independent School District had almost no staff for the purpose. After a string of daylight burglaries committed by a group of armed men who shot off their weapons to terrorize people, Nordling quickly organized the community to watch for suspicious persons and solicited businesses to offer rewards. The community response was overwhelming and contributed to the capture of twelve suspects.

Houston's storefronts grew like Topsy, and what they will become is not at all clear. Some divisional captains wanted to put detectives into them to take advantage of the contacts with the community. Such a move would make the storefronts more like DART teams, only at fixed locations. It might also tilt the orientation of the storefronts away from crime prevention. An even bigger change occurred at the Canal Street storefront. In September 1984 it was moved from its old location to a new police substation several blocks away. It was just like one of the city's existing police substations. It was open around the clock, supervised by a duty sergeant, held roll calls for local beat officers, and had a computer terminal linked to headquarters. The storefront became a part of it—Civilian Coordinator, Police Aides, and all.

By late 1984 three distinct kinds of police–community facilities in Houston were all loosely referred to as "storefronts": the five spare offices doing liaison work out of multipurpose community centers and run by the department's Community Services Division; the four new police–community stations combining patrolling with community development and run by Field Operations commanders; and one community–police office attached to a scaled-down police substation that provided outreach to the community. Recognizing that some attempt at standardization was needed, the department created a task force to develop a "concept of storefronts," as Chief Brown put it.

That was especially important because the Community Services Division was being disbanded as a result of projected decentralization. In the past the division had done most of the department's community crime prevention, including organizing

"Houstonians on the March" in various neighborhoods. The department had never pushed the program very hard, allocating only five officers to it for the whole city. Chief Brown now planned to send community service officers to each DART team, as well as existing police substations, keeping only some support personnel and the crime-stoppers program at headquarters. The rationale behind that was that patrol operations and community outreach needed to be more closely integrated. Patrol stood to benefit by more extensive contacts with the public, and local communities needed to develop closer relations with officers working in the area rather than a remote headquarters staff.

The future of "storefronts" in Houston is problematic. The public likes them and would undoubtedly clamor for more. The Police Department, however, has no plans for increasing them. DART and the command stations represent the department's main strategic thrust. Storefronts are a sideshow. Their future depends in large part on whether they have more than a tangential role to play in developing close relations between police and the community under the DART strategy.

CONCLUSION

The Houston Police Department formulated and began to implement an ambitious, forward-looking plan that attempted to synchronize command structure, delivery strategies, and street behavior. Each aspect was designed to break down the wall that separated police and the several publics of the city. Opportunities were to be created for involving the public in police planning, while the police simultaneously demonstrated in all they did that they were worthy of public trust and assistance. So far, change has been initiated solely by the police; it is their vision that is shaping interaction. It remains to be seen whether the public will respond.

In terms of strategic innovation, the Houston police have returned to devices that were widely discussed in police circles in the early in 1970s, namely, team policing, decentralized command, and storefront police stations. Generally those innovations failed to develop, partly perhaps because Federal funding was gradually withdrawn. The Houston P.D. and departments elsewhere have rediscovered them and are implementing them for their own reasons, unforced by fashion or infusion of money.

Determining whether Houston's innovations are working is difficult, because change has been undertaken on so broad a front. Assuming, for example, that DART is effective, as Chief Brown and his colleagues think, is that because coverage is more intense, officers are making better use of uncommitted time, or community contacts are more extensive? DART can undoubtedly be labeled team policing, but are all elements essential to it? The same problem arises with respect to race relations: Which has had the greater impact, Lee Brown or reformed behavior on the part of individual police officers? Houston's broad-gauged plan is praiseworthy for its ambition but frustrating for systematic evaluation and for learning by other police departments.

One thing is clear: Regardless of whether rigorous evaluation of strategic innovations in American policing is undertaken, experts and practitioners must be much more careful than they have been in using omnibus terms like team policing, decentralization, community outreach, and storefronts. Many cities have experimented with storefronts over the past decade or so, but what they have done is not always the same. Even within Houston, it is not the same everywhere. Storefronts can be small police stations, bases for community organization, facilities for walk-in solicitation of assistance, fixed patrol posts, facilities for ready referral, or liaison offices with community service agencies. Deciding what a "storefront" should do is critical both for developing it efficiently and for justifying its costs. If police elsewhere are to learn from Houston, they must penetrate behind programmatic labels and pay careful attention to the operational details.

5

DENVER:
The American Standard

THE DENVER POLICE DEPARTMENT represents the American standard in police strategy. Patrolling is the heart and soul of its program. Intelligent, well managed, and sensitive to community opinion, the Denver Police Department adheres to the belief that effective police service depends overwhelmingly on the quality of uniformed patrol. The main programmatic innovations of the past fifteen years, even those resulting in the creation of specialized units, have all involved some form of uniformed patrolling. While the Denver Police Department assigns substantial numbers of officers to criminal investigation as well as traffic control, its clear emphasis is on enhancing public security and reducing the fear of crime through improvements in the conduct of patrol. The Denver Police Department merits careful study, because it exemplifies the most likely direction that strategic experimentation by American police departments will take in the future.

In order to understand that classic police strategy and its variations, we shall first describe Denver and its Police Department, then present an overview of programmatic changes in Denver's policing during the last fifteen years, and finally discuss the conduct of patrol in all the forms it has assumed there.

THE CITY AND THE DEPARTMENT

The Denver Police Department has about 1,350 officers. That qualifies it as a big-city force, but it is a far cry from New York's 25,000 or even Houston and Detroit's 4,000. The Police Department is responsible for about 110 square miles of territory containing a population of almost exactly 500,000. Because Denver's population is unlikely to grow, further expansion in the size of the force is not in the cards. The metropolitan area as a whole, however, with a population now about 1,400,000, is growing rapidly. It grew almost one-third during the last decade, while Denver's declined slightly. The city of Aurora, which lies directly to the east, is now the third largest city in Colorado behind Denver and Colorado Springs.

Denver is a "yuppie" city par excellence—upscale, professional, and young. Its economy is based on government, high-tech industry, and services, especially medicine, banking, and law. Twenty percent of the population is Hispanic, and 12 percent is black. For minorities as for whites, living standards are higher than in the country as a whole, and unemployment has been consistently below the national average. Though there are pockets of poverty in Denver demarcated by ethnicity, Denver gives a solidly middle-class appearance. Visitors are often surprised to discover that the prosperous suburb of Park Hill, with its large homes and well-kept lawns, through which they travel from the airport to downtown Denver, is predominantly black.

The Mile-High City, as Denver proudly calls itself, is on the western rim of the great plains directly in front of the looming wall of the Rocky Mountains, which is snow-capped most of the year. People who live on the high plains differ in their orientation to sky and earth from people farther to the east. It's like living on a gentle convex surface where the sky seems to fold down around the horizon, rather than at the bottom of an upturned bowl. It's the land of the "big sky." Sad to say, the glory of sky and mountains have been increasingly obscured by Denver's notorious "brown cloud," which is easily visible on most work days lying low in the dazzling blue sky. The pollution is health-threatening when temperature inversions persist for several days. The source of the brown cloud is not hard to find, although politicians seem to think so. Denver has more vehicle registrations per capita than any other city in the country, a fact that affects police strategies, as we shall see. As in all large American cities, crime rates are higher in Denver than for the country as a whole, but they are not unusually high. Its rate is comparable to Dallas, higher than New York City, lower than Detroit.

Any description of the Denver Police Department at this time must be tentative, because both it and the city experienced a sweeping change in administration in the summer of 1983. Federico Peña, a thirty-six-year-old attorney, became the city's first Hispanic Mayor, and only the second Hispanic Mayor of a large American city. Peña immediately cleaned house in a city government that had been controlled for more than fifteen years by the aging political machine of Bill McNichols. Peña quickly appointed John Simonet, a former priest, as Manager of Safety, a post that supervises both the police and fire services. Then Peña and Simonet together reached far down into the ranks of the Police Department and appointed Lieutenant Thomas Coogin as Chief of Police. Coogin, who bears a strong resemblance to McGarret of "Hawaii Five-O," was forty-five at the time. He replaced Art Dill, a McNichols appointee, who had been Chief for eleven years, one of the longest tenures in the city's history.

The department that Coogin took over, while popular with the public, had become stodgy and ingrown. Chief Dill himself in 1981 frankly described the department in the following terms: "We are not always innovative, nor progressive, nor trend setting. We are cautious, concerned, malleable, and community conscious like the people we serve."[1] A middle-ranking officer more cruelly characterized the department at the time as having "one hundred years of tradition unmarked by progress." It was widely accepted that the department was dominated by a "thinning shell of the old school." Management was from the top down, carried out by a trusted group of fifty- to sixty-year-old officers who tended to be shuffled from one senior post to another.

It has been easy in Denver to lose sight of the accomplishments of Chief Dill's administration behind the lethargy of its

waning days. The fact is that the department Chief Coogin inherited was widely perceived by the public as well as police professionals as being honest, open, efficient, and conscientiously
disciplined. That was not something that would have been said
about the department in the early 1960s. Chief Dill and his now
deprecated colleagues were responsible for rebuilding a department racked by scandal. Seven percent of the officers at that
time were convicted of various crimes, most involving burglaries from commercial premises. The city invited the International Association of Chiefs of Police to name an interim Chief
in 1963, the first time an outsider ever commanded the Denver
force. Newcomers to Denver were facetiously advised by neighbors that if they needed police assistance, they should call the
Fire Department. Furthermore, ''ass kicking'' was a hallowed
operational tradition, especially with respect to minorities.
Though Denver never exploded in fire and riot as other cities
did in the 1960s, it trembled on the brink during several hot
summer nights. That tradition, so common throughout urban
America, gradually changed under the tough-minded leadership of Chief Dill. The change is partially reflected in increased
hiring of minorities, including women, which has never been as
high as the police department wanted. In 1967 only 2 percent of
the force was black and 1.6 percent Hispanic. By 1983, 6 percent of the force was black, as compared with 12 percent black
in the city's population, and 13 percent was Hispanic, as against
18 percent in the city; 6 percent of the officers were female.

Finally, the Dill administration upgraded many of the department's operations and physical facilities. In 1976 it moved
into a handsome, prototypical police building, joined underground to the city's state-of-the-art jail. The department also
actively and successfully sought money from the Federal Law
Enforcement Assistance Administration for new programs and
was aware of the latest trends in American policing. Its vision,
in other words, was admirable. The department was neither
hidebound nor reactionary.

Building upon those solid accomplishments, Chief Coogin's
initial moves have been to revitalize senior management. He
has created his own team of division chiefs, in the process promoting many sergeants and lieutenants farther down the line
who had despaired of ever moving up. In effect, a new genera-

tion has taken command of the Denver Police Department, one that believes in executive training and crisp, clear participatory management. The organizational shape of the department has been left almost exactly as it had been. The general emphasis of the Coogin regime had been on making Denver's patrol strategy, in its existing configuration, work more effectively.

AN OVERVIEW OF OPERATIONS

Since the late 1960s strategic innovation in Denver has involved creating specialized field units, all with the stated purpose of preventing crime. They were the Community Services Bureau (1971), which did neighborhood crime prevention and directed four storefront police stations; the Special Crime Attack Team (SCAT, 1972), which targeted primarily burglaries and robberies; ESCORT (1975), a motorcycle patrol unit for high-crime areas; and the Juvenile Crime Prevention Unit (1979). Those developments seem to indicate that the Denver Police Department recognized the limitations of traditional uniformed patrol and felt the need to create new units to meet neglected needs. The reality was, in fact, that with the exception of the Community Services Bureau, all of them have done saturation patrolling, for the most part in uniform. And they still do. The difference between them and the uniformed patrol has not been tactical so much as managerial. The specialized units were proactive and flexible. They were disconnected from the 911/radio dispatch system and so did not have to respond to calls for service. They also were not assigned to fixed areas but could be shifted from place to place according to need. All those units were, in effect, directed patrols. Their crime prevention effect, like that of patrol, was to be achieved through high visibility. For the most part, then, specialization has created not new kinds of policing but variations on the patrol theme.

What those developments meant in terms of assignments is puzzling. Between 1970 and 1983 the proportion of the force assigned to patrol, including the specialized units, fell from 66 to 54 percent. If one includes as well other officers who patrol streets in uniforms, such as traffic officers, the proportion declines from 76 to 64 percent. Though the number of officers on the street fell relative to total personnel, they remained about the same in absolute terms. That is, despite a growth in sworn officers as opposed to civilians, from 1,132 in 1970 to 1,366 in 1983, the number of officers showing the flag by patrolling the streets did not change. What happened was that the additional personnel were assigned to other branches, notably administration, technical services, and criminal investigation. The creation of specialized patrol units did not mean, either, that general patrol strength declined. Since 1975 about 75 percent of the patrol division's personnel have been sent to precinct operations, and 12 percent to the specialized units. The remainder were in patrol administration and the helicopter squad.

The Denver record shows clearly that in order to understand what is going on in policing, attention must be given to how personnel are being used and not simply to changes in an organizational chart. More than a decade of innovation neither challenged the dominant strategy nor enhanced the police presence on the street. Although the Police Department did develop new field units, for the most part these units did visible patrolling. At the same time the number of uniformed officers doing patrolling of all sorts did not increase. As a proportion of personnel available in the department, it actually declined.

FORMS OF PATROL

The variations of the patrol theme that Denver has developed are, in order of presentation here, precinct patrol operations, ESCORT, and the Juvenile Delinquency Prevention Unit. The Special Crime Attack Team (SCAT) will be discussed in connection with changes in precinct patrolling.

Precinct Patrol

The largest single command in the Denver police force, as in all police departments, has been patrol. Patrol officers are everyone's stereotype of the police. They cruise the streets every day in distinctive white vehicles with blue trim decked out with an imposing strip of multicolored lights on the roof. The words "To Serve and Protect" are painted on the side, along with the shield of the department. The primary duty of patrol officers is to drive repeatedly through designated areas so as to deter crime by their presence while awaiting emergency calls for service. In 1983, 43 percent of all Denver police officers were in the patrol division. It had four district commands corresponding to the quadrants of the city: northeast, northwest, southeast, and southwest. The districts were organized in turn into beats, called precincts, each patrolled by one car during each shift.

According to Denver officers, each district had a distinct police force with a different character and set of priorities. Former Chief Dill has noted further that even the three shifts in each district were distinctive. Undoubtedly different shifts in different places do have a different "feel" to them. Police officers know they have to adapt to the character of the people they deal with. But autonomy in the exercise of command in Denver had been limited to personnel management, not to operational innovation. Supervisory officers throughout the city have been held accountable for managing a fixed and for the most part unquestioned strategic program. They have not been expected to challenge it or even to tinker with it. Their essential responsibilities have been to ensure that 911 calls are answered promptly, that special disorder problems, like gang fights and fracases in public parks, are quickly contained and eliminated, and that patrol personnel behave properly. District captains are unanimous in saying that the key objective has been to "keep their patch clean." The successful patrol supervisor stresses ready response and individual discipline. A district captain should never be out of control of either his populace or his personnel.

These were fitting and laudable goals. That Denver substantially achieved them accounted for the solid reputation of the police in the community. The police force has been, in short, a highly professional, well-disciplined force wedded to a reactive model of patrol with little scope for innovation down the chain of command.

Patrol officers on the street felt no incentive, either, to go beyond routine reactive patrol. Although exhorted many times to meet people in their precincts between calls, they rarely did, most social contacts being confined to waitresses in restaurants. Patrol officers were also supposed to park their cars and walk for a short time during every shift. Again, they never really did, as senior officers well knew. Patrol officers believed they would be judged strictly by their quickness in answering calls, their conduct in encounters with the public, and the "numbers" they generated with respect to certain kinds of proactive contacts, such as moving traffic violations, impounded vehicles, and interrogations of suspicious persons. The officers performed very well in that reactive way. By the early 1980s response time to emergencies was four minutes on the average and for calls of all sorts, seven minutes.

The district police commands in Denver deal exclusively with patrol operations. The district captains do not direct detectives, traffic officers, or any other kind of specialist. With the exception of a few burglary detectives, all nonpatrol personnel work out of either downtown headquarters or their own command post. Denver's decentralization, in other words, involves only patrol. A recent study of several police departments, including Kansas City, Missouri; Columbus, Ohio; Atlanta; and Seattle, concluded that Denver's centralization was greater than most.[2]

The district patrol commands are housed in four small, clean, relatively modern single-story buildings with flat roofs and finished basements. Each contains a few offices, a reception room with a high counter, a large squad room, lockers, toilets, a small weight-training room, and two holding cells. The district police stations are little more than bases for patrol officers going on or off duty. The public is not encouraged to come to them, except to get a few basic forms. The officers themselves don't process street work at the district stations. They drive downtown to book people, consult records, deposit property, or meet with detectives. Dispatch, too, is handled from central headquarters, not through the district stations.

Patrol officers have had almost no input into departmental decisions. A study done for the Law Enforcement Assistance Administration described Denver in the late 1970s as having a quasi-military model of administration, more so than other big-city departments it studied. Command was hierarchical and appeared quixotic in small matters, such as "personal appearance enforcement, beat assignments, choice between one-man and two-man car assignments, accommodation for officers attending schools, and the rule of seniority.'' Furthermore, Denver has not had an effective union to offset the quasi-military system. Although there was a union in name as well as a fraternal police association, the officers have had no contract with the city or the Police Department. Wages are set according to a fixed formula incorporating data obtained through a survey of pay rates in public and private employment. Assignments are made as supervisors mandate. According to departmental regulations, seniority can be considered only in making assignments to shifts, which is done every month. Officers ''vote'' the shifts they prefer, with assignments then given according to seniority. Since personnel policies are set by the City Charter rather than a negotiated contract, the police union's role in behalf of its members has been limited to assisting them in disciplinary proceedings.

Although command in Denver is more authoritative, powerful, and hierarchical than in some departments, American policing generally is highly bureaucratized, except in very small departments. That has given a distinct tone to it. The occupational world of the police officer is that of the hourly worker rather than of self-directing professionals. Police officers work fixed shifts; they punch in and out. They are acutely aware of exactly how much time they devote to the job. They discuss endlessly among themselves their accumulated sick days, the amount of overtime worked, and vacation rotations. They live in a tightly supervised, formalistic environment. They are constantly checking what they do against set rules. Perhaps the most telling item of equipment patrol officers carry is a small bottle of ''white-out,'' which is used for correcting errors in the reports they write, fitting them exactly to the form demanded by the department. ''Who's got the white-out?'' is heard more often in patrol circles than, ''Let's be careful out there.''

Superior officers are not colleagues and are rarely friends. They are seen as instruments of the system, to be placated as necessary but never trusted. The stock complaint heard in any American police force in the country is that supervisors don't know the personnel well enough to make fair evaluations of performance. Instead, they judge mechanically by ''the numbers,'' meaning the number of actions of various sorts logged on patrol activity sheets. The implication is that supervisors don't care about quality.

For all those reasons, discipline in policing is accepted grudgingly. It flows from the system through "them." It is rigid and arbitrary, not flexible and reasonable. Officers take great pleasure in beating the system, usually in a host of small ways. In particular they love to create occasions when they are free from the constraints of supervision even though on duty. Meal and coffee breaks, for example, are treasured moments, because they represent a respite from enforced routine. Officers love to sneak out of patrol and go to sporting events for a few moments free of charge, keeping in touch through their portable radios. Similarly, police officers stretch out moments of relaxation on the job, for in that way they assert their individuality within a highly structured environment. Lingering over the reading of the daily newspaper is almost a studied act of defiance. Many police offices look like high school study halls well into midmorning, as officers slowly read the paper while smoking and drinking coffee. The contrived air of relaxation, common in other government offices as well, may reflect in part lack of work, but it is also as assertion of autonomy within a bureaucratic setting.

Police officers are also very practical people. They know about motorcycles, electrical appliances, plumbing, house repairs, guns, and the price of automobiles. They like machinery and don't mind getting their hands dirty. Many officers have worked in blue-collar occupations. They empathize more with the auto mechanic and bus driver than with the teacher and doctor. They talk about real estate endlessly. Riding in a patrol car is often like taking a seminar in property values. Real estate also seems to be their preferred financial investment—that and going into a family business, at which they often work in their off-duty hours. Finally, police officers are outdoors people who love to hunt and fish. Desk work is repugnant to them, and deep down they loathe the regimentation that characterizes their occupational life. In sum, police officers are the kind of people who prefer beer to wine, softball to running, and newspapers to books.

That orientation to the tangible and resentment of the bureaucratic system are great impediments to innovation in policing. Police officers believe in the routine they know, even while chaffing under the restrictions it imposes. They would rather be secure than responsible. Moreover, they are suspicious of the abstract. If policing in the future requires more self-directing, initiative-taking officers in order to be successful, new relationships will have to be developed between police personnel and the organization. Indeed, an altogether new kind of individual may be required.

Rhetoric in the Denver Police Department has conflicted with reality with respect to what is needed in policing. Chiefs Dill and Coogin and their senior advisers are intelligent men, reasonably well informed about the latest trends in policing. Chief Dill, for example, understood the limitations on patrol-based policing. It was "bullshit," he said, to think as Robert Peel had in England that uniformed patrol could stop crime. Successful crime prevention required active cooperation between the police and the public. That insight, however, was offset in practice by the perceived pressure for making police visible. Everyone, said Dill, "wants to see a policeman." Not just any police officer, of course, but one who is disciplined, sympathetic, and honest. So policy in Denver stressed creation of a patrol force that responded to that general public expectation, even though crime prevention results were recognized as fortuitous.

Senior officers have been interested in hearing about innovations in policing in other jurisdictions. However, the reactive model has had such a firm hold on their minds that they have imbued it with all the attributes of other strategies. Told about community mobilization or team policing, captains and lieutenants would often say, "We're doing that already." They couldn't distinguish between real operational reform and their own intellectual appreciation of an idea. Nothing was really new in policing, since they had already thought about it. Their openness in discussion masked a rooted unwillingness to change the traditional approach. Everything could be accomplished by reactive patrolling, if only the individual officers would appreciate what was necessary.

Chief Coogin and his newly promoted colleagues are determined to make the visible patrol strategy work more successfully. Rather than overthrow the patrol model, they are trying to incorporate new items into it. That may seem strategically uninventive compared with reform in Santa Ana or Detroit, but it is the path most American police departments are likely to follow. The public and its elected representatives throughout the country believe in visible patrolling. Patrol officers have become the public's security blanket. Moreover, the police have sold emergency response so successfully that they now have trouble backing away from it. People expect a patrol car to come whenever they need police help. They complain bitterly when it doesn't arrive instantly. Nonetheless, Denver, like other departments, has reluctantly had to give up the cherished practice of sending a patrol car on each call. Otherwise the Denver police would be unable to manage the volume of work.

Calls for police service in Denver average about 750,000 a year, or 2,000 a day. With only about seventy patrol cars on the street at any one time in Denver, that amounts to approximately ten dispatches per car per shift. In the early 1980s a telephone crime reporting unit was created to handle nonconfrontational crimes and traffic accidents where there were no personal injuries, damage to vehicles was less than $500, and drivers were not intoxicated. The unit has been handling about 22,000 calls a year.

Finally, even though evidence suggests that random motorized patrolling doesn't work, it is not yet clear what does. It is easy to criticize the police for clinging to a failed strategy, but no one can tell them with confidence what else they should be doing. The critics are often flying by the seat of their pants too. Therefore, for political, bureaucratic, and intellectual reasons, police innovation in the United States in the next ten years is more likely to involve some form of visible patrolling than the more dramatic experiments discussed elsewhere in this book. Making patrol perform better is going to be the objective for most police departments in the foreseeable future.

The new patrol plan for Denver formulated by Chief Coogin and his colleagues stresses "directed patrol." It involves four critical elements: intensified coverage, delegation of command responsibility, team activity, and operational crime analysis.

Patrolling is intensified by having the evening shift—6 P.M. to 2 A.M. or 7 P.M. to 3 A.M.—work "solo" cars, as the late night and day shifts have done all along. In that way the department hopes to increase the number of evening patrol cars, when most calls for service occur, by 60 percent. Beats with a higher incidence of crime can then be served by two patrol cars rather than one. Beats have been redesigned and made smaller, which also increases coverage. "The way to remove the fear of crime," Chief Coogin firmly states, "is to put more policemen on the street, increasing both our visibility and availability." The new strategy requires more patrol vehicles; those were obtained by keeping vehicles in service one year longer than city policy had previously allowed.

Patrol officers in Denver, as in most places, have substantial amounts of uncommitted time devoted to random patrolling. Police officers refer to themselves as being "in service" during such periods and "out of service" when handling a call. In Denver 40 to 50 percent of the eight hours on duty is spent in random patrolling, waiting for a mobilization. The Denver department wants to increase the uncommitted time even more by having Traffic Division personnel take exclusive responsibility for accident investigations. In the past patrol officers handled about 80 percent of those. One unexpected consequence of the new policy is that traffic officers have less time for ticketing "moving violations," with a resulting decline in this important source of revenue. It will be interesting to see whether strategic vision or financial exigency prevail.

Denver's directed patrol tries to make purposive use of uncommitted patrol time. Groups of precinct officers under the direction of a sergeant analyze crime and public order problems of their sector (consisting of several beats) and then use their combined resources in appropriate ways against specified targets. Sector sergeants and many patrol officers learn how to use the computer terminals in each district station to call up data about criminal events and calls for police service. Eventually all patrol personnel are supposed to be computer-literate. Technicians known as collators, which most districts have had for several years, assist in the analysis. Rather than having precinct officers tailor their patrol activities on the basis of "gut feeling and reported crime," as the new chief of patrol says, they are supposed to develop coherent plans to be reviewed by superior officers. Even more ambitiously, sergeants will have authority to develop plans for particular problems that might involve shifting officers out of the patrol mode altogether for short periods. For example, if there has been a series of daylight robberies at convenience stores, some patrol officers can be unhooked from the 911 system and put in plainclothes to stake out likely targets. In general, then, patrol personnel are to be used as an adaptable instrument directed according to area plans developed through current analysis of local events. Denver's directed patrol plan is similar to the DART (Directed Area Responsibility Teams) program in Houston, although DART teams are composed of detectives as well as patrol personnel.

The amended patrol strategy rests on a crucial assumption, namely, that certain forms of crime are "patrol preventable." That phrase peppers the conversation of senior officers in the Denver department. The "patrol preventable" crimes are believed to be robbery, burglary, sexual assault on the street, purse snatching, and theft from autos, though not, oddly, auto theft itself. Although aware that research has failed to demonstrate that patrol actually prevents such crimes, they believe it can at least displace criminal activity, creating uncertainties for the criminal and thereby increasing the likelihood of capture.

Detailed knowledge of the areas by precinct personnel is essential to formulate and carry out practical plans of action for each sector. Accordingly, the department has lengthened the time periods officers are assigned to particular shifts. Previously, assignments had been made monthly. People with higher seniority could "bump" people on shifts they preferred, which caused changes in car assignments as well. Under the new policy, officers are assigned for six-month periods, providing enough stability for successful team coordination. Because Denver has no contract with its personnel, the change, which would cause upheaval in many departments, has been done by administrative fiat.

Besides depending on the unquestioned assumption that there were "patrol preventable" offenses, Coogin's staff realized that several problems had to be solved if directed patrol was to succeed. For one thing, although patrol units had substantial amounts of uncommitted time in the aggregate, those came in fairly small lumps, like five or ten minutes between calls. If those blocks of time couldn't be combined, directed patrol would be very perfunctory. Combining could be accomplished best by exempting whole units from responding to calls for a shift and having outside cars cover their beats. That would violate the integrity of beat boundaries, but it was being done frequently anyhow when a patrol car was too busy to handle all the calls in its area. The difference was that it would be done now as a matter of policy rather than expedience. That was the reverse of what Houston tried to do with its DART personnel. One reason for the difference appears to be that Houston's beats were much larger than Denver's—5 square miles on the average, as opposed to 2.8—so that Denver officers could more effectively cover for one another without straying far from home base.

Officers also have to learn to think proactively and to use the computer as a tool. In the past officers had listened inattentively at roll calls to information, usually anecdotal, about crime in the district. The information provided rarely suggested patterns and was not focused on specific beats. Officers therefore did not really plan what they would do; they simply based their patrolling on instinct and past experience. The department's computer facility can provide relatively current information about crime patterns, broken down if necessary by city blocks. The system cannot yet, however, deliver information that might help officers respond to particular calls for service, such as whether the caller is a repeater or whether weapons have been involved there in the past. In any case, computer terminals are available only at the district police stations. The department does not plan to put them in patrol cars.

The police department had hoped to move to computer-assisted-dispatch (CAD) in 1976. That allows dispatchers to know the placement and availability of patrol units at all times. Unfortunately the department failed to provide for emergency backup to their power supply when the new police headquarters was built. When power failed, patrol operations became blind. Providing backup power is very costly, and the city has not yet approved it. Houston is doing it now at an estimated cost of roughly $5 million. So the Denver Police Department has been forced to rely on the city's computer, where it stands ninth in line for service.

Directed patrol is not really a new idea in Denver. Two independent commands within the patrol division specialized in it for years. They were the Special Crimes Attack Team (SCAT), already mentioned, and the Special Services Unit (SSU).

SCAT was created in 1972 under a grant from the Law Enforcement Assistance Administration. Its original purpose was to "attack" the problem of burglary through the coordinated action of patrol officers, detectives, and technicians. Based on their own analysis, they saturated areas having a high incidence of burglary anywhere in the city, trying to catch and successfully prosecute offenders. Originally composed of thirty-four officers, SCAT grew in strength to a maximum of forty-four in 1974. It was successful enough for the department to move it onto its own budget in 1975 after the Federal grant ran out. By 1980, however, disenchantment with the unit had set in, not because it wasn't working as expected but because Chief Dill and his colleagues thought directed patrol of the same sort should be done by all patrol officers. They disliked the separateness of the unit, not its mode of operation. Because SCAT officers were especially dedicated and had very high morale, they tried to save the unit by nimbly developing a new mission. They targeted career criminals, "sitting on them" until they could be caught committing an offense. Even though they produced some notable successes, SCAT was doomed. It was judged to duplicate the activities of the department's career criminal unit. That is ironic, because the unit never numbered more than three officers. While several police departments, such as Washington, D.C., and Minneapolis, have established new units to watch career criminals, in the hope of catching them in a violation of the law, Denver's police have virtually eliminated that capacity. In any case, SCAT was abolished in the interregnum between the Dill and Coogin administrations in the summer of 1983.

The Special Services Unit (SSU) was created in 1968 to handle situations requiring particular skill in the application of force, notably riots, hostage takings, and barricaded suspects. It was Denver's version of what have become known generically as SWAT—special weapons attack teams. Because riots and hostage-takings are relatively rare, SSU has had lots of time on its hands, notwithstanding its demanding training requirements. So in its spare time, which has amounted to 90 percent, it has been doing saturation patrolling. At the invitation of district captains or on its own initiative, SSU saturated an area with a particularly acute street crime problem. Its officers patrolled in uniform but in unmarked cars. As far as the districts were concerned, SSU was a gift and was heartily appreciated. Unlike SCAT, SSU's future was assured, because it had a unique mission. Its strength has remained steady at about forty officers since the unit was created and in all probability will remain so. SSU, like SCAT, generated an impressive record of enforcement actions. They were always proactive, though not always serious, indicating that there was a great deal of street work to do that fell through the cracks of reactive patrolling. The only modification that the Coogin administration made was to change the name from SSU to METRO, which stands for Metropolitan Enforcement Tactical Response Organization. Police departments, like the military, love acronyms. Buried somewhere in any police payroll there must be an officer who specializes in dreaming them up.

The Denver Police Department has had experience with directed patrol not only in specialized units but within district patrol operations as well. In the latter days of the Dill administration a small-scale experiment in directed patrol was tried on an around-the-clock basis in two beats. The idea came from Dennis Weller, a former police officer who had directed the Denver Anti-Crime Council in undertaking the most imaginative research on policing being done in the city. In some ways it became the department's unofficial think tank, a function that could not be performed by the department's own starved and unimaginative Research and Development Office. Two beats were chosen for directed patrol in March 1983. They were chosen not for their representativeness but because they were patrolled by officers who were intelligent, active, and interested in innovation.

It may be worth commenting parenthetically that this kind of practical, applied research is what police departments need most and are best equipped to carry out. Elaborate studies involving careful controls, rigorous sampling, and sophisticated impact measures are too demanding, and hence costly, for most departments to attempt. Furthermore, police departments can't wait for others to do the research they need: They must know if changes in tactics or strategies using existing personnel and resources can be made to produce beneficial results in the kinds of areas in which they are already working. The police need research that provides insights better than the intuitions on which they normally operate. The standard of comparison in police research should not be the optimal designs dear to the hearts of academic methodologists, but procedures that represent an advance over "gut feeling." The Kansas City Preventive Patrol Experiment in 1971–72, for example, was done well enough to give any police administrator pause before continuing unthinkingly with random motorized patrol. The criticisms of it, while often just, obscured the fact that there was no evidence at all for the contrary point of view, namely, that random motorized patrolling was useful. The Kansas City study may have been flawed, but it was much better than the hunches police were relying on in their random patrolling.

The directed patrol experiment in Denver began in March 1983 and continued for about three months. Current crime analyses were provided weekly to the precinct patrol cars by the Denver Anti-Crime Council. In practice, that proved overly demanding, and analyses were given biweekly. Although the quantity of activity produced by the patrol units—such as number of arrests, on-view enforcement, and proactive contacts—increased, it was not clear that patrol activities had really changed. The well-known Hawthorne effect may have occurred, where productivity rises because people know they are being studied, not because of new procedures.

The point is that the Coogin administration's move to directed patrol throughout patrol operations was preceded by considerable experimentation. The new emphasis on directed patrol does not break with strategic tradition in the department but simply marks its expansion to patrol operations throughout the city. That does not mean the move is insignificant or easy to accomplish—it is an ambitious undertaking fraught with uncertainty. The Denver Police Department continues to place faith in visible patrol. In the new variation, however, it will be done more intensely and on a broader scale, will be based on enhanced analytic capacity, and will make teams out of all patrol personnel.

Directed patrol as it was being developed in Denver was attractive for managerial reasons, too, quite apart from its likely impact on public safety. Retirement regulations were changed recently to require officers to serve until age fifty-five before retiring. They used to be able to do so with full pension rights after twenty-five years. The result has been "compaction," meaning that people now serve longer and thus block chances for promotion. Twenty-seven-year-old sergeants and thirty-two-year-old lieutenants will occupy those ranks for a long time. So police administrators have faced an important morale problem. They have to find ways to keep officers from "burning out" doing the same thing year after year. Directed patrol, it was hoped, would provide a partial answer by giving subordinate personnel greater responsibility. By encouraging officers to manage patrol operations themselves within particular areas, their interest in and enthusiasm for police work could be kept alive, even though they did not advance in rank. Another way to provide a variety career was to rotate personnel through special units, like METRO and ESCORT. That was not feasible, however, for all officers in the patrol division, or even for a majority. So directed patrol, especially if delegation of command occurs effectively, might give the patrol officer a new zest for the work.

The Coogin administration also shows renewed interest in foot patrol. Denver is a highly mobile town with few densely populated areas. Even in Five Points, the heart of the black area of the city, the air smells mostly of greenery, especially after rain, from trees lining the streets and from long grass and weeds in yards and on the parkways between the sidewalks and the street. Like many other cities, Denver eliminated the last of its foot beats a generation ago. Senior officers suspected that the police were losing touch with the public but couldn't find ways to break down the impersonality created by patrol cars. Although they urged officers to park and walk in high-crime areas, it didn't work. Some foot patrolling was done, however, on an *ad hoc* basis. For example, Juvenile Delinquency Prevention Officers were assigned to walk beats in downtown Denver during the Christmas season beginning in 1980. One district created what might be called a foot patrol car. Four officers would go in a single patrol car to places where teenagers congregated on summer nights. That might be at a shopping center, a public park, or a fast-food restaurant. The officers would park their car and patrol the area on foot, mixing with the unruly crowds of youngsters. Those officers were "hitters," adept at rousting people for infractions of public order ordinances. Finally, in a few locations, such as commercial strips, foot patrols would occasionally be sent when particular problems arose, such as derelicts panhandling or sleeping in doorways.

The new foot patrol idea, implemented for the first time in 1984, is to designate foot beats and have one car in each district serve them on a random, rotating basis. The patrol car goes to one beat, parks, and its officers walk for about an hour. Then they move on to another beat. The reasoning is that few areas require foot beats all the time. It is simply not cost-efficient to tie personnel down in that way. So the department hopes it can reap the benefits of foot patrol without the public, especially its criminal elements, noticing that coverage is episodic. The department has no trouble getting volunteers for the foot patrols, generally from among the older officers. As the Deputy Chief of Patrol notes, "The new generation of police officers hasn't walked beats and doesn't know what they are like." Older officers, however, remember them with fondness and look forward to more supportive and less stressful interaction with the public.

Denver actually provides police service to one very important part of the city exclusively through foot patrols and has always done so. That is the airport. The exception proves an important rule: Foot patrol has obvious advantages in areas where there is heavy pedestrian traffic. If American streets were more intensely used by people on their feet, foot patrols would return quickly to policing—or if not foot patrols, then horse patrols, and for the same reasons. Denver created such a unit in August 1984 to patrol the new downtown mall. There is great enthusiasm currently in American policing for them, reflecting the resuscitation of pedestrian areas in large cities.

Escort

ESCORT is a force of about twenty-one officers who try to ensure that order and safety are maintained on the streets of the Capitol Hill section of Denver. ESCORT, which was created in 1975 (as usual under a Federal grant), stood for "Eliminate Street Crime on Residential Thoroughfares." The acronym is so apt that one wonders whether it was invented first and appropriate words fitted to it. Chief Coogin, however, disliked the name. As a lieutenant assigned to ESCORT, he had been angered by the calls the unit kept getting from unattached men who thought it was a dating service.

ESCORT officers are volunteers who patrol the streets on small motorcycles, Kawasaki KZ 440s. They do not respond to 911 calls except as backup for precinct officers. Their activities overlay those of the district patrol units. Police coverage is so dense in Capitol Hill that during one shift we observed, when the dispatcher requested units to respond to a knife fight in a parking lot, thirteen officers showed up within three minutes on six ESCORT bikes and riding in four precinct patrol cars.

The ESCORT officers use their small motorcycles to cruise parking lots, parks, alleys, and even sidewalks when necessary. The officers are mobile and accessible, able to interact with people in ways that are not possible from inside a patrol car. They frequently stop and talk or banter with people as they slowly glide past. ESCORT officers delight in slipping up beside people who think they are alone and unobserved. ESCORT officers do what police are beginning to refer to as "order maintenance." That involves controlling behavior in public places in order to demonstrate that a normative-legal order exists even in areas fraught with high crime and a turbulent street life.

Capitol Hill is situated in the heart of Denver, just to the east of the downtown's upwelling of glass-and-steel skyscrapers. Although ESCORT's designated patrol area covers more than a thousand square blocks, its attention is concentrated on a few blocks north and south of East Colfax Avenue, the city's main east–west axis, just to the east of the State Capitol building with its distinctive gold dome. Capitol Hill is an area of cheap rooming houses and multifamily houses bisected by the East Colfax commercial strip, which is packed with fast-food restaurants, porn shops, bars, convenience stores, and theaters. Pepper and salt in racial makeup, its primary characteristic is exploitation of both people and property. Buildings are crowded and dilapidated. Homes for battered women, shelters for juveniles, and halfway houses for paroled criminals are scattered throughout the neighborhood. The streets are vibrant and alive late into the night, pedestrians plentiful. But the tone overall is sad, tawdry, and cruel. America's marginal people collect here, desperately seeking or selling—hookers, transvestites, bums, black youth, druggies, unwed mothers, transient manual workers, homeless families, and runaway kids.

One such is a man named Virgil, well known to Capitol Hill officers from repeated encounters over many years. Virgil is probably fifty years old, unshaven and dressed in Salvation Army clothing. Chronically unemployed, he drinks too much and, as one officer has said, "His elevator doesn't go all the way to the top." His problem one night is that his "girl friend" has locked him out of her apartment and, Virgil claims, appropriated his belongings. The police refuse to force the door and tell Virgil to seek a civil remedy. Later in the evening the officers get a call that Virgil is causing a disturbance at a bar. Sure enough, he is. He has found his girl friend there, drinking with friends. She, too, is poor and fiftyish, but she is sensible and employed. The officers take Virgil out on the street and warn him sternly about causing any more trouble that night to anybody, especially his girl friend. Actually, only one of the officers delivers the lecture; the other has to get a coat hanger from the bartender to open the patrol car door, which had been shut and inadvertently locked as the officers rushed into the bar. The keys are still in the ignition and the motor is running. As one officer copes with that embarrassment, the other makes his parting point to Virgil in an especially homely way. "Pardner," he says, looking down on Virgil benevolently, "think of life as a shit sandwich. Some days you have to take a big bite, some days a small bite. Today, you have to take a *big* bite." And with that, he steps majestically into the now opened patrol car and drives away, leaving Virgil standing goggle-eyed on the sidewalk.

Sex is for sale in every form along the Colfax strip. What is striking, however, is not its perversion but its joylessness. Cruising shame-faced johns; mini-skirted hookers with hard faces and slack bodies; slender, effeminate young men, the "chickens" waiting to be picked up by male homosexuals; transvestites laughing, prancing, fooling; and gay couples flaunting their life-style. On every side people are single-mindedly seeking sexual pleasure, but no one seems to be having much fun. Sex in Capitol Hill, it appears, has become desperate, risky, and furtive.

ESCORT officers are specialized in the enforcement of laws dealing with behavior in public places. One might call this skilled harassment. Working the streets' busy hours, 10 A.M. to 2 A.M. divided into two shifts, ESCORT officers are told to "find a rock and kick it." That means combing the streets for minor violations by people who live persistently in the narrow space between respectability and criminality. Particular attention is given to the "bad apples," whom officers soon know as well as their own colleagues. Those people are hit for any infraction that can be found, from rowdyism to use of drugs, from propositioning to illegal parking, from procuring to causing a disturbance. ESCORT is deterrent policing with a vengeance.

While it may seem arbitrary to categorize people as "assholes," a favorite police epithet, a great reality of policing is the discovery that there are people in the world who are incorrigible—incorrigibly evil, ready to harm others without compunction, or incorrigibly incompetent, needing help perpetually, especially in their personal relations with others. Police officers may, of course, misclassify people. But for the most part they spend much of their daily life dealing with people with whom they, or the system, have already dealt many times. How the people got this way the police don't know or especially care. Their job is simply to protect society from the incorrigibles and, often, the incorrigibles from themselves. Being labeled an "asshole" is both a moral judgement and a fairly well-defined descriptive category.

The art of ESCORT's work consists in using every handhold in the law to maintain failing moral discipline. Law, not force, is the key to its activity. ESCORT officers are nitpicking experts in the law, especially minor violations of the municipal code. For instance, one evening at roll call several ESCORT officers had a long discussion about whether they could arrest people for being naked in public. Evidently that afternoon two male gays had walked stark naked through Cheeseman Park holding hands. Getting out well-thumbed copies of the municipal ordinances, which every officer carried, they read aloud and discussed passages they thought could be used. They finally decided that nudity itself was not an offense. An arrest could be made only if a sexual act was involved or a member of the public agreed to file a complaint for disturbing the peace.

ESCORT officers are frustrated generally because of the repeal during the last few years of many public order regulations, notably laws against loitering, drinking, and being drunk in public. Such laws are needed, they say, to provide leverage over the "bad asses" on the street. July 1, 1983, was a red-letter day in their eyes, because that was when they could again arrest for loitering. The City Council had been persuaded that the police needed such power. ESCORT's personnel were concerned, however, that the District Attorney's office would refuse to prosecute or judges to hear. Nonetheless, the ordinance empowers officers to give more people "the ride" even if they cannot give them "the rap."

Since such powers can obviously be abused, ESCORT's operations have to be carefully monitored. We saw an instance where timely intervention would have prevented a serious assault but could not be justified under existing law. Two ES-CORT officers pointed out six black youths who had settled down about 7:30 in the evening to drink beer from stacked six-packs on a busy corner of East Colfax near a Denny's Restaurant. The officers predicted trouble would arise before the night was over, a remark we dismissed as unsupported prejudice. The officers, it turned out, were right. About eleven o'clock we received a call about an assault behind the Denny's Restaurant. A middle-aged wino had been beaten and his wallet stolen. Witnesses identified the drinking youths, who by then had fled the scene. The ESCORT officers vainly searched the area and helped paramedics put the bloody and befuddled wino into an ambulance.

Although the ESCORT operation raises important questions about the proper role of the police in society, one must never forget that the maintenance of order in places like Capitol Hill serves as well as afflicts its polyglot population. No neighborhood should be allowed to become a no-man's-land. The people most likely to be hurt in such situations are not prosperous, educated professionals. They are the very people at the bottom of American society who are so commonly viewed as a problem. But they, too, have a right to a secure life. They need police protection every bit as much as people who practice mainstream life-styles. But because their needs occur in unprepossessing surroundings and take unusual forms, they may also require a different type of police response.

We encountered two people of that sort one night when the dispatcher notified our patrol unit that two drunks were trying to force their way into a house. Hearing the police cars coming, the two middle-aged drunks had taken refuge in some juniper bushes. They were dragged out by a police dog and lay, as we arrived, on the ground, thoroughly frightened and keeping as far away from the dog as they could. As we took them to the station, one announced loudly, "Officer, I want you to know I'm a foogitive from justice, I am a dangerous man." Getting nothing out of the officers, he demanded to know where he was being taken. "Jail," one officer said laconically. "No you ain't. You're taking me to the river." After listening to this for awhile, one officer said, "Paul, can you swim with handcuffs on?" After thinking about that for a moment, Paul replied, "Sheeeit yes!" Later, asked if he had ever been arrested before, he said "Uh huh." "What for?" "Bein' drunk . . . just like I am now." As far as one could tell, there wasn't an ounce of harm in either man. They had simply been worked over by life and lost. They are one kind of incorrigible, making problems for others and getting into trouble themselves. Who takes care of them? More times than not, the police.

It's hard to tell if ESCORT has been successful. It has certainly been popular, and the department has been asked continually to expand it to other neighborhoods. As one would expect, ESCORT officers generate impressive totals of proactive enforcement. They are surely a felt presence. The department believes ESCORT has been effective in reducing crime, although the evaluation has been rough-and-ready. For example, during ESCORT's first twenty months (1975–1977) reports of rapes and both simple and aggravated assaults declined significantly. Burglaries declined too, but only slightly. Despite a continuing high incidence of crime, many politicians and business people credited ESCORT with stabilizing transitional areas that otherwise would have become blighted and uninhabitable.

Working with ESCORT highlights a quality in policing that is invisible to outsiders but profoundly affects the psychology of its practitioners. Policing in the United States is very much like going to war. Three times a day in countless locker rooms across the land, large men and a growing number of women carefully arm and armor themselves for the day's events. They begin by strapping on flak-jackets, designed to stop most bullets, under their regulation blue, white, or brown shirts. Then they pick up a wide, heavy, black leather belt and hang around it the tools of their trade: gun, mace, handcuffs, bullets. When it

is fully loaded, they swing the belt around their hips with the
same practiced motion of the gunfighter in Western movies,
snugging it down and buckling it in front. They fasten it to their
trousers with leather loops. Many officers slip an additional
small-caliber pistol into a trouser pocket or a leg holster just
above the ankle. Inspecting themselves in a full-length mirror,
officers thread their nightsticks into a metal ring on the side of
the belt. Finally, they pick up individual radios, checking to see
if they are properly charged, which they also fit into a metal
bracket on the belt. In ESCORT's case, the officers complete
their preparations by pulling large, cushioned plastic helmets
with retractable visors down over their heads. In every sense of
the word, going on duty as a police officer day after day is
"heavy." Heavy physically, heavy in anticipation, heavy in
meaning.

What is also striking and more than a little frightening is
that the people going to this peculiar kind of war are very often
hardly more than kids. They come out of police academies
fresh-faced and naive. Many have never held a job. Most are
unmarried. Yet they are sent out to deal with hard-core criminals, junkies, wife abusers, violent drunks, and psychopaths.
We give a massive pistol to these tender-faced children and ask
them to handle people whose life experiences they can't begin to
understand. Dressing them to kill, we expect them to keep order
so that we may live in security. What a colossal act of faith on
our part; what tremendous responsibility on theirs.

Crime Prevention

The Denver Police Department has acted on the view that
crime prevention is best done by the officer on the beat. Specialized crime prevention programs are all right in their place,
but a cooperative relationship between police and citizens depends essentially on the impression made by every officer
throughout the force. If officers respond to citizens sympatheti-
cally and effectively, then the public will provide the kind of
support to the police that would most assuredly prevent crime.
Crime prevention has tended to be seen as community relations.

Special crime prevention programs have been undertaken for the department by the Community Services Bureau. The bureau was originally named, revealingly, the police Community Relations Bureau, and it was responsible for both liaison with the community and the training of police officers. In the early 1970s police training was split off, and the revamped bureau concentrated on liaison and crime prevention. Since the bureau reported directly to the Chief, it would appear to have been a high-priority operation. That was not the case. Under Chief Dill, the head of the bureau was excluded from the weekly staff meetings attended by all division chiefs as well as the head of the Bureau of Internal Affairs, whose status was exactly the same as the CSB's. One former head of the bureau thought Dill excluded him to protect him from the disdain of the front-line commanders. One of Chief Coogin's first actions was to transfer the bureau to the Juvenile Division. Too many units, he felt, were reporting directly to him.

Since 1971 about ten officers have been assigned yearly to the Community Services Bureau. This is not a negligible commitment in a force of about 1,300 officers. Detroit's headquarters crime prevention unit, which has attracted national attention, was only fractionally larger on a proportional basis. If Detroit's mini-station personnel are included, as they should be, then Detroit's investment in crime prevention is much greater.

The Denver Police Department has always been willing to try new programs, especially if Federal money is attached. So, almost despite itself, the standard crime prevention programs have been undertaken: Operation ID, Neighborhood Watch, and Crime Stoppers. The Crime Stoppers Program solicits information about particular crimes through radio and television announcements. Callers' tips are received anonymously via phones in the Community Services Bureau, and rewards are given if the information leads to arrests and indictments. More unusual among crime prevention programs, the Community Service Bureau created four "storefront" police offices in 1971. A single plainclothes officer was assigned to each of them during daylight hours. Since the department never really figured out what to do with them, they were premises without a mission. Some officers simply sat in them giving candy to kids and talking to people who happened by. Others tried more actively to build rapport with the local community, usually by attending meetings of neighborhood groups. Because the storefronts never recruited volunteers to help staff them, the storefronts of the busiest officers were closed most of the time. As one officer said, "When we were available, no one came. When we were out, we couldn't be found."

The storefronts, like the Community Services Bureau as a whole, worked in a vacuum, not integrally related to the ongoing field operations of the department. As one storefront officer said, "I kept sending in bullshit statistics about the numbers of meetings attended, but no one cared about what I was learning." District captains didn't cultivate them, and some didn't even know where they were. The contempt for them was palpable. When we asked one bright, experienced storefront officer about the reaction to her by district personnel, she quietly reached into a drawer and without a word handed us a copy of an article entitled "Why Does Officer Friendly Eat Lunch Alone?" Fairly or unfairly, crime prevention officers were perceived as the department's walking wounded. The Community Services Bureau was a place no one wanted to go.

The Coogin administration concluded, correctly, that the storefronts weren't providing a service that couldn't be done more cheaply from headquarters. So the storefronts were abolished in late 1983 and the officers reassigned as "Community Detectives" to the district patrol stations.

In short, the Denver Police Department did do crime prevention, and its senior officers could talk intelligently about its importance. It probably did as much as most large cities. But the programs were peripheral to field operations and unintegrated into the dominant strategic plan. One promising new development was an invitation to the Community Services Bureau to send a representative to the weekly meetings of the Denver Planning Commission. Although representatives from the Fire Department attended for years, it was belatedly recognized that city planning should encompass security needs as well.

The dominance of the patrol paradigm in Denver can be seen even more clearly in the way the Juvenile Delinquency Prevention Unit has developed since its creation in 1979. Again sponsored by the LEAA, it is a kind of ESCORT for kids, performing directed patrol against juvenile delinquents. Its approximately fifteen officers drive patrol cars with "Juvenile Crime Prevention Unit" stenciled on the side. In the winter, the patrols concentrate around the city's schools and, in the summer, wherever kids congregate: parks, shopping centers, drive-ins, "hot rod alleys," and "low-rider" hangouts. Like ESCORT, the district patrol captains consider them a free bonus, helping to share the load. They represent another flexible patrol force that the department can send, like ESCORT and SSU, to trouble spots that the district commanders can't handle with their own reactive, beat-tied cars.

CONCLUSION

Policing in Denver typifies what is both classic and good among the country's large departments. Active, visible, flexible patrol is the centerpiece of the department's operations, supplemented by expert criminal investigations. The department believes that patrol officers must deter crime through their presence, demonstrate that public order will be maintained, and respond quickly and effectively to calls for service. Furthermore, in all that they do officers must encourage willing cooperation from the public. Although the Denver Police Department has experimented with special programs, it has acted on the view that policing could be no better than what was done by the many officers in blue uniforms who were sent into the community every day and night. Recently it has sought to reform its broad-gauged patrol operations by incorporating lessons learned by specialized, directed patrol units. It has started to delegate command to lower levels, to form patrol teams that will assume responsibility for policing in particular areas, and to base patrol activities on analysis of crime problems.

The Denver Police Department understands that, for its strategy of policing to work, its personnel must be well-trained, adequately paid, and closely supervised. Implementation of a patrol-based strategy requires that senior administrators work to shape behavior generally in the department and not simply in a few elite units. This strategy, then, might be considered narrow, but not unambitious.

Since patrol-based policing is the stock in trade of most American police departments, its success relative to better-publicized and flashier innovations needs to be determined. Barring persuasive evidence about the greater utility of other approaches, Denver's program sets a standard for the likely future of American policing.

6

OAKLAND:
Keeping It All Together

GERTRUDE STEIN'S FAMOUS APHORISM "There's no *there* there" is not as apt as it once was, but Oakland still struggles for a positive identity. Situated 12 miles across the bay from San Francisco—a twenty-minute drive from City Hall to Civic Center—Oakland is all too easily overshadowed by cosmopolitan San Francisco and also by adjacent Berkeley with its renowned university, colorful characters, and innovative restaurants. Yet Oakland is naturally at least as inviting as Berkeley and far more comfortable than San Francisco. Recall that Mark Twain's coldest winter was a summer in San Francisco. Oakland is about 10 degrees warmer in the summertime. Moreover, Oakland has hills every bit as visually spectacular as Berkeley's, with large, architect-designed, single-family dwellings that rival Berkeley's in attractiveness and price.

Oakland enjoys another environmental advantage. Lake Merritt is within walking distance of downtown. With a circumference of 3.2 miles, Lake Merritt is the largest urban salt water lake in the United States. From a distance the Children's Zoo, duck preserve, Roman Temple, Scottish Rite Temple, and even the Alameda County Courthouse contribute to the lake's aesthetic appeal for strollers, picnicking families, and joggers. The *Bay Area Runners' Guide* cautions, however, that the

natural beauty also attracts "macho hormone cases, liver cases
. . . dudes." The Oakland Police Department acknowledges
that Lake Merritt and other Oakland parks have become ha-
vens for drug dealers. Oakland's challenge during the 1980s,
and therefore the Police Department's assignment, is to figure
out how Oakland might live up to its considerable potential.

In this chapter we try to explain how the Oakland Police Department is attempting to do just that, despite past problems of
racial conflict and continuing problems of urban decay, marked
by a growing and menacing street drug-selling presence. Any
Oakland police administration is limited in what it can do by
geography, history, and economy. Thus the department must be
understood in light of historical and demographic constraints.

Oakland is a big but not very dense city. It spreads out over
79 square miles, with Berkeley to the northwest and San Lean-
dro, a predominantly white working-class suburb, to the southeast. The East Oaklands Hills offer breathtaking views of the
sun setting over the Golden Gate Bridge. The farther one de-
scends from the hills, however, the more one experiences a decline in the size and attractiveness of housing. East 14th Street,
the main flatlands connection to downtown, is busy with auto
repair shops, liquor stores, bars, and small restaurants. Litter
punctuates the sidewalks, and urine odors occasionally assault
the sensibilities of the strolling shopper. At night East Oakland
seems desolate and forbidding. The eastern flatlands are the
highest-crime area in a city that produced 117 homicides in
1984 and nearly 7,000 serious assaultive crimes.

Oakland would be even larger and significantly more affluent but for one odd and significant feature of the city's geography. Oakland entirely surrounds mainly white and affluent
Piedmont, the Beverly Hills of the Bay area. Geography would
dictate that Piedmont be part of Oakland, providing a tax base
for schools, police, fire, and other public services. Politics dic-
tated otherwise, and Piedmont residents are thus freed from the
obligation of supporting Oakland's needs.

Oakland reported a 1980 census population of 339,337, a
decrease of 22,224 from 1970. The 1980 census was expected to
show a movement back to the city by young urban professionals
attracted to Oakland's benign climate, natural beauty, low
housing costs relative to Berkeley's, and proximity to San Fran-

cisco. Some of that movement did occur and contributed to Oakland's status as the most racially integrated city in the United States. Nevertheless, the outflow of whites far exceeded the inflow during 1970–80. The U.S. Census Summary for 1980 documents that the white population was reduced by 83,820, (39 percent), while the black population rose by 34,571 (28 percent) and the other nonwhite population showed an increase of 27,025, or a whopping 116 percent. Those shifts resulted in a population that in 1980 was reportedly 46 percent black, 35 percent white, and 10 percent Hispanic. In 1985 thousands of Asian refugees—Vietnamese, Cambodians, and Laotians—have moved to Oakland, and the city's Chinatown, with bustling markets, restaurants, and shops, has expanded greatly. Oakland is now a booming polyglot city.

Still, blacks are the dominant ethnic group. Since nonwhites tend to be underrepresented in Census counts, one hears unofficial estimates of a black population exceeding 60 percent. Whatever the actual percentage, there is no doubt that Oakland in 1985 is a city where blacks are politically powerful. Oakland has a black Mayor, four black City Council members (out of nine), a black City Manager, and a black middle class second in size only to Atlanta's. The Chief of Police, however, is white, and so are 61 percent of the sworn members of the Police Department. There is no requirement that Oakland police reside within the city, and only 13 percent actually do.

Race relations have long presented a problem for the Oakland P.D., particularly around the issues of police brutality and use of deadly force. The Black Panther party was founded in Oakland during the 1960s explicitly to defend the black community from what was perceived as police harassment. A loosely organized group, the party nevertheless achieved substantial symbolic significance among black youth during the 1960s and early 1970s. Relations between the police and the Panthers were worse than acrimonious and sometimes broke into armed conflict. Following the conviction of Panther leader Huey P. Newton for manslaughter in the death of a white policeman, a small group of Oakland police fired into the Black Panther office with rifles and shotguns, presumably because they felt that a conviction for first-degree murder would have been more appropriate.

There can be no doubt that hostile relations between police and community crested in Oakland in the mid-1960s, as they did in other places in America. The 1968 Report of the National Advisory Commission on Civil Disorders, on the basis of surveys conducted by them and others, found that "Negroes firmly believe that police brutality and harassment occur repeatedly in Negro neighborhoods. This belief is unquestionably one of the major reasons for intense Negro resentment against the police."[1] In Oakland there was frank recognition among ranking officers that black militants were expressing some of the community's most deeply held hostile feelings, even though the militants were more volatile and outspokenly oppositional than others were prepared to be.

At that critical juncture, 1967, the City Manager appointed a new Police Chief from within, Charles R. Gain. Gain, who is white, was unquestionably a reform Police Chief. He brought to the Police Department a civilian administrator, a female legal adviser, a family crisis intervention program, a landlord–tenant investigation program, a consumer fraud unit, conflict management training, and a peer panel of officers to review and analyze "critical incidents" showing unusual conflict with the public on the part of the officers involved. From the standpoint of community relations, however, Gain's most significant changes involved internal affairs investigations and the introduction of a restrictive use of deadly force policy. He took citizen complaints seriously and discharged thirty-eight policemen in six years following internal affairs investigations. Gain became a media favorite and often made public statements explaining a philosophy of police professionalism that stressed police compliance with the rule of law and service to all segments of the community.

Gain's administration was widely accepted and even lauded by various representatives of the black community—radicals, of course, could not accept any police chief. On the other hand, many rank-and-file policemen were to find themselves in both open and private conflict with him. At one time the Police Officers' Association (POA) voted no confidence in his future as Chief of Police. Some attributed rank-and-file dislike to Gain's severe, if not authoritarian, management style; others to his progressive policing philosophy. When he resigned in 1973 his successor, then Deputy Chief George Hart, organized a retirement dinner for him. More than 800 persons attended. Representatives of minority groups warmly praised the Gain administration. The POA sent a representative who spoke in terms that at most would be described as polite.

George Hart inherited a Police Department that had been hailed in the national media as a "near paragon of virtue," but it was scarcely that. The department had experienced six years of often deep antagonism between the Chief and the rank-and-file. Police administrators can often manipulate their troops into not doing certain things, but it is not so easy to move them toward more appropriate behavior. How do you tell whether cops are doing their job? Statistical checks are a necessary but insufficient means, and the department's statistical competence was at an all-time low. The Oakland P.D. had once enjoyed a highly sophisticated automated data processing system, but the city ordered it to sell off portions of the departmental ADP system in favor of a citywide central system. Unfortunately, the new centralized computer turned out to have all sorts of bugs. As a result the department lost much of its capacity to check on individuals and programs statistically. Chief Hart regards that period as a terrible hurdle for his administration.

Moreover, the mid-1970s were a time of economic retrenchment. Cities and states were experiencing fiscal crises, as was the Federal Government. Many of Charles Gain's innovative programs had benefited from Federal and state support, which was decreasing rapidly. As the department had to cut manpower by more than 100 between 1972 and 1979, virtually all of Gain's innovative programs were cut from the department budget. Gain's successor, George Hart, says that the "critical incidents" program was perhaps the most valuable of those cut. "But," he explains, "we couldn't afford it. The peer review panels usually occurred on days off, and the union required that we pay each panel member time and a half. I figured that each panel cost about $3,000. We simply couldn't afford to continue this worthwhile program." Hart adds that his toughest task has simply been holding the department together through budget and personnel cuts of the 1970s. "It's true," he says

somewhat ruefully, "we don't have a lot of programs. But its
tough to have innovative programs during a period of economic
austerity."

HIRING AND PROMOTION POLICIES

In addition to cutbacks, Hart faced the problem of dealing with
underrepresentation of blacks and women in the department.
Although the department had made considerable efforts to recruit ethnic minorities, the overwhelming majority of Oakland
police, nearly 85 percent, were still white males in a city that
was becoming increasingly black. Hart, who is attuned to the
constituencies that surround him, acknowledged that he simply
had to hire blacks and minorities. It is clear that Oakland, with
its increasing black and minority population, would not permit
a white police chief to retain his job unless he expressed sensitivity to the need for minority hiring. Hart does say forthrightly
that the minority hiring mandate was clear and justified. "You
can argue the merits of affirmative action all day long," he
says, "but everyone should recognize that when I was appointed Chief, I was given that mandate."

Local hiring was part of the affirmative action mandate.
Oakland had formerly—as part of its legalistic "professional"
image—hired nationally, not only from colleges like Michigan
State and Kent State but from Southern schools like Tulane and
Florida State. Many black residents saw those people as outsid-
ers, even "rednecks," seemingly an army of occupation.

Things looked markedly different from within the Oakland
P.D. "I was involved in the process," George Hart recalls,
"and I remember well when the insensitivity issue was raised.
It never occured to us, and we were probably naive. We took
great pride in our national recruiting and felt we were really
getting some top-notch people from around the county." Strict
local hiring was tried, but the "population was not there to
draw from in terms of qualified candidates," Hart says. "We
got into a situation where, quite frankly, we hired people who
did not belong, who could not compete, who should not have
been there. We were forced and did learn to give individualized

instruction, but I recognize we had some real problems." The department has stopped recruiting nationally, with priority given to Bay Area residents and then to Californians. Hart says he would like to resume national recruitment, which might now be accepted, given the changes in the country and particularly in the South.

It is questionable whether the politically influential Black Police Officers' Association would accept such a change. The Black Police Officers' Association is headed in 1985 by Sgt. Ceta Floyd-Peoples, an attractive, articulate 1975 graduate of U.C. Berkeley's School of Criminology. The BPOA was formed in the early 1970s to increase black hiring and promotion and to ease tensions between the black community and the police. According to Sgt. Peoples, relations with the community have definitely improved, a betterment she attributes to "getting more blacks and other minorities into the department with a different perspective, a different way of meeting and greeting people." There is no doubt that the intake of minority officers has increased. On the average more than 60 percent of new recruits have been minority members since 1973, with a low of 55 percent in 1977 and a high of 76 percent in 1979. As a result the Oakland P.D. has increased its minorities from 15.30 percent in 1973 to 39.51 percent of sworn officers in 1983. Such percentages, of course, are not yet entirely reflected in the higher ranks. In 1985, however, Captain Marvin Young replaced John Ream as one of the department's three Deputy Chiefs.

Perhaps even more important, the overall quality of white officers has improved, according to Sgt. Peoples: "Officers that make up the majority of the department now, who are young officers, who were raised in the sixties, who saw the peace movement, the Civil Rights movement, and that sort of thing, are sensitized to the reality that there are different people in this world. Because of that, bigotry is not as prevalent as it was twenty years ago, when I was growing up in Oakland. That is not to say that there are no racists or certain things that are unfair, but I don't think the magnitude is as great as it was."

Still, affirmative action and minority hiring have been a stiff, twisting road for the Oakland P.D. and perhaps especially for the Chief, who has experienced barbed criticism from all sides. Affirmative action is at least as searing an emotional is-

sue in policing as it is in other organizational settings. Oakland's Police Department for some years had been guided by a
conception of hiring and promotion according to demonstrated
merit rather than political clout as, say, in police departments
closely allied with political machines. In those circumstances,
affirmative action is easily interpreted as representing everything bad—unfairness, capitulation to political pressure, interference with ambition. On the other side, advocates of affirmative action could argue that its absence had led to a constabulary with few local roots and little understanding, a legalistic, crime control–oriented conception of police work, and
slight interest in serving the community. Thus, blacks claimed,
the department was insensitive to black community needs, was
hiring too few minorities, and was not promoting them fast
enough, while whites countered that hiring—and especially
promotion—should go to the most qualified.

After much discussion Hart and others had gotten the POA
to agree to promotion on the basis of a "band of five" princi-
ple. (One of his high-ranking officers says that Hart is "master-
fully skilled" in negotiating with the POA.) For example, in
1983 there were two openings for the position of captain. Formerly, the Chief would have had the discretion, under civil service rules, to promote two of the three top-ranked lieutenants.
Now he could promote two of the top five. He selected the first-
ranked, a white male, and the fifth-ranked, a black male. The
second-ranked white male was furious (as were other white
males who identified with him). But eventually this highly qualified applicant was promoted when other captaincies opened
up, and he calmed down. It is important to stress that the white
lieutenant who was passed over is widely regarded in the department as anything but a racist. Moreover, he held the black
lieutenant in high regard. But he saw the promotion as a violation of the more generalized normative prescription that people
should be promoted in order of demonstrated merit. However
defensible a policy of affirmative action may be in broad historical and community perspective, it is hard for an individual—
who has merited a place in line—to step aside for someone because of race or gender. There might be more sensitive *methods*
to introduce affirmative action—e.g. to offer credit for years of
community residence or knowledge of black history and culture, all of which are legitimate criteria for promotion in a city

like Oakland. Surely such a system would alter the structure of the promotion line without undermining norms of merit.

In any case the black lieutenant, by then a captain, was promoted in 1985 to Deputy Chief. Several high-ranking members of the department regarded that as an inevitable adjustment to the racial realities of the city and are predicting that the Deputy Chief will be the next Chief.

CIVILIAN COMPLAINT BOARD

The worst year for the department, the absolute low, was 1979, when nine black males, including a fifteen-year-old, were gunned down and killed by Oakland police. All of the shootings were investigated by the Alameda County District Attorney's office, the U.S. Attorney, and the Police Department's Internal Affairs investigators and found to be justifiable. Nevertheless, the shootings resulted in widespread dissatisfaction with the Oakland P.D., particularly in the minority community. Local black organizations, such as the NAACP and the Oakland Community Organization, as well as city agencies, received many complaints from Oakland citizens. As it had been in the 1960s, the Police Department was once again becoming the focus of community mistrust.

According to community activist Margaret Pryor, the city was in such turmoil that city officials decided to hold a public hearing in the Oakland Auditorium. Pryor says she was terrified by the anger and resentment the several hundred people attending held. "I felt unadulterated hatred in the auditorium. You could almost slice it," she remembers. She says the Mayor wisely recessed the meeting as the anger and resentment reached a really frightening pitch.

That meeting led to the formation of a Mayor-appointed committee, which recommended the formation of a Civilian Complaint Board (CCB). The board, composed of seven members—three women and four men; four blacks, one Hispanic, and two whites—is appointed by the Mayor. The CCB employs two staff people, one of whom is an investigator.

By all accounts, the CCB does not enjoy impressive investigative resources. The sole investigator usually solicits information through the mail and over the phone, because personal visits would stretch him too thin. Accused police officers rarely appear, since the board has no authority to subpoena them, as they do for civilian witnesses. The Oakland Police Officers Association has agreed in writing that it will not discourage its members from appearing before the board, but "not discouraging" is scarcely the equivalent of actively cooperating. Interviews with persons in and around the board concede that the board has not had much impact upon the Oakland Police Department. From within it is considered a necessary public relations annoyance, something to be put up with, but with no real clout. From without, even from members of the board, it is regarded as "another avenue of public scrutiny" rather than as an authoritative sanctioning force to be reckoned with. For that to happen, everyone agrees, would require substantial changes in authority and resources, and nobody expects that to happen soon. The Police Department and the union would wage a fierce political battle against such a development. For the time being, "Internal Affairs" will remain internal.

George Hart is acutely aware of the explosive potential of charges of excessive force against the Oakland Police Department. He and his staff would like nothing better than to develop a predictive device to ferret out problem cops, potential users of excessive force. The department has experimented with various weighted scales to identify those people, but so far the predictive devices are more an aspiration than a reality.

The number of complaints received by the CCB declined between 1981 and 1983. In 1981, 125 complaints were filed, 109 in 1982, and 66 in 1983. Although the board sustained twenty-six complaints during the three-year period, Deputy City Manager George Oini declined to uphold even a single ruling, on grounds that not even in one complaint could a preponderance of evidence be found to indicate that the complaints were justified. Internal Affairs has received a declining number of complaints about officers' use of excessive force, and the City Manager's refusal to sustain the Civilian Complaint Board in even one case is regarded in the department as something of a vindication of the Oakland P.D.'s success in controlling police use of excessive force.

At the same time, critics of the department contend that both Internal Affairs and the City Manager's office are not trustworthy. James Chanin, an attorney whose law office is a focal point for citizens' complaints, advises complainants to avoid Internal Affairs. "I don't send anyone to IA," says Chanin. "I've had some bad experiences with them. I just do not believe them capable of finding against their fellow officers. The standards they use are so high that you cannot get the number of convictions in IA that are deserved." Chanin points out that in rape and spouse-assault cases Oakland officers will take the word of the woman. "But," he adds, "they don't use the same standards with their own officers. If someone comes in with black and blue marks and says this officer beat me, they will not seriously entertain the notion that the officer could have done it—or even if they do, there's no set of circumstances where they'll find the complaint substantiated." Department brass in turn deny the truth of Chanin's allegations.

DEADLY FORCE

George Hart maintains a mediational leadership style that serves him well in the hothouse of Oakland city politics. A graduate of U.C. Berkeley who wears tweed jackets to the office and smokes a pipe, Hart is warm, engaging, modest, and above all patient. He once explained to an undergraduate seminar at Berkeley how he had spent nearly two years bringing his officers around to accepting a use-of-deadly-force policy that police in most cities would reject out of hand. He pointed out that most of the time the deadly force issue is framed in terms of whether police should be permitted to shoot any fleeing felon or to fire only in defense of their own lives or the lives of others. "But," he added, "that's not the real issue." He explained that Oakland P.D. policy for years (since Gain instituted it in 1968) had been that policemen should not be permitted to shoot any fleeing felon. That would have allowed trigger-happy police to impose capital punishment for minor property crimes. If police in Oakland shot every teenager who was running away from a marijuana arrest or an attempted auto theft, Oakland P.D. might have had several riots on its hands.

"The more difficult issue" Hart added, "concerns defense of life." Everybody agrees that if an officer or citizen is actually being shot at, the officer is entitled to return fire. "But suppose someone walked into this room, fired his gun, killed three people, threw the gun on the table, and ran away. Should a police officer be entitled to shoot at him as he is fleeing?" Hart's answer is that the officer should not for several reasons: He might injure innocent bystanders; he might be using unreasonable force to effect a capture; but most important, a defense-of-life policy without that limitation simply isn't a defense-of-life policy. Instead, it's a policy of permitting police to punish on the street.

Had Hart merely announced the restrictive deadly force policy without preparing the troops for it, he might have had an internal revolt, as Charles Gain, his predecessor, had when he first announced that police should not be permitted to shoot all fleeing felons. Gain was said to have held liberal and humane values outside the department but to have been an authoritarian within. Hart, by contrast, is of a piece. What you see is what you get inside and out—a quiet, thoughtful man with firmly held values, tempered by a deep appreciation of *realpolitik*.

On the other hand, Hart is criticized as overly cautious. Some of Hart's critics felt that he waited too long to announce the restrictive deadly force policy, that he procrastinated. Hart acknowledges that the deadly force policy was long overdue but points to an event that "complicated everybody's thinking." An Oakland motorcycle officer chased a speeding automobile onto Berkeley's Telegraph Avenue. The automobile's occupant slammed on the brakes, jumped out, and pumped two shots into the pursuing policeman. The assailant turned his back to the policeman, dropped the gun, and began running away. The wounded policeman fired and shot the man in the back, killing him. Hart says, "This happened hours before I was going to announce the new deadly force policy. But I realized that under our proposed policy the officer might not have been entitled to shoot, since he wasn't defending his life—the man was running away, and he wasn't menacing anybody else. Yet in my gut I felt the officer was entitled to shoot. I wanted to draft a policy that would deter policemen from shooting at the proverbial 'furtive movement' or 'glint of steel,' but I didn't want to go too far. This incident gave me a lot of trouble in drafting a policy."

There remains a certain confusion about what the Oakland P.D. deadly force policy actually is. On the one hand, it is clearly a defense-of-life rather than fleeing felon policy. But the more restrictive defense-of-life policy remains informal, no memorandum has been issued explaining it. Moreover, different ranking officers understand it differently. The Chief stoutly maintains that he will finally issue the more restrictive policy "by the time your book is completed. Anyhow, everybody on the street understands that shootings will be thoroughly investigated, and they'd better be able to justify defense of life."

BEAT HEALTH

Hart's and the Oakland P.D.'s policing philosophy—the aspirations for the department—is contained in a memorandum he issued two years after he became Chief entitled "Beat Health." The memorandum is in some ways as interesting for what it does not prescribe as for what it does. Beat health does not suggest a fundamental reorganization of the Police Department into local districts, with considerable authority offered to the commanders of those districts, as is contemplated in Santa Ana's team policing scheme.

Oakland did have a form of team policing, called a district patrol plan, during the 1970s, but it was discontinued. One ranking officer felt that it was a pretty good idea, but that a certain tension inhered between the added authority given to district sergeants in matters of deployment and scheduling, and loss of authority to the higher ranks. "The sergeants were just ecstatic about it," he said, "because they had a great deal of control over resources." Sergeants had some flexibility in terms of responding to developing crime and disorder problems, as well as the responsibility to make sure there were sufficient officers available to handle calls for service. Some sergeants did a good job of managing resources, while others apparently did not. Some would lay off too many men and have trouble managing calls for service. After about a year and a half the Oakland P.D. reverted to a more hierarchical, centrally controlled system, which basically removed responsibility from sergeants.

Would it be possible to reinstitute team policing in Oakland along Santa Ana lines, where an officer might be assigned to the same beat for a couple of years? The answer is no. Provisions of the "Memorandum of Understanding"—the labor contract between the police union and the city—could make team policing just about impossible. There has been a tremendous change during the past fifteen years across the country in the authority of police management to control shifts and duty assignments. No longer can the captain—or the Chief of Police in most cities—inform a police officer that he or she will be working in the patrol division, at a certain time schedule, assigned to a certain place for the next two years. "You can't do it in this department" we were told, "simply because he or she has the option of submitting a reassignment request card. If that person has seniority in the department, the request must be granted."

Oakland's seniority system not only precludes the possibility of team policing, it results in other management rigidities. It is understandable that, as in other institutions, officers would like to be able to choose when and where they would like to work for the next couple of years; as professors become more senior they are more likely to ask for and be assigned the most desirable teaching hours and offices. In the university setting that may mean that students will discover that senior professors tend to teach at similar hours of the day, say 10 A.M. to noon. In the Oakland P.D. there is a concentration of high-seniority people—which some officers equate with less productivity, less assertiveness—on the day watch, a mix on the 3 P.M. to midnight watch, a few on the dog watch. Yet, as one captain pointed out, "It's critically important that on the dog watch, where you've got basically new employees, to have some fairly capable, seasoned people. But if an opening should come up on day shift, the department is obliged to honor the most senior request."

Given the limitations of altering the officer's occupational environment, as team policing does, "beat health" is supposed to modify the perceptions of the patrolling officer by changing his values and priorities. The beat health concept stands in contrast to earlier conceptions of the police role defining the job of the patrolman as "law enforcement"—searching for and apprehending criminals. Beat health legitimates the expansion of the patrol officer's role to encompass such concerns as conditions contributing to neighborhood blight; unsanitary conditions and the security of buildings; and the needs of people who live, visit, or do business in the beat area.

Beat health is part of a more general department policy of proactive policing, which envisions the patrolman as a neighborhood crime preventer. Sgt. David Krauss, who is the Chief's aide and therefore a spokesperson for the department, says that "proactive policing is crime prevention. It's the same as putting stronger locks on your doors, forming a neighborhood watch program, joining a neighborhood security patrol. It means using crime analysis data to learn where you should deploy your officers, and what areas and what type of crime you ought to concentrate on. It means identifying suspicious persons and making field contacts. If the department wants crime to fall, it can't just wait for the phone to ring. The patrolmen's tour can't be governed by the 911 system."

The beat health concept envisions the patrol officer, in the first instance, as a set of eyes. Those eyes will take in the same scenes, irrespective of the officer's conception of his role; but what the officer perceives to be important varies with role conception. Moreover, the officer's vision is not supposed to be limited to what he can see from the patrol car. He is supposed to get out and walk periodically and to read local newspapers, neighborhood throwaways, and handouts of community groups and social agencies serving the beat. The officer is also encouraged to become active in home alert, neighborhood improvement, and community action groups in the beat area and to find out about noncriminal aspects of the beat: medical facilities, employment opportunities, merchant associations, and social service people who also work in the area. As in so many police departments, however—Houston and Denver come immediately to mind—philosophy is one thing, behavior another. The department has no systematic data-gathering capacity to find out whether the "Beat Health" injunctions are being followed.

In reading the "Beat Health" memorandum, one is struck by the parallels in thinking between it and the famous Wilson and Kelling article "Broken Windows" published years later, particularly that article's stress on the decaying neighborhood as a causal factor in the development of street crime.[2] The department strongly recommends that police involve themselves in cleaning up environmental eyesores—an abandoned refrigerator on a public lot littered with trash, garbage dumped in a vacant lot or park, abandoned vehicles, defaced or damaged property. In no part of the city is that mandate felt more forcefully than in downtown Oakland.

DOWNTOWN RENEWAL

Oakland, like many other American cities, is in the process of renewing its downtown area. Oakland's downtown is sometimes described as the Twilight Zone—when you're in it you don't know what next will happen to you, particularly after dark. It used to be that after executives and secretaries returned to their suburban residences, the only signs of remaining life were litter, bums, and menacing-looking teenagers. Downtown Oakland has not been entirely transformed, but signs of change are everywhere. Two of the most dramatic occurred when IBM moved its western headquarters to Oakland, creating 500 jobs and a new downtown plaza, and when the Hyatt Regency opened its doors in May 1983 next to the new Convention Center. Still, the X-rated Pussycat Theater marquee, offering such treats as "Insatiable" and "Up and Coming," greets Hyatt Regency guests as they exit its fashionable doors. Downtown Oakland unquestionably retains memorable features of its recent tawdriness.

Like every redeveloping city, Oakland faces a problem of what to do with the human beings—"the undesirables"—who occupy unsightly residences and dot public spaces. Part of the issue is housing relocation, finding adequate shelter for the elderly, welfare mothers, alcoholics, and others who are poor and disadvantaged in various ways. When that issue is not satisfactorily resolved—and it usually isn't—it may or may not become a concern for the Police Department. Always a front-line problem for the Police Department, however, is what might be called residual street deviance, the continuing presence of people whose appearance and behavior suggest enough threat or unpleasantness to incline others to avoid those streets. When IBM brings in 500 new employees, their potential economic benefit may go unexploited. Sizable numbers of them might brown bag their lunch instead of patronizing local restaurants. Those who might be interested in shopping for skirts, shirts, or jogging shoes may be loath to venture into the streets for their purchases. What can and should the police do about the problem? The Oakland Police Department has adopted several related strategies under the general rubric of a "Fourth Platoon," a mobile patrol force that includes canine patrol, helicopter patrol, mounted patrol, small vehicle patrol (dirt bikes, motor scooters, and small motorcycles), and foot patrol; two Special Duty Task Forces; and the RID program (see following section).

It is all costly and cannot be accomplished without financial support. All police departments must make do with limited resources. If the departmental brass allocate resources to beef up public safety in the downtown business area, communities in other areas of the city will find themselves with a reduced police presence and will certainly complain.

The central business community and the Oakland Police Department, acutely aware of the problem, worked out a partnership whereby the private sector subsidized the Oakland P.D. Such a partnership, however, generates its own concerns. To what extent can the department retain its autonomy if the private sector pays for enhanced policing? Will that set a precedent for other less affluent areas of the city? Do the less affluent within the downtown area lose their capacity to influence department policy within the area? Will they simply be displaced to other areas of the city? Will crime committed by "undesirables" be displaced to other areas of the city? All of those problems of equity and power must affect any private–public policing arrangement.

Although aware of all those issues, those in the Oakland P.D. who have been involved with it regard the partnership as a success, as do outside observers like the sociologist Albert J. Reiss, Jr., who has evaluated the program for the National Institute of Justice. Reiss lauds the business community and the Police Department for providing "dynamic leadership and commitment" for making the program a success.[3]

RID

To whom the streets belong in our society is not simply a matter of police and business community strategy. Its discussion invites broader consideration of constitutional law and policy. In *Papachristou* v. *City of Jacksonville*,[4] the Supreme Court in 1972 struck down an old-fashioned vagrancy ordinance for failing to give due notice of what it prohibited and for encouraging arbitrary and erratic arrests and convictions. Besides assailing the ordinance for sidestepping around the probable cause requirements of the Fourth Amendment, the Court declared it impermissible to make a crime of walking or wandering. There seems to be a constitutional right to public streets and sidewalks extending to "poor people, nonconformists, dissenters, idlers," and "so-called undesirables" who cannot be required to comport themselves according to an officially approved life-style.

Whatever one may think of the Supreme Court's juxtaposition of "dissenters" and "idlers," there can be no doubt that the problem of street deviance demands a rather fine sensitivity to the delicate interplay between the sometimes conflicting requirements of law enforcement and the maintenance of public order. The problem is not quite as the Court constructs it; it is not so much that loiterers may be planning a robbery as that loiterers may be responsible for an *aggregation* of minor incidents, some of which may be criminal and some not. Law enforcement can deal with individual persons committing individual acts, but certain kinds of loiterers repeat nuisance offenses and downgrade public places. An annoyingly aggressive panhandler, for example, can repeat his offense many times, but the average citizen will not bother to report the offense to the police. At the same time the police don't ordinarily enjoy the resources to observe decoys who are being panhandled and then make an arrest. Besides, local courts would not ordinarily impose severe enough sentences to deter the panhandler.

The 911 emergency system prioritizes calls according to their seriousness. Obviously an armed robbery must be responded to immediately. Annoying incidents, however, may not even be illegal. A man who exposes himself to a woman on the street has committed an act both obscene and illegal. But what about a man who stands at bus stops or street corners pursing his lips, making obscene noises and gestures, offering unsolicited invitations to erotic liaisons? That sort of unpleasant, even threatening behavior is the kind that the RID program encourages women to report. RID stands for Report Incidents Directly, a program designed to circumvent the 911 priority system. The RID program is not a big deal. Postcard-size forms were developed and distributed to office buildings in the downtown area. The forms contained the obvious questions: What happened? What did the person or persons who did it look like? and so forth. Respondents were asked to mail the cards to the Oakland Police Department or hand them to any officer or security guard. No precise tally was made of returned forms, but the department estimates that several hundred were turned in during 1984. After an active return of forms during the program's beginning, returns began to decline either because of lack of interest or, more likely, because police had been able to deal with some of the problems the forms referred to.

FOOT PATROL

Foot patrol, sometimes enhanced by cops on horseback, motor scooters, even ten-speed bicycles, are all used in the greater downtown area to deal with what Captain Pete Sarna, head of the Fourth Platoon, calls "soft crime." How the Oakland police have chosen to deal with soft crime is certainly not lacking in controversy. Sarna is a thoughtful man who reads widely on the police and other social organizations and who clips *New York Times* articles on police-related matters. He comments—when asked by us to do so—about an article in the *Express: The East Bay's Free Weekly*, a surprisingly well-written free newspaper that subsists on advertising. The article laments the treatment of Skid Row inhabitants in downtown Oakland. The Hyatt Regency is described as a "rhomboid, pristine, modernistic tower" in sharp contrast to the old, rundown residential hotels, empty lots, demolition sites, and out-of-the-way places to sleep that used to be accessible to "winos and bag people."[5]

Sarna doesn't appreciate that viewpoint at all. "That article," he says, "mentions certain behaviors as essential to the
Skid Row life-style. If the author means urinating in public, being loud and abusive in public, panhandling, and things of that
sort, well, they may be essential to the style of life, but they are
also for the most part unacceptable and unlawful."

Oakland foot patrolmen and women, with whom we walked
on morning, noon, and night shifts in downtown Oakland and
in the Fruitvale district of East Oakland, share Sarna's perception. Poverty is not a crime, they say, but a fine distinction is
drawn between the reputable and disreputable poor, as public
officials have done in England and the United States since the
beginning of industrial capitalism. Of course, not only public
officials share that view. The overwhelming majority of the
public shares it as well, including both the rising bourgeoisie
(today we call them yuppies) and the reputable poor, black,
Hispanic, and Asian residents who want to shop and work in
Oakland without being exposed to fetid odors, loud noises, or
abusive remarks.

It is interesting that another article in the same free weekly
is written from the perspective of the soft-crime victim. The author, Tom Johnson, writes:

Seems like every time I've gone out this week I've run into
some crazy person. Some guy came up to me on the street the
other day and said he didn't like my face. I pushed him out of
the way but he stood there screaming at me as I went on up the
street. I could hear him for blocks. And last week I saw these
four teenagers setting fires on a BART train. And the bus is
like a goddamn zoo, always someone screamin' about how he's
gonna rape some woman, or how abortion is murder, or how
Jesus is comin' back to burn up all the sinners. It's getting so I
think twice before I leave the house![6]

Whether Johnson's remarks are to be taken as writer's license or fact, the feelings expressed are not uncommon, particularly among persons whose incomes demand that they use
public facilities for transport and recreation. Those who can afford to travel by automobile, belong to private country or athletic clubs, and reside in more affluent neighborhoods are less
likely to experience disturbing encounters.

Foot patrol seems to be part of the answer to disturbance. The foot patroller is constrained by the law, which means that he or she is reined in by the twin constraints of observation and complaint. We have seen arrests made of people who were weaving down the street or sleeping in the street or "sack-sucking"—drinking whisky out of an open bottle encased in a brown paper bag. But what does a patrolman do with a man who is standing at the edge of a mini-park in downtown Oakland, dressed in dirty clothes evidently obtained from a Mission or a surplus store, shouting about the imminent return of Jesus? "Nothing I can do about him," says the foot patrolman, "He's not really breaking a law." He is not accosting people, he is not asking them for money, he is what has become a natural part of many urban scenes, a residual street deviant who is ignored by passersby.

By contrast, with another foot patrolman, Sherman Bennett, we see a black man in his twenties standing at the back of a restaurant and bar in Jack London Square. His back is turned and the patrolman mutters, "I wonder what he's doing." We walk toward the man and see that he is fiddling with the zipper on his pants.

"What were you doing?" asks the officer.
"I was taking a leak. Didn't mean any harm."
"Why didn't you use the restroom in the bar?"
"I didn't have any money to buy a drink."
"Do you have any identification?"

The young man empties his pockets. Nothing there. The officer grows suspicious. "What's your name?" he asks.

"Byron Dawson."
"Where do you live?"

The young man gives an address in San Jose.

The officer turns on his radio and inquires whether warrants are outstanding for anyone with that name and that address. The dispatcher says there aren't for a Byron Dawson but there are for a Brian Dawes, who lives two blocks away from the address the young man has given.

Now the officer is visibly suspicious. He unsuccessfully tries to persuade the young man to admit he is Brian Dawes. The of-

ficer calls his patrol supervisor, Lt. Krathwohl, who arrives on
the scene within five minutes. He agrees with the officer's suspicions, tells him to arrest the young man, and explains the arrest: "We don't know who you are and we think we'd better
take you in, arrest you for urinating in public. If you'd taken
your leak in a less public place we might not have arrested
you."

The young man protests, but to no avail. The real purpose
of the arrest is to find out, through fingerprints, whether this is
the man wanted on three burglary warrants. The young man
continues to protest, but the names of Oakland residents he
might know do not produce answers to the officer's phone calls.
The young man behaves more erratically, begins to curse quietly. "You have devil eyes," he says to us. The officer laughs at
the mutterings and takes the young man back to the Oakland
City Jail for booking. The next day we find out that the officer's
suspicions were correct: The young man was wanted on the
burglary warrants.

We learn two elemental points about foot patrol. One, appearance and demeanor count for much on the street. The
other: Arrests for nuisance violations can sometimes produce
felony suspects.

Much of the time, however, foot patrollers do not make arrests as a way of preserving public order. They admonish. One
of the best at this, as well as at making arrests, is Sue Hoffman,
a petite yet sturdy, attractive, straightforwardly businesslike
woman in her late thirties, capable of either making arrests or
telling people to behave themselves when she feels it appropriate. In walking with her, we noticed no less "respect" given her
than other foot patrollers. The badge, the gun, the uniform—
most of all, the interactional poise—lend her all the authority a
police officer could expect. She and the department take the
view there is nothing wrong in saying to someone suspected of
being a street drug dealer: "There's no legitimate reason for
your being here. Please leave."

But officers are not always so polite. Even when they are,
the patrolman's admonition may be felt as "harassment." The
foot patroller is above all an observer who knows who belongs
and who doesn't, who are the regulars and the transients. A
somewhat more idealized version of foot patrol is offered by
Wilson and Kelling when they say, "The essence of the police

role in maintaining order is to reinforce the informal control mechanisms of the community itself.'' Here they are discussing what they call ''the standards of the neighborhood.'' The problem is that downtown Oakland is not a neighborhood, a place where people live, except for the ''winos and bag people.'' Clearly, Wilson and Kelling are not suggesting that the standards of the ''disreputable'' poor be served. In such non-neighborhood conditions standards become vague, ambiguous, hard to define.

Foot patrolman Chris Rye told us confidently that he knew things were in order when he ''owned the street,'' by which we took it to mean that he regulated street deviance. We watched him patrol the street and talk to people who look vaguely deviant. While we were observing, a young man walked toward us and asked for spare change. Clearly the patrolman only partly owned the street.

To be fair, however, we talked with four merchants on the same street, identified ourselves, and asked whether they liked having the patrolman around. They waxed enthusiastic and said the street was enormously improved over what it had been. Are the standards of the neighborhood those of the merchant, the owning or renting resident, or the street wanderers and walkers? Police everywhere naturally gravitate toward the standards of established institutions and reputable citizens.

PROSTITUTION AND DRUG DEALING

There can be no question that drug dealing and prostitution are Oakland's most serious and persistent street problems. After all, this is a city with an overwhelmingly minority youth population that has a low income and is unemployed or under-employed. Young men can earn far more dealing dope than washing cars, if those low-level jobs were even available.

Although prostitution and drug dealing have traditionally been labeled as victimless crimes, that is true only in a narrow sense. When consenting adults perform sexual acts in private, whether for love or money, those activities could properly be regarded as victimless. But the conceptual niceties of sociological and legal reasoning are challenged by the phenomenon of street prostitution. To citizens who reside on streets populated by prostitutes, the presence of the ladies of the night—in Oakland not uncommonly of the day—is a species of environmental pollution. That is especially so when sexual liaisons become visible to children or passersby.

The Oakland Police Department counters street prostitution at the behest of predominantly black community organizations. That is, of middle-class and working-class persons who are offended by the presence of prostitutes in their neighborhoods. The police employ two strategies. One is arguably illegal harassment; the other is legal female undercover officers who discourage men—often nonresidents—from seeking assignations on the streets of Oakland. Both foot patrolmen and those occupying vehicles stop and talk with night ladies. We have ridden around with such patrolmen, and the ladies usually turn out to be teenage girls, the cousins and sisters of the young men who are dealing dope down the street.

Oakland street prostitutes have to be bold to advertise their services. It is rare to find a prostitute dressed in neat, conventional attire, and little imagination is needed to identify street prostitutes. Cops and ordinary citizens can spot a hooker a block away. For a courtesan, an ambiguous appearance might generate hesitancy, even embarrassment, on the part of the lustful male, and that's not good for business. So a streetwalker's body language is virtually unmistakable. If "probable cause" were simply to mean more probable than not, police might have a tenable argument to arrest on a combination of appearance and demeanor. At the same time officers do "harass" such women by inquiring what they are doing on the street, telling them to move on, and arresting them if they set foot in the street and wave to occupants of a car on the clearly fictitious, absurd grounds of "directing" traffic.

So a game of social and legal fictions develops. Hookers pretend they are strollers, and cops pretend hookers direct traffic. The cop does so not to punish but to discourage. To the police the prostitute is not a "dissident" or an "idler" but a person conducting an illegal business, annoying the neighbors, and often supporting a pimp and a drug habit. To police, prostitutes do not represent the disreputable poor but the disreputable semiaffluent.

Simplistic variables like income and education simply cannot capture the complex reality of the social stratification of this most racially integrated of all American cities. Affluent whites live in the hills alongside some affluent blacks. There are lower-income whites, working people, students, and artisans living in the flatlands. There is a small affluent black middle class and a much larger black working class composed of people who own small homes and go to churches. The "criminals" are usually young people between thirteen and twenty-five who may be the sons and daughters of respectable Baptists. Unemployed black entrepreneurs may well become street drug dealers.

The proceeds from drug dealing have a ripple effect on the middle class. Proceeds may be used to pay off mortgages, buy furniture, put food on the table, and send children through school. At the same time local residents, members of black-dominated Oakland community organizations and the black churches, pressure the Police Department to move the drug dealers off the streets.

We have ridden around with drug enforcement squads when they have made controlled street buys and subsequent arrests. The typical catch of the day is a seventeen- or eighteen-year-old black male who may reside in the neighborhood where he is dealing drugs. These are neighborhoods where residents use the drugs, particularly marijuana, that are being sold out on the street.

During the mid 1980s law enforcement authorities—both county prosecutors and city police—began to experience growing and persistent pressure to control drug dealing in the Oakland streets, particularly dealing that was open, flagrant, and increasingly dangerous. Lieut. Al Perrodin, head of the Oakland Police Department's Homicide Division, estimates that in 1984, of 117 homicides, approximately 32 were drug-related. According to the 1984 Uniform Crime report, published by the FBI, Oakland's homicide rate is the sixth highest among the nation's cities, following Gary, Detroit, Miami, New Orleans, and Richmond. "Most of the drug-related homicides," Lt. Perrodin says, "occurred right on the street. The victims were either known drug dealers or users, with drug paraphernalia visible nearby." He adds: "The homicides were flagrant. Anybody who lived or worked in the vicinity had to be terrified."

The shootings generated prominent newspaper and TV coverage throughout the Bay Area. Oakland, which had never enjoyed an image as a peaceable and safe community, began more than ever to appear as a drug-infested, dangerous city. It was not the sort of city to which big businesses or middle-class professionals would gravitate for profit or residence.

A special duty unit, known colloquially as the "Drug Task Force," was created to address the growing street problem of illegal drug trafficking in the city. The unit was formed after the Chief called a "think tank" meeting among senior officers and asked, "What haven't we done, what have we left out?" The discussion suggested an appraisal different from the Vice Squad's reliance upon informants and its "up the ladder" concern for bigger dealers. Instead, it was proposed that a unit be formed to target enforcement in areas identified through community complaints about neighborhood, park, or street corner drug dealing. Those complaints, coupled with knowledge of beat officers, provided a more than abundant data base for identifying thirty initial locations where street drug selling was conspicuous. As the unit's presence became more widely known in the community, additional locations were reported by citizens. The informants were not required to give their own names but were asked to cooperate in naming the drug sellers or, if the sellers' names were unknown to them, to identify them through a physical description. Certain locations turned out to pose continual problems, e.g. the "tree streets" (Walnut, Oak, and so on) of East Oakland, and were worked regularly.

We spent a weekend with the Task Force, day and night, to observe how it was organized and how it functioned.

Headed by Lieut. Ray Birge, who oversees a related Special Duty Unit as well, the Task Force is composed of a sergeant and ten patrolmen, selected for aggressiveness, physical prowess, street smarts, and willingness to work irregular hours. Patrolman Mike Baldassin, for example, played for three years on the San Francisco 49ers' special teams and is said to be the only Task Force member who can be counted on to catch a fleet young drug dealer in a flat-out foot race. Two of the ten members are black and usually pretend to be drug buyers.

Sgt. John Sterling, who can scarcely squeeze his towering 6 foot, 8 inch frame into the compact undercover cars, is the key man. He holds daily briefings, selects personnel, and decides which locations to target. The Task Force moves as quickly as possible, hitting a half-dozen, even ten locations in one shift.

The Task Force's typical and successful tactic is the buy-quick-bust (BQB). An area is selected, and four undercover cars park so as to surround the location where it is expected the buy will occur. A scout is sent in to report whether "action" is happening or the area is a "ghost town." If the latter, another location is selected by the sergeant, and the entire force moves on to it. Assuming there is action, one of the black officers makes a buy—most Oakland drug dealers are black or Hispanic and are wary of white buyers—while the other "spots" and reports when the buy goes down, along with a good description of the seller.

Sometimes other officers will spot as well from behind steps or bushes, or from tops of roofs. For example, we "spotted" on one occasion with Baldassin and his partner, Barney Rivera. To get to the spotting location, we drove along the freeway at night, parked, climbed a barrier, tramped down a hill through deep foliage, and then hid behind bushes and trees to observe the buy from a block and a half away. The observations were made by Baldassin, who was equipped with a special telescope facilitating night observations.

When a buy occurs, the other officers move in. On our first BQB we were riding with Sterling and Officer Terry McCrea. The suspect spotted our brown Chevrolet—it's hard to miss 6 foot, 8 inch Sterling, in uniform, behind the wheel—and took off running. Sterling hit the brakes hard, flung open the doors, and ran. We followed. McCrea shouted, "Stop, or I'll shoot," which was in fact an empty threat. A split second later we heard what we thought were three distinct shots and assumed someone was firing at us. Actually, the shots were coming from a backfiring car. The suspect, who also thought he was being fired on, hit the ground. He was overcome with fear and wet his pants. He turned out to have been released eleven months earlier from San Quentin, where he had been confined after an armed robbery conviction.

The buy-quick-bust seems an effective tactic. The Task Force uses marked money for the buy, the possession of which is clear evidence of a sale. Such arrests result in a sure-fire charge and conviction. Overall the District Attorney's office charged 86 percent of the unit's 449 arrests between December 10, 1984, and May 31, 1985. Those who were not charged usually had been busted following identification from a surveillance point, such as a roof of a building, or identification by an undercover man blending into a crowd.

The BQB is, however, the principal Task Force tactic. Others are used when the Task Force is understaffed on a given day, particularly when lacking undercover buyers. The BQB is superior to the Vice Squad's "Buy-Bust" strategy, where buys are made and warrants later secured (a street seller has no privacy rights and so warrants are not needed) or where a time lapse occurs so as not to "burn" the buyer.

Still, there is no real way to control the drug trade. Everybody understands that, perhaps especially those who enforce the drug laws. The street drug Task Force can contain drug sales occurring in streets and parks, making those locations more accessible to residents and families. In a sense that is a big achievement. For Sgt. John Sterling there is no ultimate success. Sterling is gratified when he sees children playing in parks and playgrounds. "Parks," he says, "are for kids. When I see families and kids in the parks, I feel we've accomplished something." Lieut. Ray Birge writes, in a memo to Chief Hart dated March 19, 1985, with scholarly caution:

The true measure of success is not in the number of arrests. The actual measurement is far more difficult to quantify. The test will be the amount and type of street drug dealing that continues to occur. This is probably more accurately reflected by citizen satisfaction and simple visual survey of the neighborhoods than any other means.

Still, in a city like Oakland, "citizen satisfaction" can be an idea tinged with ambiguity. Drug sales are in many ways the linchpin of an underground economy, the proceeds of which serve to shore up an overground economy that in turn fails to provide jobs and opportunities for minority youths.

In a sense the real class conflict in Oakland then becomes projected as between blacks in the overground and those in the underground economy. Whites at every level are more closely integrated into the overground economy. That is not to say that there are no whites in the drug trade. But one rarely, if ever, sees a white drug salesman on the streets of Oakland as one would, for example, on the streets of Berkeley or San Francisco. Oakland's drug trade is predominantly black. When arrests are dismissed or taken to be relatively unimportant crimes by the district attorneys, black Oakland residents complain bitterly that even when the police make arrests, the dealers are the next day back on the streets.

RECENT CRITICISM AND SUPPORT

Oakland is a city experiencing the ironies that many other cities also have come to live with. The black residential community complains that its streets are being neglected by the police. The police respond with more aggressive enforcement, which may be translated into "harassment" by low-income black citizens on the street. Six lawsuits were filed on May 14, 1984, seeking more than $4.8 million in damages from the city of Oakland. The suits all alleged discrimination against blacks and use of excessive force to make arrests by Oakland officers. Oliver Jones, an NAACP attorney and one of a group of lawyers who won a $3 million Federal judgment against neighboring Richmond in 1983, says that in the past two years "there has been a steady upsurge of racial abuse and excessive force by Oakland police officers." His partner, James Chanin, adds, "What I see or have seen from this office—and we get complaints from the NAACP and the ACLU plus referrals from other lawyers—the Oakland Police Department is periodically very bad. One period was in 1979–80, and even in 1981. Another was late 1983 to 1984."

Just about the same time those lawsuits were filed, for three days in mid-May 1984 KRON-TV (Channel 4) presented a series of investigative reports charging the Oakland police with "brutality and harassment." KRON organized its story around five police officers, including a black Oakland policewoman, Teresa Jeffery, who said, "I have all of my brothers and sisters living in Oakland, and I am afraid for them making a vehicle violation . . . hey, if they run a red light they may get beat up." The other officers on the program made similar charges. Oliver Jones was shown supporting the charges and pointing to the people who have filed lawsuits as victims of police brutality.

KRON's investigative reports drew various responses. The Mayor and the City Manager backed the Police Department but agreed to investigate further. We did some further investigations ourselves and concluded that the documentary presented a simplistic approach to a complex situation.

For example, KRON commissioned a scientifically drawn survey of three hundred Oakland residents to determine "how the Oakland community perceives the quality of its Police Department." The documentary reported three principal findings from the telephone poll. Two of the findings were highlighted by graphic headlines: "A Double Standard of Justice" and "Too Much Force."

Every student of survey research understands that if you change the wording of a question you may well turn up a different response. The KRON survey violated that fundamental tenet of survey interpretation. Respondents were not actually asked about double standards of justice or too much force. Those surveyed were asked to agree or disagree with several statements. One was: "The Oakland Police Department treats everyone the same regardless of race." People answering the question might well have figured that people are often treated differently because of race. Different treatment does not necessarily imply a "double standard of justice."

The question of "too much force" is even more complicated. Respondents were asked to agree or disagree with: "When Oakland police have to deal with someone, they use no more force than is absolutely necessary." Thirty-two percent of white respondents and 23 percent of black ones—27 percent of all those surveyed—didn't answer the question. No other question drew as many failures to answer. By contrast, only 3 percent of the respondents didn't answer the following question: "If I were stopped by an Oakland police officer, I'd feel intimidated." The results were not reported on the program, yet both white and black respondents, by nearly three to one, said they would not feel intimidated.

On the only direct question—"Do you approve or disapprove of the job the Oakland Police Department is doing?"—82 percent of white and 74 percent of black citizens voiced approval. That seems an overwhelming vote of confidence in the performance of Oakland police. It is hard to reconcile that level of approval with charges of widespread brutality, racism, and harassment of minorities. A close look at the survey does show, however, that although the Oakland P.D. generally enjoys public confidence, white citizens are more approving than blacks.

The Oakland Police Department surely has some problems—and some problem officers. But there is too much support from significant members of the black community to suggest that the kinds of charges leveled in the most recent of the controversies were justified. Following the KRON controversy, Pastor J. Alfred Smith of the largest church in East Oakland's flatlands, the Allen Temple Baptist Church, wrote to Councilman Frank Ogawa that he had often been critical in the fourteen years of his pastorate of the sensitivity of the Oakland Police Department, but that his members had not recently reported any instances of police brutality in East Oakland; that his own experiences had been positive; that the Oakland police had been responsive to the pleas of the community to deal with drug problems "that are rampant in East Oakland"; and that he had discovered in recent years a "better-trained police officer and have felt that I have not done enough to give that officer support."

Sergeant Ceta Peoples, head of the Black Police Officers' Association membership, agrees. She sees the new black police officer as someone who will assess issues on their merits. "Our association," she says, "will continue to aggressively go behind charges. There is no way we're going to support an obviously misleading interpretation of the Oakland Police Department."

CONCLUSION

The Oakland Police Department has in many respects resolved the problems it was facing during the late 1960s. Blacks and women are no longer unrepresented in its ranks, and it is affirmatively acting to promote minorities to positions of authority in the department. At the same time it might be argued that the Oakland Police Department has not really transcended the

problems of the 1960s. It is still responding to those. That may
be because it is so easy for critics to evoke images of those earlier days, images which have to do with police misconduct and
Police Department response to that misconduct. As a result the
department often finds itself in a defensive and negative posture of fending off criticism, an overall stance that directs attention away from organizational creativity and innovation.

In general, the Oakland Police Department provides the
community with essential patrol services and a fair measure of
public safety. The department's main problem is with its strategy of so-called proactive policing. It finds itself in the catch-22
position of being damned if it does and damned if it doesn't. To
the extent that officers patrol aggressively in response to community demands to keep the streets safe and attractive, the department is liable to invite accusations of harassment and even
of brutality.

It might be possible, with large-scale structural changes like
the ones we have seen in Santa Ana, to reduce some of the of-
fensiveness of proactivity, that is, to engender community support through positive organizational efforts between minority
communities and the police. Some of that is occurring, but
without the drive and commitment observable in Santa Ana—
or in Detroit, and Newark, with their mini-stations.

Substantial structural change within the Police Department
seems formidable and unlikely. Chief Hart is satisfied that everything that can be done is being done. "I take pride," he
says, "that the department is doing a commendable job." He
questions whether further change is necessary and bridles at in-
vidious comparisons between his regime and that of his predecessor. The Oakland department used to be considered one of
the most, if not the most, innovative in the nation. Hart is not
much interested in novelty and experimentation. "The innovation of the eighties is to survive," he argues. Thus, there is little
taste for new programs. Hart does not enjoy a high profile in
the community, trips around the country, meetings, seminars,
or jaunts to Washington. He sees his job as maintaining a func-
tioning department.

Similarly, the rank-and-file have won considerable gains
through the union and have no particular interest in generating
change. For change to occur in policing, it might be better to

have a really terrible department—characterized by corruption, racism, and laziness—which can be transformed from top to bottom. Oakland is not, nor has it ever been, a terrible department. On the contrary, it has long been considered one of the better ones in the United States. Thus it was always easy, particularly given Oakland's reputation for innovation during the Gain era, to think about minor tunings rather than major changes.

Response to controversy, rather than a larger vision and planning on the basis of that vision, seems to fuel movement within the department. Sometimes, as in the introduction of downtown foot patrol and related problems, the department encourages a middle manager to work with the business community. It could be said that the business community is easy for a police department to work with, but that would be too glib.

In fact, the department has clearly been responsive to minority communities as well. Out of an authorized component of 992 positions—635 sworn and 357 nonsworn—minorities made up nearly half the total work force and 39 percent of the sworn staff. The department has aggressively recruited minorities, and minority promotions within ranks have gone up as well.

There are surely advantages to a responsive leadership style, particularly in a department that in many respects is very good. Department morale is higher than in many police departments. Besides, cops, like soldiers, love to gripe about the inadequacies of higher ranks.

At the same time there are disadvantages to the "If it ain't broke, don't fix it" philosophy. One is this: The transmission of positive values invites and thrives on dynamic leadership, yet a "response-complaint" style does not require or generate that sort of leadership. Another occurs around the perception of problems. Things may not be seen as requiring repair until they are badly broken, and by then they are harder to fix. From the vantage point of positive innovation, a cautious responsive leadership style implies that the vision of what the department might look like in five or ten years is an essentially similar version of its current self, almost a substitution of management by complaint for management by objective. In such circumstances it is harder to motivate in any given direction.

7

NEWARK:
Innovation Amidst Burnout

ALL THAT SEPARATES Manhattan's World Trade Center from Newark's Gateway complex is a fifteen-minute, inexpensive train ride. A Gateway Hilton Hotel guest can take an elevator to the lobby, breakfast in the Hilton coffee shop, walk through an enclosed bridge, and take the PATH train to the big city. Our traveler can go about business, enjoy a meal in Manhattan, return in the evening, and entirely avoid contact with the City of Newark. That would be a mistake, because knowledgeable Manhattan residents—but only a relative handful—drive to Newark's Portuguese Ironbound district for mussels and paella. Most New Yorkers, however, as well as most residents of New Jersey suburbs, avoid the sidewalks of Newark because of the city's almost legendary reputation for mean streets. That reputation is not undeserved. Things have improved downtown recently, but most streets remain uninviting.

Newark has never won awards as one of America's model cities. It has been consistently at the other end of the scale. Robert Curvin described it as "the metaphor of America's urban crisis."[1] George Sternlieb likened it to a sandbox where the poor are left to busy themselves.[2] Norton Long labeled it a reservation for the unwanted.[3] And David Shipler characterized it as "the real truth about America, the nation's subconscious finally stripped of its rationalizations and platitudes."[4] Yet, as we shall demonstrate, it has been possible through initiative and executive vision for Newark's Police Department to be innovative and resourceful.

Newark's record of public safety has long been dismal. Between 1965 and 1973 the Newark homicide rate was about three times the national average.[5] Dorothy Guyot, who studied Newark crime during the 1970s, reports that the homicide rate was accompanied by increases in violent and property crimes, surpassing the rate in other cities.[6] There has been some decline in crime in the early 1980s.[7] For example, Newark's crime rate per 1,000 dropped from 126.1 in 1981 to 112.8 in 1982. Its violent crime rate similarly declined from 38.0 in 1981 to 33.6 per 1,000 in 1982. Homicides dropped from 166 to 118, while burglaries fell from 10,700 to 8,760. But those are still huge numbers. In that same year Santa Ana experienced 814 burglaries and 28 homicides.[8] Newark had 10,515 larcenies to Santa Ana's 1,800 and 3,779 aggravated assaults to Santa Ana's 330. Square inch for square inch, Newark could contend for the title of crime capital of the Western world.

THE ECOLOGY OF NEWARK

Newark's extraordinary inclination toward crime is shaped partly by its density. Newark is a very small city. Strictly speaking, Newark's population of 330,000 is crowded into 23.5 square miles. Actually, the meadowlands and the airport occupy about one-third of that space. "I've got 3.3 square miles in my district and about 130,000 people," says Captain George Dickscheid, a forty-two-year-old white man who has been in the department since 1965. It goes without saying that the overwhelming majority of Dickscheid's "people" are poor, black—and young. Dickscheid is regarded by the Director and his colleagues as one of the department's top cops, one of several to whom visiting researchers are sent when the department wants to show its best face. Dickscheid's district includes the high-rise towers of the Reverend William P. Hayes Housing Project, where the 1967 riot began. It is worth quoting from the Report of the National Advisory Commission on Civil Disorders describing the beginnings of the riot to comprehend the potential for animosity between police and west district residents: "From the dark grounds of the housing project came a barrage of rocks. Some of them fell among the crowd. Others hit persons in the line of march. Many smashed the windows of the police station. The rock throwing, it was believed, was the work of youngsters; approximately 2,500 children lived in the housing project."9

Newark's high rises stand fifteen stories tall. Residents who are victimized by gangs of youths fear reporting crime to the police. "I've visited various cities around the country," Dickscheid says, "and in all of them public housing projects present a crime problem, a problem of defensible space. The high rises in this city are an even worse problem." Patrolmen hate the high rises. Patrol cars have been hit with bottles and trash, and even fired upon, from distant windows. Radio communications are difficult inside the buildings. The department is reluctant to send a single officer to the tenth floor of such a building to handle a disturbance call, because "you may not hear from him again."

The high rise problem is presented to us vividly one morning as we are being driven by a sergeant from the Director's office to the West Precinct house. We are passing a high rise when we hear sirens and see flashing lights. An armed robbery has occurred just a few miles away in a neighboring suburb. The robbers, three young black males, are being pursued by police. They drive their car into one of the interior roads of the high-rise housing project. They abandon their car—a stolen vehicle—and disappear into the building. We observe as police question residents who might have seen the young men. Nobody will admit to having seen anything. The young men simply vanish into the sanctuary of the labyrinthine structure.

Still, the high-rise apartment buildings appear more substantial than the low-rise residences of the west district. Worn, shabby, and old, like most of those in the black neighborhoods of Newark, the buildings are often tidy and well-tended; at other times they are neglected and desolate. Newark contains some attractive streets and houses on the better side of the railroad tracks, the predominantly Portuguese Ironbound district. An enclave of stately residences brightens the far north, where the Police Director resides alongside local professionals, business people, and the stirrings of a few Manhattan white-collar workers seeking exceptional value in housing. In much of Newark, however, housing is depressed, weatherbeaten, and rundown. We observe from a police car burned out dwellings whose boarded and blackened windows offer compelling testimony to the straitened circumstances of local residents. When abandoned houses are razed, the remaining empty lots are often scattered with litter and waste, further contributing to an impression of urban decay.

NEWARK'S HISTORY

If the social landscape of Newark leaves much to be desired, so does its history of urban governance. Between 1917 and 1954 Newark was run by five Commissioners elected at large. They seemed continually to be jockeying for the patronage coincident with controlling city departments. The historian Charles A. Beard wrote that the commission two years after its inception was "extravagant, inefficient and potentially vicious."[10] The rise of civil service curbed some of the power of the Commissioners—employees could not be fired after a change in Commissioners—but new Commissioners could still hire political supporters and shift incumbents around to more or less choice jobs, depending on political support.

The history of the Newark commission system is also a history of intermittently exposed corruption. Votes were falsified on a large scale, commissioners were periodically investigated in connection with scandals: the purchase of swampland by the city at a price much higher than the assessed value; extortion from city milk suppliers; kickbacks from city employees; and extortion by the Board of Adjustment. Corruption became an entrenched tradition.

THE POLICE DEPARTMENT

This brief discussion of the appearance of Newark and its traditions are necessary for understanding the limits of contemporary reform. The Newark Police Department historically mirrored the inadequacies and characteristics of the rest of city
government. "Like the commission government," Guyot
writes, "the police department was ill-organized, unproduc-
tive, and overstaffed."[11] It was undoubtedly also corrupt. In
1948 the Police Department's 1,236 officers were double the urban average for officers per capita. The 1948 annual report was
nothing more than a loose-leaf collection of reports from more
than a dozen units. There was not even a consecutive number-
ing of pages. The physical plant was horrendous, yet some of
the same precinct houses remain in use today. If they were out-
dated by 1948, by 1985 they can only be described as archaic,
minimally serviceable ruins.

The fact that the Newark Police Department was a lamenta-
ble organization before and after World War II does not mean
it had no room to decline. And so it did until 1958, when Mayor
Leo Carlin appointed New York Assistant Chief Inspector Joseph Weldon to the position of Police Director. Weldon was a
Patrick Murphy protégé who introduced some modern administrative techniques during his four-year tenure from November
1958 to June 1962. Weldon overhauled the patrol force. He
used unmarked cars to saturate high-crime areas and substi-
tuted civilians for patrolmen to carry the brunt of writing parking tickets.

Weldon instituted other changes intended to upgrade the
professionalism of the department according to the prevailing
theories of the day. A tenth-grade education would no longer
suffice to join the department; henceforth a high school di-
ploma or its equivalency would be required. Weldon expanded
recruit training from seven to twelve weeks and established an
Inspections unit and an Internal Affairs unit. The department
upgraded its record-keeping by employing a statistical analyst
and its first computer. As a result crimes no longer went unre-
corded and, of course, the crime rate rose substantially. But the
department's most severe problem was the tension felt between

the increasingly black and Puerto Rican population of Newark and the local constabulary. In 1950 blacks made up 17 percent of Newark's population but only 2 percent of the police force. By 1960 the proportions were 34 and 7 percent.[12]

Not only were blacks underrepresented, but white police moved out of the city. Prior to 1962 two years of city residence was required for applicants to join the Police Department; once on the force, recruits were required to reside in the city. During the 1950s police began to evade the residency requirement surreptitiously by maintaining two addresses (a similar evasion occurred in Detroit). In 1962 the PBA won a court decision allowing officers to maintain two addresses. Police, fire, and teachers' unions banded together in the 1970s and successfully lobbied the legislature to outlaw residency requirements altogether. As a result Newark has been, and continues to be, policed by a force of outsiders.

THE 1967 RIOT

White police flight mirrored a more general exodus, which began in the 1950s and accelerated between 1960 and 1967. During those years more than 70,000 white residents deserted the city. White flight precipitated a dramatic six-year change in the racial makeup of the city: from 65 percent white to 52 percent black and 10 percent Puerto Rican and Cuban. Newark had become a predominantly black city, while whites in Newark retained political power. Then came the 1967 riot, which drove even larger numbers of white residents out of the city. Dorothy Guyot writes: "The 1967 riots mark a watershed in Newark's history. Before the riots, Newark looked to the past, a white man's town for 300 years; afterwards Newark looked to the future, a black man's town."[13]

THE 1980s

The Newark Police Department of the 1980s is neither a black man's nor a white man's. The term "integration" cannot, however, convey the complexity of the Newark Police Department's racial dynamics, much less the relation between those dynamics and the rest of the City of Newark. The city was in bad shape after the 1967 riots. Most of the remaining whites just gave up on Newark, fearing for their businesses, their safety, and their very lives. The South Ward, which had a substantial Jewish population, became almost entirely black. The West had been mainly black before the riots. Anthony Imperiale organized a North Ward Citizen's Committee to oppose black incursion. Imperiale, an ex-Marine, a black belt in karate, and a racist— he referred in his speeches to "Martin Luther Coon"—was able to organize a small corps of vigilantes who forcibly stopped blacks on North Ward streets and drove them from the neighborhood. Eventually, however, Italians left the North Ward, and in 1985 it is populated primarily by blacks, Puerto Ricans, and Cubans.

Kenneth Gibson became Newark's first black Mayor in 1970 after a bitter and racially divisive runoff campaign. His election, wrote Robert Curvin,

. . . represented a profound change in the political leadership of that city. It was not only a shift from white power to Black power, although, on the surface, this was perhaps the most significant aspect of his victory. It was much deeper than that. Gibson rode to victory in front of a mass movement of Blacks, aided by an interracial force of reformers. Civil rights activists, young and old idealists and the fiery Black nationalist, Imamu Baraka, and his followers, were all united in forging Gibson's victory.[14]

Gibson's opponent, Hugh Addonizio, was certainly not a racist and was considered a liberal when he served in Congress. Above all, he seems to have been a classically corrupt Newark politician. He was convicted and sentenced to ten years' imprisonment for extortion of firms doing business with the city and for income tax evasion. Addonizio's trial took place during the runoff campaign. He was on trial during the day and campaigned at night. He lost, and Newark had its first black Mayor.

The new Mayor's most sensitive and important appointment was that of Police Director. Gibson understood that although the city was predominantly black, the Police Department was predominantly white. Gibson's first appointment as Director was a white man, John Redden. The City Council unanimously opposed Redden. The PBA influenced the white councilmen to oppose Redden, because he promised to revamp transfer policies. The three black Councilmen stood against Redden because he wasn't black. Gibson faced them down with his huge public support and appointed Redden.

Gibson's political strength could not so easily overcome the recalcitrant deficiencies of the City of Newark. He could dampen racial tension and build bridges between the black community and the downtown business community. He could also generate Federal and state subsidies to the city. Nevertheless, when a *Fortune* editor undertook a survey ranking fifty large American cities in 1975, Newark stood "without serious challenge as the worst."[15]

Both street crime and racial tension continued to undermine the city. Director Redden resigned when the Mayor allowed Kawaida Towers, the Imamu Baraka–sponsored high rise at the edge of the North Ward's Italian neighborhood, to initiate construction. Redden opposed the decision as "narrow, selfish, political" and resigned.

The Mayor appointed Edward Kerr as the first black Director of the department. Kerr was not an overwhelming success and resigned after one year. We were told by a high-ranking white officer that the Kerr appointment was made "to test the waters," to see whether it was possible to have a black Director of this mainly white department.

In July 1974, Gibson appointed another black Director, Hubert Williams, whose tumultuous and innovative directorship lasted for more than a decade—and set the agenda for the Department's future. Williams came to the directorship from a civil service position as a sergeant, but more importantly from administrative experience as director of the Federally funded Impact program. Williams is a complex man and was a controversial Director, heartily disliked by many of his officers and staff and warmly admired by others. We were given free access to his office and spent parts of fourteen days with him, plus a side trip to Atlantic City to attend the 1983 National Association of Black Law Enforcement Executives conference.

Williams is a powerfully built man in his mid-forties with a full head of jet black hair and a goatee beginning to go gray. His face carries a look of alert intensity. He seems ready to pounce upon, consider, and express an opinion about any idea or proposal. His office is open and busy. Aides are sent scurrying looking for documents, making appointments, reservations, and contacts. The Director is the boss, the man in charge, and everybody knows it. Williams is proud of running a tight ship. "When people work for me," he says, "I put them through the fire and take them out again." A former speechwriter who left the department met Williams later at a social occasion. "He told me, 'There were two traumas in my life. One was the death of my mother, the other was you,'" Williams recalls. But Williams is not all fire. At times he shows warmth and compassion for the speaker and his problems. At such times he seems the ideal mediator, a task he occasionally performs in industrial labor disputes.

Whatever he may be, Williams is not simple. His complexity is illustrated by his attitude toward black officers in the department. Williams is not uniformly beloved by black officers, certainly not by those whom we accompanied on patrol. They complained that Williams is *too* fair. They charged that blacks had been discriminated against for years and that blacks deserved more than equality of treatment now; they deserved affirmative action to make up for the years when whites—particularly Italians—enjoyed the political spoils.

Williams might have replied that the past wasn't so significant, that his current policy was to be fair. Instead, he drew a more complex distinction: between fairness toward assignment and fairness toward discipline. He said that his assignment policy deliberately favored blacks as evidenced by the fact that about half the detectives are black in a department where only 21 percent of the force is. At the same time, he said, rules and policies of the department apply equally to everybody: "When blacks are charged with breaking the rules, they get the same hearing and the same treatment as whites, and vice versa. When I am judging I am color blind. When I am promoting, I am color conscious."

The traditional and underlying problems of the City of Newark affect the Police Department in several continuing ways. During the 1970s the city was for a time favored with Federal funds via the Law Enforcement Assistance Administration. The LEAA's Impact on Crime Program brought $20 million to Newark (recall that a youthful Williams administered the program). Dorothy Guyot argues that the Impact program was largely a disaster because its requirements did not fit the needs of the city. Although it would have made more sense, according to an evaluation of Newark's Impact program, to have invested in community crime prevention projects or in a centralized police facility, which had long been beyond the reach of the city, LEAA insisted on installing a complex 911 system and subsidizing the hiring of new officers.[16]

The 911 system undermined public confidence in the police instead of increasing it. The 911 emergency number is supposed to encourage citizens to call police. The citizens did. So many called that the switchboard became overloaded. To remedy overload, the department installed an answering machine. Operators monitored the tapes and hung up on those they regarded as insignificant. Callers learned to call the switchboard, but that too became overloaded. By 1983 the nonresponsiveness of the Newark police had become almost legendary, and citizens had learned to adapt to it, but not uniformly. The most recent policy is: If a call comes in about a family dispute, which may involve a beating, it receives a low priority. Indeed, the dispute may be resolved between the time the call is received and the police arrive some two or three hours later. But some citizens have learned to construct stories conforming to the department's priority system. "People have now learned," a sergeant on patrol says, "that if they get on 911 and say 'There's a man with a gun at Manchester and whatever,' they'll get service. . . . When we get there we find out it's a bullshit street argument; there's nobody with a gun."

If the department felt it had enough manpower to cover citizen calls, there would be no concern about responding to "bullshit street arguments." The seriousness of such encounters varies, of course, with the conception of what is a meaningful public disturbance. A loud street argument may not call for a quick police response in Newark, but it certainly would in Santa Ana. Only part of the reason can be attributed to Newark's objectively far more serious crime problem. After all, a street argument that evokes a citizen's call is at least a breach of somebody's peace and perhaps more—it could evolve into a fight or a shooting. Indeed, the most serious crime we witnessed while riding patrol was a homicide that escalated from a street argument between two Puerto Rican men, one of whom claimed that the other had insulted his wife. The wife stepped between the two men to quiet the disturbance and was stabbed and killed while protecting her husband. Following the stabbing, five patrol cars arrived on the scene, their officers holding back neighbors and jamming the small apartment of the victim's family.

The Impact on Crime Program also funded salaries of newly hired police, as stipulated by LEAA guidelines. When the money ran out, the new police had to be fired. Whether they were really needed is another, and more interesting, general issue. Among Newark police, white and black, low-ranking and high, there is an almost culturally ingrained belief that Newark police are understaffed and overworked. Our observations, however, suggested that that was not necessarily so. When we compared Newark with Oakland, where the homicide rate is even higher than Newark's, we found that Newark has a significantly higher ratio of police to population. The two cities are similar in size of population: Oakland, 339,000; Newark, 330,000. But in 1984 Oakland had 611 sworn officers to Newark's 1,073. Each has about the same number of civilians: Oakland, 297; Newark, 257. But Newark has 111 lieutenants to Oakland's 23.

Nor does Newark have a clearly higher rate of reported crime to justify the larger size of its police force. In 1983 Newark did report *more* robberies—5,287 to Oakland's 3,460—but *fewer* burglaries (Newark, 7,660; Oakland, 11,987) and *far fewer* larceny thefts (Newark, 9,281; Oakland, 19,378). Each city recorded about the same number of felony assaults: Newark, 3,375; Oakland, 3,231. It could be argued that with its combination of poverty and density, Newark may be a tougher city to police. On the other hand, the Oakland police have to cover a lot more ground. On balance, it appears that the Newark police are less efficient in combating crime, that the high crime rate to number of police ratio is at least in part attributable to inefficiencies within the Police Department. At the same time it should be noted that the crime rate was reduced by 25 percent between 1980 and 1983. The department is "extremely proud" of that reduction.

One answer to the persistence of the "understaffed/over-worked" syndrome might be that Newark has always been overstaffed and that traditional overstaffing has generated somewhat bloated expectations of what the department's size ought to be. At its peak the department numbered 1,640 sworn officers and 183 civilians.[17]

The 1970s layoffs might be another reason. As a result of reductions in Federal and state funding and the city's straitened economy, the Mayor decided to lay off municipal workers across the board, including the police. Everybody we interviewed agrees that the layoffs were, if not traumatic, a source of serious trouble for the department. They generated considerable mistrust between the rank-and-file officers and department brass, particularly the Director.

The Director is sometimes viewed as a "puppet of the Mayor" by the rank-and-file with respect to any dispute between the mayor and the police unions. There is a certain sense in which any such charge is merited. The Director is appointed by and is responsible to the Mayor and is always available for a telephone call from the Mayor's office. The Director can influence and advise on issues of police budget and policy but ultimately must comply with the Mayor's decisions.

In any case, the layoffs have to be seen as a self-inflicted wound upon the department. Both the Mayor and the police unions share some of the responsibility. The Mayor seems to bear the initial responsibility. A study by Guyot and Dede charges that "Mayor Gibson . . . set the stage for a layoff by irresponsible budgeting prior to his reelection in May 1974."[18] But the police unions also contributed by their intransigence. They refused to give up certain prerogatives they had gained through earlier negotiations and refused to cooperate with a plan whereby officers would take five days' unpaid leave in return for no layoffs. Moreover, they engaged in a "Fear City" campaign in retaliation against the layoffs. The campaign involved urging private businesses to hire security guards, since the police could, it was said, no longer protect them. Whether rank-and-file sympathizers smashed the windows of forty-six police vehicles—eight of which were unmarked—has never been determined.

The layoff's results are, however, felt years later in both the average age of patrol officers and the morale of the patrol force. The department laid off the 332 people with the least seniority. That meant, of course, that the youngest and most energetic police officers were laid off. It means that the average patrolman in 1984 is more than forty years old. We rode with patrolmen and were impressed by their attitude: "We have a job, we'll do it, but we're not going to break our asses." There may be some advantages to that attitude. On the one hand, these older white patrolmen rarely harass anybody; on the other, they do little active policing.

The attitude of such patrolmen is not, however, universal. There are patrolmen who remove themselves from their cars, walk on portions of their beat, and contact citizens. Most patrolmen, however, seemed to be tied to the 911 system. Under that system there are some busy times, but fewer than the average patrolman claims. We talked about the issue with Captain Charles Knox of the South precinct. Knox, like Dickscheid, is another of Newark's top cops in whom Hubert Williams takes great pride. Knox is wiry, expressive, intelligent, black, and well-tuned-in to stable elements of the local black community. We have toured the South precinct area with Knox and with the patrol cars he commands in the South precinct. Once a middle-class, predominantly Jewish neighborhood, the South precinct lost the remains of its Jewish residents after the 1967 riots.

We ask Knox, "What happened here today in this precinct? Was there any action last night?" (June 22, 1984).

Knox replies, "Nothing really significant. Just kind of a routine day. . . . The only thing of significance was that last night we had a guy chased into a building. Shots were fired at him. We recovered some of the spent cartridges. During the twenty-four-hour period we had two street robberies, two burglaries in businesses, and one burglary to a home. That's not bad for twenty-four hours. Not bad at all."

We calculate—and comment—that if there are six cars to a shift and two men to a car, and this is a routine day—fairly typical, we feel, of the days and nights we have ridden on patrol—there seem to be an adequate number of patrolmen. We conclude that, in calculating manpower needs, patrolmen seem to recall their busiest days. Knox does not dispute that reasoning.

He comments, "That's right. You have to remember with this manpower question, you talk to the unions they're going to clamor for more men, that's why they're in existence. You talk to the police officers, they're going to relate back to how it was when we had a heck of a lot of manpower. But the fact of the matter is . . . nobody is overworked. If anybody is overworked," he adds with a smile, "it's me, going to community meetings all the time. Not that I'm complaining. It's my choice."

Newark, like other East Coast police departments, employs two-man patrol cars. Given the salary, pension, and fringe benefits of officers, that becomes a costly system to maintain. To a West Coast observer, the two-man car seems an anachronistic relic, particularly in a relatively small city like Newark. Besides, patrol is divided into four districts, and within any district you can drive from here to there in a flash with lights and sirens running. It would obviously be safer, more efficient, and less expensive to have nine cars patrolling each precinct than six, with each car occupied by one officer. The patrolmen, however, *feel* safety in proximate numbers, even though there is demonstrably no evidence of greater safety, and even though greater safety could be achieved with more cars and fewer police in a given area.

REFORM AND INNOVATION

Newark is a place where one would least expect innovation in the Police Department. Its dismal history—an eroded economy, racial tensions, a century-long tradition of urban mismanagement, even corruption—scarcely predicts anything but more of the same. Yet, although Newark hardly stands out as a model of modernity, given its limited resources and entrenched, often intractable underlying constraints, the Newark Police Department has done well recently. It has possibly done more with less than any other police department in the United States. Still, before it could accomplish anything innovative, the department needed to reform. "You need," Director Williams says, "to look at where this department has come from. We used to be steeped in corruption, excessive force was routinely being used by officers, the department's reputation was something less than professional, to be kind about it."

Systems of accountability and control are fundamental to the success of any department. A corrupt police department is not anomic, in the "normlessness" sense. Corrupt cops do not so much run wild as operate according to hidden norms, unacceptable to the general public, such as the legendary "blue code of silence." Even when a department is not corrupt, we find variation from written rules. Under previous administrations, Police Directors were expected to and in fact did support officers, right or wrong. Director Williams says that he will support officers if they're right and will also support them if they are wrong, provided their conduct is reasonable under the circumstances. "But," he adds, "if police officers are wrong and their conduct is unreasonable, they will be treated like any citizen and will be prosecuted vigorously by the Police Department."

Like many departments, Newark's formerly did not use an Internal Affairs unit to investigate complaints. Squad bosses investigated shootings as well as other violations of rules and regulations. Shootings are now investigated solely by two Internal Affairs officers, whose first duty is to get immediately to the scene and conduct an investigation, notify the Director of the shooting, and file a written preliminary report to him within twenty-four hours. As in other police departments, Newark's operational deadly force policy is not, however, exactly the same as its written policy. Williams explains that the guidelines policy has been amended several times, although it is basically a defense-of-life policy. "The reason," Williams says, "is that written policies give notice to the world, the good and the bad. I talked in the community about our policy of restraint and after a while criminals in the street were beginning to become more obstinate and arrogant, challenging and daring our police officers, saying they weren't allowed to shoot. We don't want to convey that kind of message. Our public posture is that we will cut you down if necessary—but everybody knows our reputation for restraint."

If one prong of reforming the department involved changing the norms regarding use of force, the other involved keeping the officers active. Police management can vacillate between the poles of restraint and productivity: on one side restraining officers from being overly aggressive, on the other ensuring that officers actually produce some positive results. "For the last seven years," Williams says, "we've been streamlining our organization, instituting control and accounting procedures to improve operations. . . . We've lost 34 percent of our officers since I took over in 1974, yet our arrest rate per officer has increased about 14 percent. Summons issuances have gone up over 87 percent, field interrogations are up, and sick leave has gone down by more than 30 percent in the last five years."

Williams is an active manager reforming the department, but he is also an innovator and a politician. In 1984 Kenneth Gibson organized Jesse Jackson's campaign in Newark. Williams supports Gibson and Jackson. Politically, then, Williams would have to be identified with the left wing of the Democratic party. At the same time, as we shall see, he employs aggressive crime fighting tactics in Newark, tactics that might not be permissible if not used by a black administrator in this black city.

TRUANCY TASK FORCE

The Truancy Task Force illustrates an effective, aggressive, innovative program that is scarcely conceivable for Oakland and might be very controversial in Detroit. In Newark it is a source of pride. The program was developed by Williams in cooperation with Executive School Superintendent Columbus Sally, also black. Downtown merchants complained to the police that stores were being shoplifted and purses snatched from customers during school hours. The Police Director and the School Superintendent agreed that there were plenty of youths cutting school and making trouble downtown. Not only is the prototypical "criminal" in America as well as in Newark a fifteen-year-old black male, but daytime downtown crimes are especially attractive to young men, who, as at least one scholar has noted, tend to commit crimes in groups.[19]

The Truancy Task Force is the response of the two agencies, the police and the schools. The Task Force is composed of a couple of lieutenants, a sergeant, a patrolman, and the downtown pickpocket squad. The pickpocket squad, assigned to an 8-to-4 shift, actually used to accomplish little before noon, so there is slight additional manpower cost to the city, always a concern in Newark, when the squad is assigned to the Truancy Task Force.

The Task Force divides the city into four districts and assigns a bus to each. Each bus has a driver, two teachers who serve as truancy officers, and a police officer. The buses tour the streets of the district and stop any youngsters who are seen walking the streets. If identification shows the youngster to be over sixteen, he or she is released. If under, the student is consigned to the bus. The bus is filled, or nearly filled, with truants within an hour and is driven to a central location. The kids are let out and assigned to school social workers, who question the truants about why they are not in school, with whom they reside, and so forth. The school social workers, called intervenors, follow up on the kids, get in touch with parents or guardians, even bring them into court and charge them as disorderly persons (an offense that carries a $25 fine), if they find the kids persist in playing hooky.

At first the Task Force generated considerable suspicion. It is no small program. Approximately 8,000 youngsters were apprehended in 1983. There were some complaints that the officers were using Gestapo-like tactics, rounding up people on the street solely on the basis of their status as youths. Moreover, the plainclothes police are armed, another point of contention. But the program is vigorously defended by the Police Department and supported by the schools. Police officers are armed to protect the truant officers, who, without police assistance, might be hesitant to order a group of truant fifteen-year-old males into a bus against their will.

The Director perceives the Truancy Task Force as a model, positive innovation for three reasons: It's good for the kids; it makes for a safer city; and it shows how cooperation between agencies can benefit the area. It is good for the kids because "youngsters who are out there on the streets when they should be in school usually get themselves mixed up in some kind of illegal activity." It makes for a safer city because when several thousand kids are not committing crime, businesses, homes, and individuals are protected.

Williams is continually and seriously concerned about Newark's youth. This is a poor city with high youth unemployment. One need only drive through to observe young men hanging around on street corners. Obviously the Police Department cannot be expected to develop an economy to put kids to work. But Williams believes in working with other agencies, particularly the schools, that will guide kids to a positive track. "We are working with the Board of Education," he says, "to enhance the self-esteem of Newark youth by opening up the schools at night, putting in programs that might break the cycle of failure. People that fail develop a failure attitude. You need to break that cycle by introducing success into their lives."

POLICE PRESENCE

If police are perceived as oppressors, nothing is so desirable as their absence. But if police are seen as protectors then, the more police are seen to be visible, available if needed, the better. We observed four "innovations" by the Newark Police Department involving a neighborhood police presence. The two most dramatic—"sweeps" and "roadblocks"—seemed of questionable value, although they arguably could claim to have achieved some success in deterring street crime. Two others, "storefronts" and "bus inspections," are virtually noncontroversial. Our limited observations in Newark, as well as in some of the other cities we studied, suggest that both of those are desirable innovations, adaptable by large and middle-size police departments across the nation.

Sweeps

Of all Newark's innovations, the sweep by far is the most controversial. A sweep is an intimidation tactic designed to clear the streets, particularly corners believed to be hangouts for youths who are thought to be thieves, robbers, and dope dealers, and to deter the aforesaid "undesirables" from continuing to hang out on those favored corners and thereby discouraging the traffic of other legitimate citizens.

The theory of the sweep is clear. To understand its problems and limitations it might be worthwhile to discuss a couple in which we participated. Both occurred on early summer nights.

The sweep is a quasi-military tactic. There is considerable police involvement in preparatory organization. Sgt. John Dough, an exceptionally literate officer who normally works in the Director's office but is assigned to special sweep teams, explains: "One of the underlying features of this whole activity is operating as a unit, rather than individual action. As a unit, you have to have a game plan and map out your method of operation beforehand. Otherwise it's spasmodic."

The concept of the sweep envisions police cars surrounding the area, while a van, driven by bilingual officers, twice announces over a PA system, in both Spanish and English, to those assembled that they are violating a statute requiring them not to block pedestrain traffic. They are further told that if they do not move on, they will be subject to arrest or interrogation. Each police car is given a specific assignment. One, occupied by a lieutenant, observes individuals who do not move after the warning is given. Other cars are prepared to move in and question, search, and arrest.

One sweep takes place on a crowded corner that has an all-night grocery store. It is no ordinary grocery store, however. It is not possible to operate a grocery store at night in Newark's inner city without extraordinary security. In fact, customers do not actually enter the store. They tell the clerk what they want, pass the money through a slotted door, and receive groceries and change. A nighttime Newark grocery store has more security than a suburban bank.

The store is a magnet for bystanders. Women in summer dresses and shorts and men in sleeveless shirts—mostly T-shirts and undershirts—congregate on the corner. The warning is twice given, and most of the bystanders disperse. Those who remain are ordered to "assume the position" against the wall. Their outer clothing is patted down, and they may have their pockets searched for drugs or weapons. Some drugs are uncovered, but in this sweep and another similar one (near a liquor store) no weapons are found.

If such a sweep is legal, it is only marginally so. No lawyer committed to traditional constitutional conceptions of Fourth Amendment rights of citizen privacy would regard the sweeps as anything but unlawful. Statutes forbidding loitering are unconstitutional, and the "warning" is an evasive device intended to afford the police an arguably legal position. Those who remain after the warning are supposedly blocking pedestrian traffic and therefore are subject to arrest and to a search incident to the arrest. Yet the police have no legal "probable cause," no reason to believe that a crime has been or is about to be committed, and thus should have no right to search. Moreover, following the warning, those who remain are not blocking pedestrian traffic, since the area is now uncrowded.

Even if the sweeps were to be considered legal, serious questions would remain as to their tactical usefulness. Given the fact of a clear warning, those holding drugs or weapons—serious criminals—will doubtless leave the scene. Those who remain are innocent, law-abiding, or impervious to police warnings. They may be drunk, stoned, stupid, disbelieving, brash, unable to make up their minds whether to stay or to leave, or all of the above. Some people—usually young black males—do not move. After all, this is their turf. Those who do choose to remain are thrust up against a wall and frisked. For most of those who remain, around 15 to 20 percent of the original crowd of twenty to eighty people, being frisked is no novel experience. They've been through it before. Amazingly, the police sometimes do confiscate drugs and weapons, despite the clear warnings to disperse. For whatever reason, on hot summer nights in Newark young men do not always behave with what to an outside observer would be rational self-interest.

The police themselves interpret the sweeps positively. The Newark police feel that they are not seen to be a serious presence on the streets. The sweeps demand discipline, command, control, a show of authority. They convey an impression of police activity, if not aggressiveness. The police act, they do not *react*. The sweeps provide a rare opportunity for the police to be totally in control of a street situation.

Whether sweeps make a similarly positive impression upon the neighborhood residents is questionable. One of those remaining after a sweep was a neighborhood resident who, as it happens, was also a young Newark policeman. We expressed to him our own skepticism about the efficiency of the sweep—we didn't discuss its legality—and he agreed. "The dope dealers," he said, "will probably return tomorrow or the next night. The department doesn't have the manpower to do this over and over again. Still, it might do some good. Nothing else seems to work." The sweep may just as well be interpreted as a symbol of police frustration ("it might do some good; nothing else does") as an effective law enforcement strategy.

Roadblocks as Symbolic Interaction

Roadblocks are also symbolic, and expressly so. The implementation of roadblocks in Newark, particularly in the neighborhood of Lincoln Park, roughly a half-mile from downtown, are primarily intended to show a police presence while carrying out a police assignment. As Director Williams explained to us:

"The roadblock is basically designed for two purposes. One, the officers are carrying out a routine police function—checking to be sure people are not inebriated and that they have proper credentials to drive vehicles. The other one is to demonstrate in a clearly emphatic way that the police are here. They're very visible, and they're in control of the streets. This gives people a sense of security, that the police are visible, proactive, and involved in the public safety function.

"Now these police are very specially trained people, so they're not going about doing their functions cumbersomely. People are willing to accept some inconvenience if they know it's for a legitimate purpose, and there's nothing more important to the public today than their own security and protection."

A young black man, mid-twenties, dressed in a shirt open at the collar, appearing respectable and concerned, asks an observer, "Why are there so many police here with guns?" with evident suspicion. He is referred to Lieutenant Harold Gibson (the Mayor's brother and an attorney), who is in charge of the roadblock. Gibson replies: "There's a road check here. We're checking up to see whether drunken drivers are going through your community." The young man smiles, slaps Gibson's hand in appreciation, and says, "Hey, that's great. Thank you."

Lincoln Park is very close to the heart of the city, a quarter-mile from the city center. On an ordinary summer Friday night, the park would be sparsely populated. It is dimly lighted and most residents would fear entering it. Those using it might be drifters or drinkers, street-trained and street-hardened.

The roadblock attracts more people to the park. Partly, the roadblock is itself an entertainment, with abundant police, signs and lights. Partly, the presence of police in the vicinity of the park reduces fear of its use.

Roadblocks are controversial. To many citizens—and judges—they represent an unreasonable invasion of privacy, a heavy-handed assertion of authority by police against citizens driving cars, about whom there is not even a shred of reasonable suspicion of illegal activity. In *Delaware* v. *Prouse*, [20] the U.S. Supreme Court excluded from evidence marijuana found by a police officer who, prompted neither by observance of a traffic or equipment violation nor by suspicious behavior by the car's occupants, stopped a car solely to check the driver's license and registration. The court also stressed, however, that less intrusive spot checks not involving "the unconstitutional exercise of discretion" might be acceptable. Concurring opinions by Justices Blackman and Powell suggested that roadblocks involving every tenth car (or every car) would be constitutionally acceptable.[21] The Newark roadblock sought to adopt those suggestions by stopping every fifth car, irrespective of the appearance of the driver or occupants or their status in life. Thus, if an off-duty police officer was driving, he would also be stopped.

The Newark P.D. has not undertaken a systematic survey of those who have been stopped or of citizens generally. The department believes that citizens look with favor on the stops. There is increasing recognition by the public that drunk driving is a serious problem and that a police presence is desirable. Most people, like the Supreme Court, also do not seem to express the same privacy interest in automobiles as in dwellings. They realize that drivers are licensed and cars registered, and seem to acknowledge the state's interest in seeing that papers are in order and that drivers are sober.

Clearly the roadblock is an inconvenience to drivers, but it may be symbolically important and necessary, particularly in a high-crime city like Newark, where the Police Department's reputation for efficiency and concern has not been esteemed. In other cities, e.g. Oakland and Santa Ana, roadblocks might be perceived with greater suspicion and annoyance, especially near the center of the city. Although a properly constructed roadblock is probably a legal tool for law enforcement, it will not necessarily prove acceptable in every setting; it will prove most acceptable when its purpose is fully communicated to the public. Without explanation, it appears to be a highhanded tactic.

Inspecting Buses and Subways

Some innovative ideas are costless, effective, and obvious once you see them. One example is the removal of toll booths from the San Francisco side of the Bay Bridge, while doubling the toll on the East Bay side for those entering the city. Annual toll revenues are about the same, but half the payroll for toll takers is eliminated, as well as the inconvenience to motorists of stopping at toll booths going and coming. One wonders why that simple efficiency was not implemented when the bridge was built. Either no one thought of it, or it was considered too radical a notion.

Like the one-way toll booth, a clearly constitutional innovation that almost any police department could adopt on a virtually cost-free basis is the subway and bus inspection system now in practice throughout the City of Newark. The idea was developed by Captain George Dickscheid of the West district. Dickscheid had been receiving complaints that many citizens were afraid to ride buses. Occasionally bus passengers would be robbed or molested. More often they would be annoyed or threatened. Behavior in a confined space like a bus can be very threatening indeed.

Dickscheid's simple idea was this: Patrolmen should from time to time stop their cars, flag down a bus, enter it, and ask the driver if everything is all right. The police should address the passengers with the same question. If the answer is negative, the police should remove, and possibly arrest, those committing crimes and other forms of public order disturbance. We observed several such bus stops. There were no problems in the buses we entered, but it was also clear that riders appreciated police concern for their safety and heartily approved. Riders smiled at the police, and there was even some applause. According to Angelo Pezzino, Chief of Security for New Jersey bus transit operations, the bus inspection program resulted in a 40 percent reduction of incidents during 1983. Statewide data show an overall reduction of 23 percent.

The bus inspection program offers a singular example of the crime prevention strategy that operates apart from the prioritized system of citizen-initiated responses through the 911 system, is not at all invasive of citizen privacy, and is virtually cost-free.

Storefronts

All the experiments instituted by the Police Foundation to re-duce fear were carried out in Captain Dickscheid's West dis-trict, partly because Dickscheid was so highly regarded by the Director and partly because his district was the most densely populated and crime-ridden in Newark. Any law enforcement innovation that might work in Newark's West patrol district should commend itself to other inner-city police districts in America. One can scarcely imagine a locale in which it would prove more difficult to innovate successfully.

As part of the Foundation's fear reduction project, the New-ark Police Department opened a "storefront" community cen-ter at 767 South Orange Avenue, in a peninsula jutting out northwest from the city. The peninsula is surrounded on three sides by the neighboring towns of Irvington on the west, East Orange on the northeast, and Bloomfield due east. The "store-front center" was located there for another reason: The area is notably dense and rundown, with a population of approxi-mately 66,000.

The so-called West District Community Service Center is an old Victorian building with fading white paint, long ago aban-doned by its owners. The community it serves includes about a twelve- or thirteen-block area marked by small retail stores, di-lapidated residences, and sectarian churches, sometimes two or three to a block. Inner-city Newark residents seem inordinately

pious. More cynical observers—among police interviewed—
suggest that the presence of so many sectarian churches should
be interpreted less as an expression of piety than shrewd, perhaps deceptive, parsimony. Anyone who maintains a residence
as a "church" lives, after all, property-tax-free. Given the
rather broad interpretation of "religion" in our constitution, it
is relatively simple to claim a flock and a ministry, or, rather, it
is difficult to disprove such a claim.

At any rate, this is the setting for the West District Community Service Center. The center consists primarily of a main entry room about 15 by 35 feet, containing three desks, couches,
and several dozen chairs. Community meetings are held in this
room.

Four sworn police officers are assigned to the center. The officers sometimes engage in foot patrol and also check out complaints of muggings, narcotics sales, public drunkenness, and
other unseemly and illegal street activity.

More important, the department, the captain, and the officers involved envision the center as a community resource.
Inner-city neighborhoods in places like Newark do not necessarily enjoy a sense of community. As in Santa Ana, police visits,
the organization of individual blocks, and the formation of
block associations all introduce a sense of community where
none may previously have existed. The police assigned to the
center are responsible for meeting everyone in the community,
going from door to door and introducing themselves. They organize community meetings and also conduct special meetings
on subjects they think might be of interest to the community.
They might, for example, bring in a narcotics specialist to talk
with local citizens who want to learn more about illegal drugs.
They have organized Cub Scout and Boy Scout programs.
Whether or not any single program component achieves a reasonable impact may prove less significant than the message that
the police are active and caring community officials who employ force when necessary and various forms of education at all
times.

Five small businesses opened within 1983, the year of the
center's initiation. The business people are all black or Hispanic, as are the residents of the area. Those retail establishments, such as a bicycle shop, candy store, and small grocery,

provide the sort of amenities urban neighborhoods have always needed but are sorely lacking in post-riot Newark. Without the police center, those stores apparently could not exist.

"How do you feel about the police being down in the street?" we asked the grocery owner.

"To me the police center is beautiful in the neighborhood. Things would be much badder if we closed it."

The bicycle merchant echoes those sentiments: "People, they don't be running wild around here any more."

Both merchants indicated that the center impacted a six-to-eight-block area, and since its introduction into the neighborhood merchants were considering opening new stores and opening them earlier and closing them later.

"The people in the neighborhood appreciate the police being here," the bicycle merchant concluded. The seven or eight merchants and customers we talked with unanimously and enthusiastically approved of the storefront's presence.

Consider the police role here. The police are, in effect, community service social workers—who can use force, even deadly force, when necessary. The center might not be successful without higher affirmation of the officer's role. The Director and the captain support the conception of the police role that the center embodies. For example, the captain does not consider the center a threat to the dignity and work of the main precinct house. On the contrary, he regards it as a positive asset and communicates that feeling to the precinct patrolmen who ride in the radio cars. Thus, unlike the Detroit "storefronts," the Newark neighborhood center is integrated with the precinct itself. Patrol car teams frequently drop in at the storefront, and check out complaints received there. "It's a close working relationship," says one of the storefront officers. "We don't feel as though we're an outpost—not part of the precinct." Such integration seems to be a critical feature of the success of the innovation.

After reviewing the center and its impact, we commented to Captain Dickscheid that the center presented a kind of paradox. Here was this old building, entirely lacking in modern equipment or technology. At the same time this sort of directed movement into the community seemed like a wave of the future for urban policing. Dickscheid replied:

"I don't think the answer is in equipment and facilities. Those are nice and perhaps enhance some programs to a degree. But the key, so far as I'm concerned, is communication between the police and the community. We try to emphasize developing a relationship with the decent people out there. Ninety-five percent of the people are decent, and you've got maybe 5 percent who are crumbs.

"Communication changes the working cop's understanding of priorities. The 911 system, the computer, tells them that robbery, burglary, and homicide are the most important thing. True, they're important. But the officers are beginning to find out that it's also important not to ignore the car speeding down the road or the kids hanging out on the corner. The community cares about those things."

CONCLUSION

Even in a city with as unpromising a history of urban governance, racial tension, and economic decline as Newark, it is still possible for creative police management to initiate interesting, even exemplary programs.

There can be no doubt that by 1985 the Newark Police Department had achieved notable improvement and, more important, recognition of that improvement within the City of Newark itself.

Relations between the business community, the Mayor, and the Police Director had long been marked by distrust, leading to charges and countercharges. The Chamber of Commerce had little confidence in the Police Department and the Mayor's hand-picked Director. Largely through the initiative of Chamber President Richard Schoon, the city initiated a management study of the Police Department, conducted by the "big eight" accounting firm Touche-Ross & Co., a member of the Chamber and a firm also active in the Newark business community.[22] The study began in 1983 and was released on August 1, 1984. The results of the study were feared, among many of the top ranking officials in the department, as a potential hatchet job.

The Touche-Ross report begins as any study of Newark's Police Department must, pointing to the city's history of civil disturbance, its sociological complexity, its diverse neighborhoods, and its "dual personality" as a place where the residents remain but "a large percentage of the business community leaves at 5:00 P.M. each day."[23]

The report also cites the poverty of the city (Newark's per capita income was $4,525 in 1980, while countrywide it was $7,538) and the decline in police positions.

Contrary to expectations, however, both within and outside the department, the Touche-Ross report generally lauds the department's management "during a time of unrelenting reduction in resources."

"Few . . . organizations could react as effectively in tailoring the services to meet a continuing workload," the report says.[24]

The report's main criticism refers to what is clearly the department's main problem: not so much an absence of positions as a filling of available positions by an old guard of officers who look forward to retirement more than to active, on-the-job duty. The department is top-heavy in rank and age. Out of 1,073 sworn personnel in 1983, 111 held the rank of lieutenant. Of 844 nonranking police officers, only 80 were under age thirty, while 449 were over forty.[25] That sort of age-rank distribution would pose obvious problems for any police department, as it does for Newark's. This department's problem is not so much losing sheer numbers of officers as it is being able to recruit young, enthusiastic ones who are in touch with the community and who look forward to patrolling its streets.

Fortunately for the department, nobody has ever accused Director Williams of lacking in energy, ideas, or ambition. His will be a tough act to follow. "The Newark Police Department is flexible and innovative," the Touche-Ross report states.[26] The report concluded that the department needed upgrading in three areas: patrol operations, attrition management, and information management. No one disputes that, including the director and the department brass.

Still, the Newark Police Department, like many old-line departments, is highly sensitive to politics and the vested interests of generations of senior officers. Even the most gifted Director is of course limited by the resources and the possibilities for change he inherits. Considering those resources and the constraints of the City of Newark—street crime, street litter, poverty, abandoned buildings, trash-strewn vacant lots, a transitional central business district, old and dirty police cars (some of which have been replaced)—the department has made genuine and demonstrable progress during the past decade.

Moreover, there is hope within the community that Newark has hit bottom and is on the rise. The Touche-Ross report and the Director agree that Newark's biggest problem is its environmental image. Newark does not attract the middle class, yuppies, or big business, but it does have certain natural advantages, mainly its proximity to lower Manhattan. As Director Williams put it, "The bottom line is investment opportunity. These cities on the Eastern Seaboard are being viewed as good investment opportunities now. . . . Businesses can get good tax advantages, all the utilities are laid; some of the problems of the past no longer exist, and they're dying for business to come in." There is, of course, a natural alliance between business, policing, and the middle class. As that alliance is forged, as it has been in Newark, we begin to see the development of large office buildings, condominiums, low-cost modular housing, and even lofts for artists to relocate from Manhattan's increasingly expensive Soho district to Newark's riverfront. Newark now has several groups, particularly the "Newark Collaboration," linking downtown with other neighborhood interests and public services. In a phrase, Newark is shaping up. The city is not yet a boom town, but it is a city of hope, rising from the devastation of the 1967 riots. Whether downtown renewal will pull the neighborhoods along remains to be seen. Still, many of the old scars have healed. It is clear that there is more unity of purpose—between neighborhood and downtown, between police and business interests—than the city has experienced in decades.

Much of the hope and unity can be attributed to changes in the police. The Newark Police Department no longer symbolizes excessive use of deadly force, brutality, and entrenched corruption. It has opened its doors to innovative strategies, research, and management skills.

Just as this research was concluding (May 1985), Hubert Williams was appointed President of the Police Foundation, to succeed Patrick V. Murphy, and Charles Knox was appointed Newark's Police Director. Williams' appointment in itself signifies the new respect the Newark Police Department has gained in the national community of policing. As in every city, Newark's fortunes are closely tied to the quality of its Police Department. Brutal, corrupt, and inefficient police destroy the image—and reality—of a city. Well-trained, research-minded, humanistic police reduce crime and fear of crime. Basic services—police, schools, fire, sanitation—define a city. As the quality of the Police Department continues to rise, the image of the entire city should accompany the ascent.

8

PROSPECTS FOR POLICE INNOVATION

"THERE IS SOMETHING NEW on the streets of Brooklyn," *Newsweek* magazine reported in January 1985. "The police are walking the beats again." Cops are walking beats in Boston, Newark, Detroit, Houston, Minneapolis, Orange County, and many other places around the nation. *Newsweek* describes the new breed as "part blue knight—and part social worker, as likely to organize a block association as bust a junkie. At bottom, the strategy embodies an insight few chiefs ever dared admit to in public: the cops can't keep the streets safe by themselves."

The new popularity of foot patrol signifies a larger movement away from reactive crime control to positive crime prevention strategies. Where the latter dominate, as in Santa Ana, police strive to mobilize the entire community in its own defense. But for that to happen, the department must first entertain a strong vision of policing as a community-based enterprise. The New York City Police Department appears to be moving ahead with community-oriented policing. It will surely discover, however, as other departments have, that despite vision and commitment from precinct leadership, community-oriented policing involves fundamental changes in the perspectives of patrolmen.

What obstacles stand in the way of implementing a community-oriented crime prevention policy? Perhaps the most important are those within traditional police organizations. All organizations resist change, but one is hard put to think of any more resistant than the police. It is not easy to transform blue knights into community organizers. The typical police department is paramilitary, regulated by the civil service, unionized, and opposed to lateral entry. Alongside those contraints is a tightly knit police subculture marked by a "we-they" mentality that mistrusts working with outsiders. Rollcall Sergeant Yablonski of TV's "Hill Street Blues" uses a rallying cry that any thirty-year veteran will find familiar and comforting: "Let's do it to them before they do it to us." Whatever their precise meaning, those words surely express an insider/outsider vision typical of traditional police culture. The words also suggest why it is difficult for police departments to introduce a community-oriented crime prevention conception of policing throughout entire departments. Nevertheless, the trend—as the *Newsweek* article suggests—seems to point away from police insularity, away from distant and aloof "professionalism," toward community orientation.

THE ELEMENTS OF INNOVATION

The new thrust in American policing, which we loosely designate community-oriented policing, is not a single coherent program. Rather, police forces around the country are experimenting with a variety of new programs all resting on the rationale, not always clearly articulated, that police must involve the community in a practical way in the police mission.

Police forces have been prompted to that kind of innovation by their own recognition that what has been tried for so long isn't working; streets are not safer, fear of crime is not declining, criminals are not being brought more surely to the bar of justice, and faith in the criminal justice system is dwindling. Though police officers are reluctant to admit this, in their guts they know it is true, and it gnaws at them as much as it does at the public. Their growing conviction that something new must be tried has been reinforced by careful and systematic research showing that standard operating procedures aren't having the effects they were supposed to. Increasing the number of police officers, for example, does not reduce crime; random motorized patrolling does not enhance public safety; rapid emergency response neither produces more arrests of criminals nor reassures the public; and crimes are rarely solved by policemen acting on the basis of physical evidence but require victims and witnesses to identify perpetrators and give persuasive testimony.

What, then, are the elements of innovation in contemporary American policing that make us conclude that community-oriented policing is the wave of the future? There are four: police–community reciprocity, areal decentralization of command, reorientation of patrol, and civilianization.

Police–Community Reciprocity

Police–community reciprocity means that police must genuinely feel, and genuinely communicate a feeling, that the public they are serving has something to contribute to the enterprise of policing. One of the most interesting conceptual distinctions we uncovered in the research enterprise was made by a Santa Ana businessman who distinguished between the "old" and the "new" professionalism. The old professional was not especially interested in hearing from the lay public, including businessmen, to say nothing of representatives of minority groups. The old professional saw himself as someone who had received advanced training in the intricacies of the penal code, search-and-seizure law, use of firearms, interrogation tactics, and the fine points of when and how to apply the baton. His training did not, he thought, require additional input from members of the community.

If the old professional leaned toward, perhaps exemplified, a "legalistic" style of policing, the new professional inclines toward and exemplifies a more service-oriented style. But the new professionalism suggests more than the service style uncovered by James Q. Wilson in an affluent Long Island suburb.[1] The new professionalism implies that police serve, learn from, and are accountable to the community. Behind the new profes-

sionalism is a governing notion: that the police and the public
are co-producers of crime prevention.

If ordinary citizens are actually to become crime prevention
co-producers, reciprocity is a necessity. Communities cannot be
mobilized for crime prevention from the top down. Members of
the community have to become motivated to work with and
alongside professional law enforcement agents. Each area,
neighborhood, or block may have its own set of problems. More
affluent neighborhoods may care mostly about daytime bur-
glars who slip in through open doors or locked doors that are
easily opened. Poorer neighborhoods have different problems,
usually centering on the quality of street life. Complaints may
be made about prostitutes working the streets so that children
cannot be let out to play, or about gangs extorting money from
children, or about drugs being sold in the street.

To prove successful, crime prevention should focus on the
needs of particular communities. When done abstractly, as, for
example, with issuance of an advisory pamphlet from the office
of the Chief of Police addressed to all citizens, irrespective of
particular needs, very little may be accomplished. Without reciprocity, without community feedback and participation, the
police are in no position to tailor developmental resources to local needs in any sort of optimal fashion. Indeed, a reciprocal
model of crime prevention can make police intelligent tactically,
so that resources can be used more effectively. Moreover, the efficient use of resources in certain communities, combined with
an experience of police–citizen cooperation, can perhaps reduce
police fear of particular communities. Surely this two-stage hy-
pothesis is worth testing. Stage one predicts that police who are
substantially involved in reciprocal community crime prevention programs will experience significantly less fear of those
communities. Stage two predicts that lessened fear by police
will result in more effective crime prevention because of better
relations within the community and the assistance those relationships will generate.

We have spoken freely about "neighborhoods" and "communities." In actuality those forms of social organization—
implying face-to-face interaction and a sense of communal
identity—may be weak. As in Detroit and Santa Ana, the police may find they have to activate neighborhood and commu-

nity associations. In our often anomic urban society the transcendent identity of many city dwellers is that of crime victim. Their neighbors may be the very people they fear. In such circumstances police departments can facilitate, even create, a sense of community where one either did not previously exist or was faintly imprinted. A National Institute of Justice–sponsored community crime prevention study of a Brooklyn neighborhood reports that such programs create conditions for mutual assistance and self-help, and, in a word, "restore a sense of 'community'."[2]

Could it be that crime, like war and other disasters, might turn out to be America's best antidote to anomie?

Areal Decentralization of Command

A reciprocal understanding of crime prevention will ordinarily be linked closely with a strategy of areal decentralization of command. That takes many forms: fixed substations in Santa Ana, Directed Response Teams in Houston, mini-stations in Detroit, or simply the multiplication of precincts. The purpose behind all of them is to create the possibility of more intensive police–community interaction and heightened identification by police officers with particular areas.

Although areal decentralization is a feature of contemporary strategic innovation, the new commands perform very different functions when examined closely. Houston's DART program integrates patrol, criminal investigation, and intelligence collection; Detroit's mini-stations exclusively organize community crime prevention; and Santa Ana's substations function as community group meeting areas as well as locales for disseminating crime prevention information. The point is that areal decentralization is not the same as team policing, a buzz phrase in police circles. Indeed, the most important dimension upon which to distinguish decentralized strategies is the vision behind them. Have decentralized reforms been tacked onto a conventional patrol-oriented approach to policing or are they part of a larger departmental plan that involves reaching out to the community? Team policing does involve creation of small, relatively autonomous commands, but it also involves the coordinated management of police services by personnel who are assigned for relatively long periods to specific areas.

Team policing may or may not stress the intensive cultivation of local communities for crime prevention purposes. There is a tendency for senior police officers to assume that coordinating police services within small areas automatically produces close community relations. That is not so. Highly professional integrated teams can be just as attached to the old reactive crime-fighting modes as traditional patrol personnel. It is a mistake to confuse structural changes in command with reorientations of operating philosophy.

In sum, three dimensions of strategic change are frequently confused: decentralization of command, integration of service delivery, and mobilization of communities in their own defense.

Areal decentralization is necessary for the co-production of crime prevention, but it is not sufficient. Co-production rarely, if ever, occurs effectively on a citywide basis. Co-production typically begins when neighborhood groups or block organizations work with police directly. Areal decentralization facilitates all of this. Long-range assignment helps police develop special knowledge of an area or a neighborhood and, more than that, a special sort of commitment to it. That sort of commitment serves to heighten trust in police, who in turn become representatives of the neighborhood's interests.

At the same time accessibility of the police to the community is essential if local community feedback is to be more accurately comprehended and acted upon. Communication processes are subtle and easily distorted even among people who know each other well—for example, husbands and wives—to say nothing of strangers. A local patrolman would be far less likely than a specialized "emergency" tactical squad to shoot a welfare mother being evicted for nonpayment of rent.

At the same time, there is a significant potential problem with the delegation of command to relatively small areas. Where a department has an unfortunate history of corruption, decentralization could prove to be a disaster, creating exactly the conditions that facilitate further corruption. Where corruption prevails, however, it is unlikely that one would find much genuine interest in the sort of community crime prevention philosophy we have described here.

Reorientation of Patrol

Since patrol operations continue to occupy most police personnel, police departments have tried to reorient them so as to help enlist the community in the fight against crime. The reestablishment of foot patrols in many American cities is an obvious instance. Foot patrol is proactive, not reactive. It appears from our observations and other studies[3] to generate four meritorious effects:

1. Since there is a concerned human presence on the street, foot patrol is more adaptable to street happenings, and thus may prevent crime before it begins.
2. Foot patrolmen may make arrests, but they are also around to give warnings either directly or indirectly, merely through their presence.
3. Properly carried out, foot patrol generates goodwill in the neighborhood, which has the derivative consequence of making other crime prevention tactics more effective. This effectiveness in turn tends to raise citizen morale and reduce their fear of crime.
4. Foot patrol seems to raise officer morale.

In some places, especially in those experiencing much inclement weather, foot patrol assignments are sometimes used to punish. But the foot patrolmen we observed seemed to enjoy being part of a community, having the opportunity to talk with people who are not directly involved in crime problems. Citizens often smile at foot patrolmen. Auto and (especially) motorcycle patrolmen, however, usually appear as menacing strangers. Whatever else it may or may not accomplish, foot patrol seems to humanize the police.

Police departments are also trying in various ways, though they don't like to admit it, to unplug the 911 emergency dispatch system selectively for patrol officers. By so doing they free themselves for community development and crime prevention activities of their own devising. In many cities the 911 system with its promise of emergency response has become a tyrannical burden. Departments know that if they fail to respond speedily to every call, no matter how trivial, the public will become angry and complain to police, politicians, and the media. The pressure of 911 calls is often so great that few officers are available for proactive community involvement. Moreover, patrol personnel can exhaust themselves speeding from one call to another, using up the time needed for understanding the human situations into which they are injected.

Even though senior officers sometimes know that rapid response has been oversold and that it is not necessary to dispatch a patrol car to every call, they simply can't get off the tiger's back. So, cautiously, they are experimenting with measures that have the effect of reducing the 911 pressure. Some departments are directing officers to park patrol cars periodically and patrol on foot, perhaps around the block or up and down both sides of one block; others encourage patrol officers to take themselves "out of service" and simply stop and talk to people; and still others help them to prepare individualized plans for meeting local crime problems, even if it means not responding to emergency calls or even going under cover. The balancing of reactive and anticipatory modes of operation is perhaps the greatest policy question facing contemporary policing.

Civilianization

Of all the strategic innovations we encountered, civilianization was the most far-reaching and controversial. It was attractive in part because sworn police officers have become so costly. Captains in Santa Ana and Oakland earn more than full professors of mathematics or English at the University of California at Berkeley or Los Angeles. In 1985 a Santa Ana captain with ten years' tenure could expect to earn $58,545, while his Oakland counterpart would draw down $50,093. The Oakland Police Department estimated that in 1985 the total cost to the city would be $101,686 for that captain. The total 1985 cost for a patrolman: $63,821. Even in economically depressed Detroit, the total cost would reach $47,500. The Denver Manager of Public Safety proposes cutting back current police services to accommodate the costs of accumulated pension obligations.

Civilianization naturally suggests a system of stratification within policing alongside of, and in addition to, the ranking structure found in all departments. Such a system is task-based. Already many clerical and communicative tasks neces-sary to policing are performed by civilians. Few, if any, chiefs any longer have sworn officers type their letters. Civilians are being injected into other support areas as well, such as research and training, forensic analysis, and equipment maintenance. More controversial are programs such as Santa Ana's, where civilians wearing uniforms almost identical to sworn officers' investigate traffic accidents, take crime reports, mediate neigh-borhood disputes, and organize communities for self-defense.

A move toward civilianization of policing implies a reconsid-eration of the fit between assignment and the badge. When are gun-toting, high-priced sworn officers needed and when could well-trained, lower-paid civilians do as well? In addition to re-ducing the costs of carrying out certain police tasks, civilianiza-tion solves a significant strategic problem that we have already noted. It can be used to free police departments from the pres-sure of the 911 system. Where civilianization does not prevail—and it does not in most police departments—it is difficult to of-fer much more than lip service to crime prevention. By having sworn officers concentrate, however, on rapid response to emergency situations and civilians on other tasks, more officers are available to handle true and serious emergencies. Thus each individual officer should have more time to cultivate the public within his assigned beat.

An assumption behind all this, of course, is that civilians do not supplant sworn officers. Civilianization in Houston, for ex-ample, was designed in part to put more uniforms on the street, thereby making it possible for DART personnel—Houston's new breed of police officer—to initiate more proactive interac-tions of a nonenforcement sort. On the other hand, civilians may be hired to specialize in community liaison, thus allowing sworn officers to concentrate on law enforcement. No longer need they concern themselves with traffic accident investiga-tions, minor burglaries, victim assistance, victim follow-up, or teaching crime prevention to the public.

More intensive involvement by police in communities be-fore problems become criminal in nature may reduce 911 pres-sure in the long run. Today the only way to attract police atten-tion is to call 911. In cities where police are very busy, citizens have learned to exaggerate the gravity of their plight so that the police will feel compelled to respond. If police make themselves available in other ways, especially through community liaison officers deployed in posts close to every neighborhood, the pressure on the emergency telephone system should decline. In effect, functional specialization of assignments will occur. Patrol officers will no longer need to pretend that they are doing everything with equal success.

There is another reason for thinking that civilianization can enhance community-oriented policing. If civilians are drawn from within the inner-city communities that are being policed, they are more likely to possess specialized linguistic skills and cultural understandings. Those can further contribute to strengthening mobilization efforts to prevent crime. Civilians will usually be insiders, not outsiders, in the communities being policed. That fact would be important standing alone. Its significance is heightened when considered in the light of another of our findings: An overwhelming majority of police do not reside in the cities they police, to say nothing of the neighborhoods to which they are assigned. If civilians are better able to mobilize inner-city communities, they are likely to be more effective agents of crime prevention.

In sum, our investigations have persuaded us that the more a department is civilianized, the greater the likelihood that it will successfully introduce and carry out programs and policies directed toward crime prevention. If we were modeling the relationship, we would say that civilianization leads to more effective community mobilization, which in turn produces more effective crime prevention. Community mobilization is thus the key variable intervening between civilianization and crime prevention.

Civilianization is and will continue to be controversial. Few people easily accept change in the *status quo*, a shift to the unfamiliar. Sworn officers, particularly, fear that cost-saving civilianization efforts will eventually bring about overall salary reduction. It does not, of course, necessarily follow that sworn police salaries will decline with civilianization. The Santa Ana Police Department has a greater percentage of its employees civilianized than any other in the United States, yet its sworn police enjoy the highest salary scale of the cities we studied. Newark has the lowest percentage of civilians and the lowest salary scale.

Ironically, Newark police union officials with whom we discussed civilianization seem to fear most the potential of civilian *unionization* to undermine sworn police salaries. That fear is understandable. The Newark Police Department has long had a history of political interference overshadowing traditions of professionalism. It is possible that civilians in Newark, assigned, for example, to respond to traffic accidents, would demand salaries comparable to those of sworn police. But suppose the Newark Police Department could upgrade the sworn patrolman's role to that of a specialist in responding to crime emergencies, investigation, and apprehension? The Newark rank-and-file might then be better able to develop a conception of themselves as highly trained and competent professionals. As such, they might feel less threatened by those who would be set apart as paraprofessionals.

REQUIREMENTS FOR SUCCESSFUL INNOVATION

What factors account for successful innovation? What ingredients are present when innovation has "taken"? Here are four we were able to identify:

1. Most important of all is *the chief's abiding, energetic commitment to the values and implications of a crime prevention–oriented police department*. Police departments are not democratically run organizations. Everyone within them is either aware of or attuned to the chief's preferences, demands, and expectations. What is true of a police department is not absent from other organizations, such as businesses and universities. Executive leadership may, however, be even more critical in a police department because of its traditional paramilitary character: The police constitute a classic example of bureaucratic organization.

The idea that the successful executive is a conveyor of values is not new, but it has been pumped into popular life recently by Thomas J. Peters and Robert H. Waterman, Jr., in their widely read book *In Search of Excellence: Lessons from America's Best-Run Companies*.[4] It would be overstating the case to say that what Peters and Waterman found in the best-run companies, we found in innovative police departments. Besides, excellence and innovation are not necessarily the same thing. An excellent organization may not need any longer to be innovative; it may have found a formula that works superbly. Similarly, an innovative organization may be not yet excellent but simply moving in a positive direction.

Nevertheless, on a general level we observe similarities between corporate excellence and police innovation. All complex organizations develop a character or culture. Unlike business organizations, however, police departments do not begin with a blank slate. Police culture has a long and not always honorable history, including insularity, self-protection, suspicion of outsiders, political interferences, and sometimes even systemic corruption and racism. An innovative police executive may face even higher obstacles to overcome than a successful business executive.

Still, as with successful businesses, innovative police organizations require an infusion of certain kinds of traits, which are suggested by the distinction between the idea of "organization" and the concept of "institution." The distinction was conveyed years ago by sociologist Philip Selznick in his important but largely overlooked book *Leadership in Administration*.[5] Fortunately, Peters and Waterman warmly acknowledge Selznick's contribution to organizational theory. They quote lengthy passages from Selznick's book as especially seminal for understanding organizational transformation and its significance in accounting for the superiority of some businesses (and, we think, some police departments) over others. Selznick sees the "organization" (he really means the bureaucratic organization) as a bare, lean, "no-nonsense system of consciously coordinated activities—an expendable tool, a rational instrument engineered to do a job" as against the "institution," a more nearly "natural product of social needs and pressures—a responsive, adaptive organism." Really important here is the process, "the transformation of an engineered, technical arrangement of building blocks into a social organism."[6] But the transformation won't take unless the rank-and-file—workers or cops—perceive the top as more than simply a public advocate of new values. He must be—and be seen as—an active, committed exponent of them, especially in a police department. To paraphrase Selznick, the Chief must build a sense of purpose into the structure of the enterprise.

2. Our second requirement for institutional innovation is that *the institutional leader—the police department's chief—must fulfill his abiding commitment to the values he espouses by motivating, even manipulating, departmental personnel into enlisting in the service of those values.*

Organizations transforming from one set of dominant norms to another will retain members tied to the *status quo*. A tenacious adherence to older norms and values may be especially true of the internal orgnaization of police departments. "Old guards" can retain much influence, and police executives often seek to keep their support. In doing so executives who would like to institute change sometimes undermine their own chances for success. They talk and act from, as it were, both sides of the mouth. They affirm conflicting norms, depending upon audience. As a result nobody in the department knows what they really stand for—sometimes they themselves don't know—and virtually all are confused.

The Police Chief must bring the troops along. Preferably, he should be the sort of executive who succeeds by persuading that the new values are superior. That is not always easy, especially in police departments with strong unions. Self-interest in higher wages and shorter hours sometimes stand in the way of introducing innovative ideas and strategies. The reader will recall, for example, how difficult it was to bring mini-stations to Detroit and how virtually impossible it was to introduce team policing in Oakland or substantial civilianization in Newark. There is, of course, a dilemma here. In the absence of unions, police chiefs who are simply martinets can ride roughshod over the legitimate interests of the rank-and-file patrol force. Still, the vested interests of unionized police can sometimes make innovation extraordinarily difficult.

Nevertheless, an innovatively inclined police chief can gain the support of the rank-and-file. Some tactics we observed included:

a. Concentrating on influencing younger members of the department, then promoting them to positions of influence.

b. Urging retirement on members of the old guard, coupled with hiring of new officers—the more the better.
c. Discerning who among older officers might be attracted to the new values, some out of genuine commitment, others perhaps because they see that's the way the wind is blowing.
d. Employing the Chief's office as a training ground for middle management.
e. Sending trained middle managers into the field as team leaders or precinct or patrol captains and lieutenants, spreading the word.
f. If all else fails, using the power of the Chief's office to sanction those fighting innovation. (As one Chief told us after having coped with a bit of a rebellion against the new values, ''In the absence of respect, fear will do nicely.'')

3. *Once established, the integrity of innovation must be defended.* Traditionally, police departments are reactive organizations. Not without reason are they attuned to emergency service. There is often a temptation to pull personnel away from crime prevention or community liaison assignments to handle pressing situations—e.g. parades and sporting events, evacuating endangered areas, or potential ethnic conflict. Those temporary demands are not so bad. The transfer problem becomes especially acute when there are a series of sensational crimes or a media ''crime wave.'' The emergency dispatch system tends to institutionalize a reactive orientation, justifying the view of patrol commanders that their priorities should be the department's. It is easy for the scarce resources of a police department to be drained away in reacting to legitimate—but ultimately random—calls for service. One way of preventing, or at least retarding, the cannibalization of community-oriented policing is to set up separate commands. This makes the community-oriented mission easier to defend. Furthermore, if officers feel they are part of a distinct and valued program, they are more likely to take pride in it and resent reassignment to emergency tasks.

4. *Innovation is unlikely to happen without public support.* Quite obviously, departments may require additional financial resources, at least during the period when new strategies are being tried alongside the old. More important, perhaps, the com-

THE NEW BLUE LINE

munity must give innovation breathing space. Politicians and the media, especially, must be cautioned not to expect instant results, to be patient when departments won't abandon new initiatives because two schoolchildren have been abducted, residential burglaries increase, or complaints rise about slow response to 911 calls. New strategies take time to implement, and demonstration of their success takes even longer.

Public support for new strategies is difficult to develop because of the public's ambivalence about police. The public acknowledges the difficulties of policing as an occupation but sometimes fears the potential of enforcement, even harassment. Such feelings are usually most pronounced in inner-city communities composed of members of minority groups. The police experience that ambivalence keenly. Although they know a police presence is frequently requested and often appreciated, they nonetheless feel embattled, resented, and misunderstood. Like authors, they tend to recall every negative opinion in a review while paying little attention to positive evaluations.

In our experience, innovative crime prevention programs instituted and implemented with community input are apt to enjoy unexpected support from the public. Even roadblocks we observed in Newark seemed to be viewed favorably when properly introduced and explained. House-to-house visits by officers in Houston and Detroit, which we thought would draw sharp criticism, were warmly appreciated. In fact, we now believe there is an enormous suppressed demand for a face-to-face police presence. The general reaction to community contact seems to have been "Where have you been all along?" or "It's about time!" Like policemen themselves, the public is tired of police arriving after harm has been done, understanding all too well that little can be done then, particularly with respect to catching the criminal.

By contrast, proactive crime prevention activities project the police into a "co-production" posture, which incorporates citizens into the police world. The citizen who co-produces may experience some of the frustrations and limitations of trying to maintain public safety. But that is positive, since the citizen will be more likely to comprehend and identify with the problems of policing. Police could scarcely invent a more effective form of positive public relations, which, we have observed, can eventually translate into political support for police and their resource needs.

THE CHANCE FOR INNOVATION

Even if the developments we have been discussing can be shown to be positive and useful in protecting public safety and raising confidence in agencies of law enforcement, change will not be easy. On the contrary, change will continue to be inhibited by an existing *system* of interconnected impediments, each contributing something to maintenance of the *status quo*. It may be worthwhile to summarize those obstacles.

First, there is the powerful pull of tradition. Like any bureaucracy, police departments are enormously resistant to certain kinds of change, particularly those challenging cultural tradition. The sort we have discussed threatens both hallowed conceptions of police professionalism and a faith in the valued primacy of certain kinds of technologies—those that increase speed of response and capacity to use force, especially deadly force. We do not deny that the capacity to employ force is a central feature of the police role. At the same time crime control ideologies stress that capacity over the crime prevention emphasis on community organization.

Second, substantial segments of the public do not want the police to change. Police have been around, as they are, for a long time. There is discernible public support for traditional functions of the police, especially for traditional evaluation criteria, such as response time and visible motorized patrolling. The establishment of community-oriented policing will require reeducating the public about what is valuable in policing.

Third, unions will continue to be skeptical of innovation. The capacity to innovate through management does influence the balancing of union versus management power. If areal decentralization is an important element of innovation, police may be assigned to tasks and shifts that they are not keen to undertake. There will always be a certain amount of friction centering on the conflict between worker autonomy and departmental innovation. Moreover, civilianization will doubtless raise fears among unionized police.

Fourth, innovation may prove costly, particularly when the department tries to provide guns and butter. A department might be willing to move toward civilianization but feel it must retain something like its present complement of sworn officers. Or it might be willing to introduce team policing but unwilling to reduce response time. Tradeoffs will not always be necessary, particularly as innovations take hold, but transition periods could be costly. Police executives, who lead precarious lives anyhow, may not care to become involved with experimental forms during transition periods.

An apparent lack of vision on the part of police executives constitutes a fifth impediment to innovation. Many police chiefs simply don't want to change or even to hear about change. Whether that lack of vision is simply a means of avoiding trouble or an expression of command powerlessness—or both—is hard to say. But certainly there are chiefs who, though possessing vision and wanting to introduce experiments in their departments, lack either the courage of their convictions or the management savvy to overcome internal obstacles.

The incapacity of police departments to evaluate their own effectiveness is a final and significant impediment to innovation. With hardly any exception, police departments don't know whether the innovations they are trying are preferable to the old ways. For that reason we really can't advocate as strongly as we would like the developments described in this book. Our recommendations about the usefulness of community-oriented policing are based, like those of police administrators themselves, on arguments that such innovations "make sense" or on conclusions developed from field observations.

But if some of the new we have praised is unproven, so too is the old. Rarely have traditional police practices been subjected to rigorous evaluation. When they have, they have usually been found wanting. Because doubts about traditional strategies are so widespread, the burden of proof should be on those who seek to maintain them. They, after all, account for the expenditure of vast sums of public money without reassuring results. The bottom line is that neither old practices nor current innovations have so far produced magic formulas for solving the nation's crime problem.

Since police departments typically don't have either financial or human resources to undertake rigorous evaluations of strategic plans, outside assistance must be provided. That is an obvious role for the Federal Government, probably through increased resources of the National Institute of Justice. Contrary to what many people think, a considerable amount of innovation is taking place at the grassroots in American policing. The country needs to take advantage of those natural experiments by evaluating them as rigorously as possible so that other departments can learn. As it is, farsighted chiefs try new programs, but rarely do they or anyone else know whether they have succeeded. Building evaluation into new programs will also help to protect against the impatience of politicians and the public and will reassure departmental personnel that decisions about the programs will not be made capriciously by new commanders but will be based on sound intellectual reasons.

We also believe that evaluation of the success of programs must be made in broader terms than has been customary. While the fundamental objective of policing should remain the protection of the public, crime and arrest rates are much too crude and elusive measures to nail down the dynamic relationship between police action and public safety. The efficacy of the police must also be considered in terms of the elicitation of cooperation from the public, the understanding police develop of particular areas and social circumstances, the anxiety of police themselves, the changing composition of calls for police service, the effectiveness with which noncrime requests are handled, the enthusiasm of the public for working preventively with the police, and the strength of the "we–they" dichotomy felt mutually by police and public.

Although the list of impediments to change focuses on factors police can in some measure affect directly, we recognize that conditions outside their control also play a significant role in determining the chances for success of police innovation. Some of those factors are the strength and weakness of local and national economies, the proportion of immigrants in a city, racial discrimination and hatred, municipal power structures, and bureaucratic and political traditions. Police chiefs frequently cite such factors as reasons for not introducing new strategies into their departments. In some instances these excuses may be valid. In others they are a "cop-out." They mask a critical lack of strategic vision on the part of the Chief or the department. Some police administrators simply don't know or are overwhelmed by the idea of introducing reforms involving community feedback, cooperation, crime prevention, and command decentralization. Some administrators are afraid of change in any form. The Chief, for example, wants to hold things together, not shake things up with the potential for releasing underlying, perhaps festering, conflicts within the department and the community.

In such circumstances the Chief is likely to talk a better game than he plays. Time after time we have described new developments in policing to staff conferences only to be told flatly, "We've been doing that for years." To hear some chiefs tell it, they discovered and implemented community crime prevention, command decentralization, and team policing years ago. There is nothing new, they suggest, that they haven't already tried. Unfortunately, the titles of programs are not the reality of programs. Knowing about programs and even enthusiastically talking them up is not the same as implementing them in practice.

Despite evident obstacles to innovation, including a great deal of self-delusion on the part of senior police officers, innovation is occurring. It is happening in every region of the United States, sometimes under the most daunting circumstances. Why should that be so? It is because police executives, just like the general public, at heart understand that more of the same is simply not getting the job done. Where success is evident, as in Santa Ana and Detroit, it has happened with a strong vision of community participation in policing, plus the management and political skills of an effective Chief to carry the vision through. But other communities, too, have accomplished a great deal.

All of the departments we studied have been innovative to some degree. Oakland has inaugurated "Beat Health," neighborhood and downtown foot patrol, plus an exceptionally solid recruit training format. Houston has introduced directed patrol and, more importantly, a set of values challenging long-held and questionable, indeed racist, traditions of the Houston Police Department. Denver, perhaps the most traditional patrol-oriented department we studied, seems increasingly open to new ideas and methods.

Perhaps no city in the United States has experienced more racial tension, more government corruption, and less economic strength than Newark, New Jersey. Yet the Newark Police Department has been able to experiment and to provide increasingly effective services to both the inner-city population and the business community. As a result the City of Newark seems finally to be rising from the ashes of the 1967 riots.

In sum, to introduce and implement new police ideas is not easy, but it is possible. More than that, it is essential if we are to achieve elementary public safety in American cities and confidence in the police by those who are being policed.

NOTES

1. COPING WITH THE URBAN
CRIME PROBLEM (pp. 1-12)

1. Pauline Morris and Kevin Heal, *Crime Control and the Police: A Review of Research*, Home Office Research Study No. 67 (London: HMSO, 1981), and R. V. G. Clark and K. H. Heal, "Police Effectiveness in Dealing with Crime: Some Current British Research," *The Police Journal*, January 1979, pp. 24–41.
2. George L. Kelling *et al.*, *The Kansas City Preventive Patrol Experiment: A Summary Report* (Washington, D.C.: Police Foundation, 1974).
3. Police Foundation, *The Newark Foot Patrol Experiment* (Washington, D. C.: Police Foundation, 1981).
4. Anthony Pate and George Kelling, "Police Patrol Research: The Lessons," unpublished paper, 1980.
5. Albert Reiss, Jr., *The Police and the Public* (New Haven: Yale University Press, 1971).
6. Police Executive Research Forum, April 1981, and William Bieck and David A. Kessler, *Response Time Analysis* (Kansas City, Mo.: Board of Police Commissioners, 1977).
7. Peter W. Greenwood and Joan Petersilia, *The Criminal Investigation Process* (Washington, D.C.: Law Enforcement Assistance Administration, 1976).
8. John J. Palen, *The Urban World* (New York: McGraw-Hill, 1975), p. 75.

2. SANTA ANA: Conservative County, Progressive Police (pp. 13-49)

1. *Los Angeles Times*, Sunday, October 3, 1976, Orange County Section, p. 1.
2. *The Executive*, Advertising Supplement, June 1982, p. 37.
3. *New York Times*, February 13, 1984, p. 10.
4. See Jerome H. Skolnick, "Police Vice Squad," in Sanford A. Kadish, ed. *Encyclopedia of Crime and Justice*, Vol. 3 (New York: The Free Press, 1983). For report and analyses of police corruption in various cities, see Lawrence W. Sherman, ed., *Police Corruption: A Sociological Perspective* (New York: Anchor, 1974).
5. See T. M. Tomlinson and David O. Sears, *Los Angeles Times Riot Study: Negro Attitudes Toward the Riot* (Los Angeles: Institute of Government and Public Affairs, University of California, 1967).
6. Donald Black and Albert J. Reiss, Jr., "Patterns of Behavior in Police and Citizen Transactions," President's Commission on Law Enforcement and the Administration of Criminal Justice (Washington, D.C.: Department of Justice, 1976).
7. Lawrence W. Sherman, Catherine H. Milton, and Thomas V. Kelly, *Team Policing: Seven Case Studies* (Washington, D.C.: Police Foundation, 1973), p. xiv.
8. For a discussion comparing integrated team policing to other forms, see Samuel Walker, *The Police in America* (New York: McGraw-Hill, 1983).
9. E. B. Hansen and David G. Salazar, "Police Service Officers: A Non-Sworn Approach," *Journal of California Law Enforcement*, Fall 1981, p. 142.
10. *Ibid.*
11. Editorial, *The Register*, September 20, 1983.
12. Editorial, *Los Angeles Times*, September 18, 1983.
13. *Powell v. State of Texas* (1968), 392 U.S. 514, 517.
14. *Ibid.*, p. 567.
15. Paul M. Walters, "Santa Ana's Police and Business Community Team-Up to Reduce Crime," *California Peace Officer*, October 1982.

DETROIT: No More Nightstick Justice in Motown (pp. 50-80)

1. John Hersey, *The Algiers Motel Incident* (New York: Knopf, 1968).
2. Letter from Mayor Coleman Young to constituents, June 1, 1983.
3. *Firefighters Local Union No. 1784* v. *Stotts*, 104 S. Ct. 2576 (1984).
4. Department of Justice, *Sourcebook of Criminal Justice Statistics 1981* (Washington, D.C.: Department of Justice, 1981).
5. This was the number on July 1, 1983.
6. Figures were taken from a computerized breakdown of assignments. They differ slightly from statistics printed in the annual reports.
7. Memo from Chief Hart, "Recapitulation of Crime Prevention Standards for Mini-Station Section," September 3, 1982.
8. *Detroit Free Press*, July 13, 1983.

HOUSTON: Old Habits Are Changing (pp. 81–116)

1. Rick Nelson, *The Cop Who Wouldn't Quit* (New York: Bantam, 1983).
2. *Ibid.*, p. 89.
3. Lawrence W. Sherman, "Reducing Gun Use: Critical Events, Administrative Policy, and Organizational Change," in M. Punch, ed., *Control in the Police Organization* (Cambridge, Mass.: MIT Press, 1983).
4. Clifford D. Shearing and Philip C. Stenning, "Modern Private Security," in Norval Morris and Michael Tonry, eds., *Crime and Justice, 1980* (Washington, D.C.: National Institute of Justice, 1981).
5. Houston Police Department, "Project DART Training Program," 1983.
6. Houston Police Department, Department of Research and Planning, 1984.

DENVER: The American Standard (pp. 117–146)

1. Denver Police Department, "Critical Issues in Law Enforcement: Selected Responses," memorandum submitted to the Police Executive Research Forum, 1981, p. 1.

OAKLAND: Keeping It All Together (pp. 147–179)

1. Report of the National Advisory Commission on Civil Disorders.
2. James Q. Wilson and George L. Kelling, "Broken Windows," *The Atlantic*, 249, No. 3 (March 1982): 29–38.
3. Albert J. Reiss, Jr., *Policing a City's Central District: The Oakland Story* (Washington D.C.: National Institute of Justice, 1985).
4. 405 U.S. 156 (1972).
5. Mike McGrath, "The Bum's Rush," *Express: The East Bay's Free Weekly*, 5, No. 40 (July 29, 1983).
6. Tom Johnson, "Disturbing Encounters, A Panel Inquiry in the Crazy Side of Street Life," *Express*, March 6, 1981.

NEWARK: Innovation Amidst Burnout (pp. 180–209)

1. Robert Curvin, *The Persistent Minority: The Black Political Experience in Newark* (Princeton, N.J.: Princeton University Press, 1975).
2. George Sternlieb, "The City as a Sandbox," *The Public Interest*, Fall 1971, pp. 14–21.
3. Norton Long, "The City as a Reservation," *The Public Interest*, Fall 1971, pp. 22–38.
4. David Shipler, "The White Niggers of Newark: The Other Side of Prejudice," *Harper's*, August 1972, p. 83.
5. FBI, *Uniform Crime Reports*, 1948–78.
6. Dorothy H. Guyot, "Newark: Crime and Politics in a Declining

City," in Anne Heinz *et al.*, *Crime in City Politics* (New York: Longman, 1983) p. 26.
7. Newark Police Department, *Crime Statistics*.
8. Santa Ana Police Department, *Crime Statistics*.
9. *Report of the National Advisory Commission on Civil Disorders* (New York: Bantam, 1968), p. 62.
10. Guyot, "Newark: Crime and Politics in a Declining City," p. 31. Most of the materials on Newark's history were learned from Dorothy H. Guyot's comprehensive study of the history of crime in Newark.
11. *Ibid.*, p. 34.
12. *Ibid.*, p. 39.
13. *Ibid.*, p. 55.
14. Curvin, *Persistent Minority*, p. 10.
15. Guyot, "Newark: Crime and Politics in a Declining City," p. 76.
16. F. C. Jordan, Jr., and R. E. Brown, *High Impact Anti-Crime Program: A History of the Newark Impact Program* (McLean, Va.: Mitre Corp., 1975), pp. 37–40.
17. Guyot, "Newark: Crime and Politics in a Declining City," p. 86.
18. Dorothy H. Guyot and Lois Dedes, "Layoffs," *Journal of Police Science and Administration*, 10, No. 4: 436.
19. Franklin E. Zimring, "Youth Homicide in New York: A Preliminary Analysis," *Journal of Legal Studies*, 13:81–98.
20. *Delaware* v. *Prouse*, 440 U.S. 648.
21. *Ibid.*, pp. 648, 664.
22. Touche-Ross & Co., *Newark Police Department Operations Review* (Newark: Touche-Ross & Co., 1984).
23. *Ibid.*, p. 2.
24. *Ibid.*, p. 3.
25. Newark Police Department, *Annual Report 1983*, p. 42.
26. Touche-Ross & Co., *Newark Police Department Operations Review*, p. 2.

PROSPECTS FOR POLICE INNOVATION (pp. 210–229)

1. James Q. Wilson, *Varieties of Police Behavior* (Cambridge: Harvard University Press, 1968).
2. William DeJong and Gail A. Goolkasian, *The Neighborhood Fight Against Crime: The Midwood Kings Highway Development Corporation* (Washington D.C.: National Institute of Justice, U.S. Department of Justice, December 1982).
3. See *The Newark Foot Patrol Experiment* (Washington, D.C.: Police Foundation, 1981) and sources cited there. James Q. Wilson and George Kelling, "Broken Windows," *Atlantic Monthly*, March 1982, pp. 29–38, offers a nice exploration of the significance of foot patrol.
4. Thomas J. Peters and Robert H. Waterman, Jr., *In Search of Excellence: Lessons from America's Best-Run Companies* (New York: Harper & Row, 1982).
5. Philip Selznick, *Leadership in Administration: A Sociological Enterprise* (New York: Harper & Row, 1957).
6. *Ibid.*, p. 5.

SELECTED BIBLIOGRAPHY ON POLICE

BANTON, MICHAEL. *The Police in the Community.* New York: Basic Books, 1964.
Pioneering work comparing police behavior in Scotland and the U.S. and exploring how social context affects police activity—particularly police attitudes toward, and interactions with, the public.

BAYLEY, DAVID H. *Forces of Order: Police Behavior in Japan and the U.S.* Berkeley: University of California Press, 1975.
Major observational study of Japanese police showing how goals, conduct, and responsibilities vary with cultural expectations. The first book to read on comparative policing.

BAYLEY, DAVID. H. & MENDELSOHN, HAROLD. *Minorities and the Police.* New York: Free Press, 1969.
Based on the largest survey of police/minority relations ever done in the United States. Describes the attitudes of each toward the other and attempts to explain those attitudes in terms of social background and experience.

BITTNER, EGON. *The Functions of the Police in Modern Society.* Cambridge, MA: Oelgeschlager, Gunn & Hain, 1980.
Republication of Bittner's celebrated 1970 monograph of the same name plus his 1974 article "Florence Nightingale in Pursuit of Willie Sutton: A Theory of the Police." Both pieces show the multifaceted nature of police work and the dilemmas this poses for police.

BLACK, DONALD. *The Manners and Customs of the Police.* New York: Academic Press, 1980.
Theoretical chapters are less than compelling, but the ethnography on police, juveniles, and blacks is unusually perceptive.

BORDUA, DAVID J. *The Police: Six Sociological Essays.* New York: Wiley, 1967.
Outstanding book of important essays by the likes of Bordua and Albert Reiss Jr., Carl Werthman and Irving Piliavin, Jerome H. Skolnick and Richard Woodworth, James Q. Wilson, and John McNamara. Allen Silver's opener, "The Demand for Order in Civil Society" remains a classic.

BROWN, MICHAEL K. *Working the Street: Police Discretion and the Dilemmas of Reform.* New York: Russell Sage, 1981.
From a study of southern California police departments. The author offers useful insights on police bureaucracy, discretion, and the dilemmas of reform.

CAIDEN, GERALD E. *Police Revitalization.* Lexington, MA: Lexington Books (D. C. Heath), 1977.
Sharp, thorough, hard-hitting description of the state of policing at the end of the decade of reform stimulated by the report of the President's Commission on Law Enforcement and the Administration of Justice (1967).

CARTE, GENE E. & CARTE, ELAINE H. *Police Reform in the United States: The Case of August Vollmer.* Berkeley: University of California Press, 1975.
Outstanding history of police reform and professionalism as traced through the life of the most significant thinker and activist of the first half of the twentieth century.

CHEVIGNY, PAUL. *Police Power: Police Abuses in New York City.* New York: Random House, 1969.
Based on actual cases, reveals the myriad ways in which power may be abused by the police in their interactions with the public.

COUPER, DAVID. *How to Rate Your Local Police.* Washington, D.C.: Police Executive Research Forum, 1983.
Short (thirty-two page), pointed presentation of appropriate and inappropriate criteria for evaluating whether local police are doing a proper job.

CRITCHLEY, T. A. *A History of Police in England and Wales, 900–1966.* London: Constable, 1967.
The most comprehensive study of the history of the British police. Combines a wealth of fact with analysis and historical commentary.

DALEY, ROBERT. *Prince of the City: The True Story of the Cop Who Knew Too Much.* Boston: Houghton–Mifflin, 1978.

Gripping and incisive case study of police corruption among N.Y.C. narcotics detectives.

ELLIOTT, J. F. *The "New" Police.* Springfield, IL: Charles C Thomas, 1973.
Powerful and controversial argument for redefining the police role so as to concentrate more narrowly on crime control as opposed to social servicing.

FOGELSON, ROBERT M. *Big-City Police.* Cambridge, MA: Harvard University Press, 1973.
Vividly written, comprehensive, and lucid history of the development of American policing, placing it within the context of the development of municipal government.

FREEDMAN, JILL. *Street Cops.* New York: Harper & Row, 1981.
Stunning pictorial essay, supplemented by brief and moving commentary, on police work as performed by patrol officers.

FYFE, JAMES J. *Police Use of Deadly Force.* Washington, D.C.: Police Foundation, 1981.
Best set of readings on the subject by America's foremost expert. Unfortunately, does not include Fyfe's careful and compelling "Blind Justice: Police Shootings in Memphis," *Journal of Criminal Law & Criminology*, 73 (Summer 1982): 702–22.

GOLDSTEIN, HERMAN. *Policing a Free Society.* Cambridge, MA: Ballinger, 1977.
Perhaps the best introductory book on American police. Well organized, thorough, and lucid.

LANE, ROGER. *Policing the City: Boston 1822–1885.* Cambridge, MA: Harvard University Press, 1967.
One of the first and best police histories of the United States, revealing the roots of contemporary American policing.

MARTIN, SUSAN E. *Breaking and Entering: Policewomen on Patrol.* Berkeley: University of California Press, 1980.
Anybody interested in understanding women in policing must read this study. Shows how cultural and behavioral expectations of women can conflict with this male-dominated occupation.

MILLER, WILBUR R. *Cops and Bobbies: Policy Authority in New York and London, 1830–1870.* Chicago: University of Chicago Press, 1977.
Fascinating comparison of police development in these two cities, arguing that each country has developed significantly different police institutions and explaining why.

MONKKONEN, ERIK. *Police in Urban America.* Cambridge, MA: Cambridge University Press, 1981.
Well-written history discussing reasons for decline in U.S. urban arrests between 1860 and 1920.

MORRIS, PAULINE & HEAL, KEVIN. *Crime Control and the Police: A Review of Research.* (Home Office Research Study No. 67.) London: HMSO, 1981.
Masterly summary of what research has shown about the value of various police strategies and practices in controlling crime.

MUIR, WILLIAM K. *Streetcorner Politician.* Chicago: University of Chicago Press, 1977.
Thought-provoking and engagingly written analysis of alternative ways police officers can employ coercive power.

MURPHY, PATRICK V. & PLATE, THOMAS. *Commissioner.* New York: Simon & Schuster, 1977.
Easy-to-read autobiography by America's most influential police professional. Essential for anyone concerned with problems of innovative police leadership.

NATIONAL INSTITUTE OF LAW ENFORCEMENT AND CRIMINAL JUSTICE. (DEPARTMENT OF JUSTICE, U.S. GOVERNMENT.) *The Criminal Investigation Process: A Dialogue of Research Findings.* Washington, D.C.: GPO, April, 1977.
Republication of study by Peter Greenwood and Joan Petersilia on the efficacy of criminal investigation in solving crimes, accompanied by rebuttal articles from the professional magazine *Police Chief.* Devastating critique of beliefs commonly held about how crimes are solved.

OSTOM, ELINOR; PARKS, ROGER B.; & WHITAKER, GORDON. *Policing Metropolitan America.* Washington, D.C.: GPO, 1977.
Definitive study of the organization of police services in metropolitan areas, demonstrating that multiplication and overlapping of police jurisdiction do not lead to inefficiency and ineffectiveness.

REISS, ALBERT J., JR. *The Police and the Public.* New Haven: Yale University Press, 1971.
Classic study of the relations between the police and the public, based on data collected for the President's Commission on Law Enforcement and the Administration of Justice, 1967.

RICHARDSON, JAMES F. *Urban Police in the United States.* Port Washington, N.Y.: Kennikat Press, 1974.
One of the most useful short histories of American policing. Well organized for easy access; thorough and straightforward in presentation.

SHERMAN, LAWRENCE (ED.). *The Police and Violence: The Annals of the American Academy of Political and Social Science* (November 1980 edition).
A special collection of articles treating police control of public violence, violence directed against police, and violence perpetrated by police.

SHERMAN, LAWRENCE W. *Police Corruption: A Sociological Perspective.* Garden City: Anchor Books, 1974.

Excellent collection of readings for understanding causes, conse-
quences, and reform strategies.

SKOLNICK, JEROME H. *Justice Without Trial: Law Enforcement in a Democratic Society.* New York: Wiley, 1975.
Oft-cited observational study of criminal procedure, urban police organization, culture, and discretion on-the-job. This edition contains an
epilogue on the politics of policing.

WALKER, SAMUEL. *A Critical History of Police Reform.* Lexington, MA:
D. C. Heath, 1977.
Readable history of American policing. Material is organized into
themes, topics, and eras so that one doesn't lose sight of the woods for
the trees.

WAMBAUGH, JOSEPH. *The New Centurions.* Boston: Little, Brown,
1970.
First and probably still best novel depicting the everyday life of police
patrol officers.

WESTLEY, WILLIAM A. *Violence and the Police.* Cambridge, MA: MIT
Press, 1970.
Landmark study introducing the idea of a police subculture and its re-
lation to justifying police violence.

WILSON, JAMES Q. *Crime and Public Policy.* San Francisco: ICS Press,
1983.
Collection of original essays on effectiveness of various policies in reducing crime. Police are one topic covered. Wilson summarizes policy
recommendations of the essays. Unfortunately, the book does not contain Wilson's seminal essay with George L. Kelling, "The Police and
Neighborhood Safety: Broken Windows," *The Atlantic* (March 1982).

WILSON, JAMES Q. *Varieties of Police Behavior.* New York: Atheneum,
1973.
Classic study showing how police conduct is influenced by the prevailing philosophy or "style" of policing.

INDEX

Adam, Officer Bob, Denver mini-station officer, 63
Adams, Officer Gary, Santa Ana, 44
Addonizio, Hugh, 186
Affirmative action, 49, 90, 152–154
Algiers Motel Incident, The (Hersey, John), 50
Applied research, 133

Balderson, Patrolman Mike, Oakland, 172, 173
Bales, J. P., Houston Director of Field Operations, 93, 94, 113
Beard, Charles A., 183
Beat health, 159–161
Beat integrity, 94, 101, 102
Beat officers, 95
Beats, 57, 123, 129–131
Belluardo, John, Immigration and Naturalization Service, 34
Bennett, Sherman, Oakland foot patrolman, 167
Birge, Lieutenant Ray, Oakland Drug Task Force Commander, 172, 174
Black community, 10, 11, 19, 48, 149, 150, 154, 170, 171, 174, 175, 177, 185, 187
Black hiring, 153
Black officers, 50, 177, 188
Black Panther party, 13, 149
Black Police Officers' Association, Oakland, 153
Black promotion, 153
Blue code of silence, 15, 194
Board of Police Commissioners, Detroit, 56, 60
Boston, Massachusetts, 21
Brann, Lieutenant Joseph, 13–15
"Broken Windows" (Wilson and Kelling), 161
Brown, Lee P., Houston Chief of Police, 82–85, 89, 90–92, 94, 99, 104, 115
Brutality, 83, 175, 176
Buy-bust, 174
Buy-quick-bust, 173, 174

Career criminals, 132
Carr, Sergeant Dan, Santa Ana, 14
Chanin, James, Oakland attorney, 157, 175
Chicago, Illinois, 21
Cincinnati, Ohio, team policing in, 23
City manager system, 18
Civilian Complaint Board, Oakland, 155–156
Civilian Coordinator, Houston, 110, 111
Civilianization, 25, 78, 99, 217–220, 222, 226
support for, 27
Civilians, in police department, 26
Civilian–sworn officer ratio, 25
Cleveland, Ohio, 11
Command, hierarchical, 124, 125
Command stations, 96, 106
Community cooperation, 20
Community detectives, 144
Community mobilization, 11, 28, 52, 53, 127, 219
Community Organizing Response Teams (CORT), 107
Community Relations Bureau, Denver: *see* Community Services Bureau
Community Sector Team Policing Program (COMSEC), 23
Community self-defense, 58, 60, 95
Community Service Center, 203, 204
Community Service Officer, Santa Ana, 43
Community Service Officer (civilian), Houston, 111
Community service officers, Houston, 94, 95, 104, 105, 115
Community Services Bureau, Denver, 121, 143, 144
Community Services Division, Houston, 111, 114
Computer-assisted-dispatch (CAD), 131
Computers, 100–101, 129, 131, 151, 184
Coogin, Thomas, Denver Chief of Police, 119, 120, 127, 129, 143

239